BURIED SECRETS

Barry Cummins is a multi-award-winning author, documentary-maker and broadcast journalist based in Dublin. He has three decades' experience working in news and current affairs with RTÉ, Ireland's national broadcaster, Today FM and local radio. Barry is the author of *Missing* (2003 and 2019), *Lifers* (2004), *Unsolved* (2007), *Without Trace* (2010) and *Cold Cases* (2011). A founding member of National Missing Persons Day in 2013, Barry hosted the annual event for a decade. Originally from Tallaght, Barry now lives in north County Dublin with his wife and two children.

BURIED SECRETS

The murder of TINA SATCHWELL and a journalist's journey into IRELAND'S MOST CHILLING COLD CASE

BARRY CUMMINS

GILL BOOKS

Gill Books
Hume Avenue
Park West
Dublin 12
www.gillbooks.ie

Gill Books is an imprint of M.H. Gill and Co.

© Barry Cummins 2026

9781804584316

Design origination by Padraig McCormack
Edited by Emma Dunne
Proofread by Sally Vince

Printed and bound in Great Britain by Clays Ltd, Elcograf S.p.A.

This book is typeset in Sabon LT Pro by
Palimpsest Book Production Limited, Falkirk, Stirlingshire

The paper used in this book comes from the wood pulp of sustainably managed forests.

All rights reserved.
No part of this publication may be copied, reproduced or transmitted in any form or by any means, without written permission of the publishers.

To the best of our knowledge, this book complies in full with the requirements of the General Product Safety Regulation (GPSR). For further information and help with any safety queries, please contact us at productsafety@gill.ie.

A CIP catalogue record for this book is available from the British Library.

5 4 3 2 1

For all missing people.
I gcuimhne gach duine atá ar iarraidh.

Contents

Prologue	1
1. Car Boot Sundays	5
2. Where, When, How	20
3. Fermoy	33
4. Ballincollig	39
5. The Grave	43
6. The First Search	55
7. Making Contact	70
8. On the Couch	81
9. Cat and Mouse	87
10. The Photos	100
11. The Shrine	107
12. Mics, Camera, Car Journey	117
13. Up to the Lighthouse	126
14. Proposal Spot	137
15. Into Christmas	148
16. The Bridge	155
17. Transmission	167
18. Castlemartyr	173

19. Face Off	181
20. Dave Knows Nothing	194
21. Incident Room	203
22. Door Knock	213
23. Discovery	223
24. Recovery	236
25. Confession of Sorts	249
26. At Peace	265
27. Court Thoughts	270
28. Seven Women, Five Men	277
29. Prime Time	285
30. Cushions and Phones	297
31. Three Options	308
32. Verdict	321
33. Life	330
Epilogue: Tina Beams	341
Acknowledgements	349

Prologue

I am six feet from Tina's body. She is buried beneath concrete, her head pointing towards the kitchen, her feet towards the bottom step of the stairs which rise above her. Tina is wearing old Dunnes Stores pyjamas and a dressing gown over them. Her decomposing body is wrapped in heavy-grade plastic sheeting and lies three feet beneath the foundations of her home.

I am sitting on Tina's couch making small talk with her husband, unaware that she is buried so near to me and that he is, in fact, her murderer. I am wearing a suit, dressed for television. It is seven months since Tina has vanished, and I am in her home to interview her apparently grief-stricken husband, Richard.

I know Tina's home was searched by gardaí five months before I entered it, and no trace of her has been found. A team of over a dozen officers spent 12 hours scouring the property for any trace of Tina. That's why I feel confident enough to sit in the house with Richard. This isn't a crime scene, I think, believing gardaí have combed every inch of the house.

Richard makes an appeal for Tina to come home. I probe him for more information. He doesn't believe anyone has hurt her, he tells me. Nor does he believe she's taken her own life. 'She's too much in love with herself to harm herself' are the words he speaks on camera. That's a very strange thing to say, I think to myself. But then again, much of the two hours I spend in the house with Richard is strange.

There are four of us crammed into the front room of 3 Grattan Street in Youghal – Richard and me, and RTÉ camerawoman Shirley Bradshaw and producer Kevin Burns. It is a very tight space in which to film an interview, made more difficult by the parrot cage taking up room in a corner by the front window. Valentine, a green-feathered, yellow-headed bird, stares back at me as I observe the layers of parrot poo stuck to the bars of the cage.

I can smell dog faeces. The couple's two dogs, Ruby and Heidi, are in a different room as we film the interview with Richard, but it seems one or both have left their dirty presence around the house for quite some time. That ever-present smell is married with a distinct scent of underarm odour. Richard is sweating.

The combination of an intense amount of dust and the various smells makes it very unpleasant being in the house. But we are guests, and Richard is facilitating us by doing an interview in the home from which Tina vanished. This is an exclusive – no one else has filmed inside the Satchwell home – and I've been chasing this interview for months.

I have one arm resting on a colourful cushion, which I guess Tina had chosen. It is cream with purple dots, and it brightens the dark couch where Richard and I now sit, our knees occasionally touching due to the cramped conditions in the room.

As I unknowingly sit so close to Tina's secret grave on this November night in 2017, I am looking for answers, when all the while the answers are within this house. But when it was searched five months ago, not a trace of anything suspicious was found. I am in the house because I believe it's the one place Tina definitely is not, but I am so wrong.

Tina Satchwell née Dingivan never left her home. She never fled with two suitcases and a bundle of cash, as her husband is about to claim when we begin our interview.

She never met with harm from a random attacker or serial killer. The truth is much simpler, and extremely harrowing, but it will take another six years after my visit to this house for the actual horror of Tina's secret grave to be revealed.

1.

Car Boot Sundays

Richard and Tina Satchwell rise early on Sunday, 19 March 2017. Today is 'car boot Sunday' so they need to get going. For years the couple have travelled across County Cork each weekend to car boot sales – both buying and selling goods. Richard lays out plastic sheeting beside their parked car and displays trinkets and clothes that the couple sell for cash. While Richard works at the makeshift stall, Tina walks the lines of other parked cars searching for bargains. She has always had an eye for fashion and rarely wears the same outfit twice. She is always looking for eye-catching clothes, and car boot sales are the perfect location to find jewellery and worn-once shoes and garments for a fraction of high-street prices. Richard likes to sell the clothes that Tina is finished wearing. He likes to haggle, and he likes to make money.

The car boot sales take place at GAA grounds or other large venues throughout the county. The earlier you get to a venue, the best position you get for selling your wares. The car boot sale this Sunday is in Carrigtwohill, half an hour's drive west from Youghal along the N25. The couple often travelled to the Carrigtwohill monthly event when they lived in Fermoy. Now that they are living in Youghal in the east of County Cork, the trips to most of their usual car boot sale events are longer, but they rarely miss any.

Richard goes downstairs and boils the kettle in the galley kitchen, which has been added onto the old house at 3 Grattan Street in Youghal. When they bought the house it was a dilapidated three-storey semi-detached home, a stone's throw from the water's edge. Ever industrious, Richard and Tina had converted the top floor into two rooms – one for the sunbed that Tina used and the other for Tina's impressive collection of bags and shoes. Much of the rest of the house was still a 'work in progress', but Richard was tipping away at the renovations himself. He had timber to refit the stairs and was already putting in new plasterboard.

The couple have been living in Youghal for 10 months, having sold their old house in Fermoy, where Tina was originally from and where her extended family lived. Richard is originally from Coalville in Leicester in the English midlands. His family are still there, but he hasn't been in any real contact with them for a long time now. He likes it just being himself and Tina. By moving to Youghal, the couple have become more isolated. Tina had told family members not to visit while the house was being done up, but she had travelled to visit them instead in Fermoy. Family members noticed that Richard was always with Tina: he drove her to Fermoy and back, and he stayed in her company all the time she was visiting.

Although they've been in Youghal since May 2016, nobody in the town really knows the couple very well. Some locals will later say they remembered Tina as a striking-looking blonde woman but hadn't ever really spoken with her. Staff at the local swimming pool know Tina in passing. She loves to swim – it was something she had done in Fermoy, and she has continued her passion in Youghal.

Richard always brought Tina to the pool, but he never went inside. He'd walk the dogs and then wait for Tina and drive them home to Grattan Street. It was just one of their many routines. Tina had once been able to drive – she had a provisional licence when they lived in England – but now Richard does all the driving.

Richard prepares two small flasks of coffee and one large flask of tea. He makes toast with blackcurrant jam and wakes Tina at around 6.45 a.m. Tina applies day creams to her face and puts on a pink jumper and brown jeggings with brown boots. She usually doesn't wear make-up when going to car boot sales.

The couple take their chihuahua, Ruby, with them. Ruby is Tina's adored pet, bought as a pup two years ago from Sara Dobson – another car boot sale attendee. Sara's chihuahua had given birth to a four-dog litter that included Ruby. Sara knew Tina would give Ruby a good home and was happy to sell her to the couple. On the day they bought Ruby, Richard haggled over the price and got a few euro knocked off.

Sara got to know Tina from occasional walks together at the car boot sales. 'She was really bubbly, and a lovely and excited person,' Sara later tells me. 'She loved handbags, just like me. She was constantly going on about animals and pets. She was a laugh. We always had a laugh.'

Sara had serious concerns about Tina's relationship with Richard. 'If I'd ask if she would walk around the car boot sales, she would ask him, and if he said no, she was staying there at the stall. Many a time she'd only look at him and she'd stay there. She didn't even ask him. It was certain looks he used to give her that she'd stop speaking. You knew there was something there. Twice I saw him grab her arm and twist it, and she was trying to pull away. I don't know what was the cause of it, or whether they were arguing, but it wasn't pleasant to see. And he was obviously hurting her. I later asked her if she was okay, and she just had her head down saying she was fine.'

Sara tried to raise her concerns directly with Tina. 'When we used to walk around I asked how she was and how was it with her and Richard. She used to always say, "I love him, I'd never be without him." That was her answer every single time. There was definitely controlling going on.'

Sara's late father, Chris, told her of witnessing one distressing incident at a car boot sale. 'My dad told me Richard was after grabbing Tina and was roaring into her face, and my dad did tell him "get your hands off her". And Richard said to him they were just having a disagreement. Next time I met her I asked her about it – "Oh, it was nothing, we were only messing" is what she said to me.'

Richard and Tina don't have any children. The couple have been married since 1989, tying the knot at a registry office at Chadderton near Oldham on Tina's twentieth birthday. Richard is five years older than Tina. Down the years they've filled their home with animals – parrots and dogs. They'd both doted on a yellow-headed Amazon parrot named Pearl, but she had died in January 2017, leaving the couple brokenhearted. They'd even arranged for an autopsy to be performed to discover the cause of death, which was later attributed to flu. A month later they got another similar parrot, driving to Portarlington in County Laois to buy her on Valentine's Day, so they called her Valentine. They also have a Jack Russell, a rescue dog named Heidi.

Tina and Richard have also spent considerable time and money in recent years trying to buy distinctive small monkeys known as marmosets. These monkeys are native to South America and about nine inches tall, with large eyes and fluffy fur. The couple have been in contact with a website that promises they will be the proud owners of two monkeys named Terry and Thelma, once all necessary costs and paperwork are covered. Richard and Tina have already sent several thousand euro across the world to the 'monkey organisation' but it is increasingly dawning on the couple that the whole thing seems to be a scam and the monkeys may never materialise.

―――

As they head for Carrigtwohill this Sunday morning, the couple leave Heidi in the living room and Tina carries Ruby out the front door in her chihuahua carrier, which matches Tina's Juicy Couture handbag. They walk directly across the road to where their silver 2005 Nissan Primera is parked. The couple pay €40 per annum for a local parking permit. The spot directly across from their house is usually free on this one-way street. The Primera has distinctive ten-spoke alloy wheels. Tina gets into the front passenger seat. Today will be her last journey, her last social outing. Tomorrow she will be dead.

Mary Tina Dingivan was born on the last day of November 1971 at St Patrick's Hospital in Fermoy. She came from a large family that lived in an old council house at St Bernard's Place on the northside of town. Tina was a kind child, remembered fondly by her primary school teacher Olive Corcoran as someone who wouldn't hurt a fly.

'Tina was a lovely, quiet, gentle child,' Olive tells me. 'I taught her at the Presentation Convent school. She was always well dressed, well turned out coming to school. Tina was more creative than academic, she'd be into art. Tina was just a lovely human being. I remember once we went to the town park on an outing and the children would have jam jars to collect things. Tina had a butterfly on her arm. I said to put it in her jar and bring it back to school and put it on the nature table. She looked at me and said, "No, I won't, wouldn't it be dead by the time we got to the school?" and she set it free. Tina was like a butterfly herself, really.'

Tina was brought up believing her mother was Florence

Dingivan, but in fact Florence was her grandmother, and her birth mother was Mary, who she had believed was her older sister. Tina found out the truth when it came time to make her confirmation and she went looking for her birth certificate. Tina remained very close to Florence right up to her grandmother's death in 1997. Florence was originally from England, and when she decided to move back there in 1989, Tina, then aged 17, followed her grandmother to Coalville, an old mining town a few miles north of Leicester.

Coalville got its name from its greatest product – for decades the coal mines were the lifeblood of the town. Richard William Satchwell was born at a time of great optimism in England, coming into the world on 21 June 1966, a month before the country won the soccer World Cup by defeating West Germany 4–2 at London's Wembley Stadium. Richard's family were one of the old families of Coalville, living on Hermitage Road on the northside of town close to the railway tracks. He had four sisters and three brothers. Richard's father, John, was a qualified teacher but also worked in the mines, which provided much of the post-war employment in the area. John's initial job was driving a large excavator; he eventually rose to the position of quarry manager. Richard's mother, Barbara, taught all her children to be self-sufficient: they were able to bake and cook for themselves. John ensured his children knew about machinery, could change tyres and fix mechanical faults in cars. Richard became a jack of all trades and master of none. He was 22 when he first set eyes on Tina Dingivan.

In my first interview with Richard, his face lights up as he describes making a life decision before he'd even spoken to Tina. The date he first spotted her is etched on his mind – 3 March 1989, a Friday. As soon as he saw her, he says, he told his brother he was going to marry her.

With her distinctive Cork accent and long brown curly hair, Tina was a unique presence in Coalville. The story Richard tells me is that he was overweight when he first met Tina, and they were friends before the relationship changed over a period of months. When Tina moved back to Ireland later that summer – in mid-June 1989, Richard followed her over, and he never left her side for many years thereafter. It is a story either of romantic pursuit or a smothering presence.

Nothing much of national note normally took place in Richard's hometown of Coalville, but in August 1994 a local woman contacted police about something that had been niggling at her. The woman was concerned that the body of her missing neighbour Jean Crowie – last seen 16 years previously – might actually be buried in the back garden of the Crowie home on Highfield Street, where Jean's husband, William, still lived. The witness told police she had been watching television reports about the recent discovery – beneath farmland, and the back garden and cellar of a house – of bodies of women and girls murdered by married couple Fred and Rose West in another part of England over a twenty-year period. Although there was no link to those horrific crimes, the woman in Coalville had been reminded of her neighbour who vanished long ago.

Jean Crowie had never been formally reported missing. When she disappeared, in June 1978, her husband told his children their mother had deserted the family home, leaving a note saying she wouldn't be back. But now in 1994, amid more heightened awareness of bodies being buried beneath houses or in back gardens of homes, the woman who came forward said that on the day Jean had vanished she had observed William Crowie digging a large hole in his back garden. Police dutifully followed up on this new lead and within days of beginning a search of the back garden they found Jean Crowie's body, with the rope used to strangle her still wrapped around her neck. The case received significant publicity in the British media, especially when William Crowie was later convicted of manslaughter rather than murder and was only given a five-year prison sentence. William Crowie said the killing had been a spur of the moment event, that he had been digging in the back garden when Jean came out to continue an argument they had been having. He happened to have a rope in his hands at the time and ended up throttling Jean during the row. After burying her in the back garden William had stayed living at the property, taking in a new partner.

The Crowie case – the most newsworthy event to befall Coalville – showed it was possible to kill your spouse, bury them within the confines of your property, keep them hidden for years and then get a lenient sentence for manslaughter rather than murder. Richard Satchwell was an avid consumer of news. Whether he followed this story from his hometown is not known, but the case of Jean Crowie was very much in my mind when Richard Satchwell's legal team would later ask a jury to consider whether his killing of Tina was possibly self-defence or manslaughter rather than murder.

In the early 1990s Richard and Tina were back and forth between Ireland and England as the couple sought work and figured out their future life together. Tina had never been in a relationship before. Richard had had one previous sexual encounter, but it hadn't been a long-term relationship. Richard and Tina moved in together and for a short time rented a home at Bunyan Close in Oldham, near Manchester. Richard would later say his family didn't approve of his relationship with Tina so staying in Coalville wasn't going to be an option, and that is why they moved a hundred miles north. Bunyan Close was a mixture of small flat complexes and terraced houses, with a local convenience store and a chipper. When the couple travelled between Cork and Oldham they always took the ferry because it was cheaper and Tina had a fear of flying. Richard got to know the extended Dingivan family in Fermoy. With his distinct English accent he stood out in County Cork, but that didn't matter to him. In 1991, on a visit to Youghal, Richard proposed to Tina as they stood on a hill and looked out over the bay. Tina said yes and the couple made plans to get married in England. With Florence living there, and other members of the family living in Derby, decisions still needed to be made about where the couple were going to settle down.

Chadderton Town Hall sits on a busy corner. Just a mile from Oldham, the old, impressive two-storey building houses offices for the local member of parliament as well as a number of function rooms. On 30 November 1991 it was the location of the marriage of Richard Satchwell and Tina Dingivan. Florence was one of two guests at the wedding, along with a friend of Tina's. None of Richard's family attended. Richard's profession on the marriage paperwork was listed as welder/fitter. No profession was listed for Tina. The creative abilities she had shown in school were not being used for work purposes. Tina had just turned 20, and she was being stifled. Her whole world for the previous two and a half years had been occupied by Richard, who smothered her with gifts and love. In advance of their wedding day he had even given her a puppy.

The married couple soon left England and settled back in Ireland. For a time they rented a flat at Bridge Street in Cork city, then another flat at Kent Street in Fermoy. They then lived in a semi-detached house at Liam McGearailt Place in Fermoy. The house was at the end of a row with a grass space to one side. Richard and Tina were a familiar sight in the locality, always together, always walking a dog. Tina's old schoolteacher Olive Corcoran often met the couple, but Richard never spoke to her. 'The one thing Tina and myself had in common as adults was fashion. She'd be beautifully turned out. I never met Tina on her own. The husband always stood beside her. Tina never stayed talking for long. Richard would put out his foot which meant they were going. One time I invited them over to a coffee shop but Richard put out the foot again and said, "We're in a hurry," and Tina scuttled off after him. And I thought that wasn't right. Maybe I'm wrong, but to me that was coercive control in play there, and I didn't like it.'

Over the many years they lived in Fermoy, Richard's strange behaviour would become more evident. In 2015 he was given an antisocial behaviour order (ASBO) after a complaint was made that he was persistently shouting obscenities at a woman in Fermoy. The order meant that if he continued with such behaviour he could be sent to jail. He stopped verbally abusing the woman. But the ASBO wasn't his first time coming to the attention of gardaí. Between 1999 and 2004 he had racked up 14 criminal convictions, all in Ireland. Half were road traffic offences, but he'd also been caught for stealing, using a false tax disc and social welfare fraud.

In the wake of the ASBO, Richard and Tina moved to Youghal, selling one home in Fermoy to buy another at Grattan Street in Youghal. The way Richard told me the story, it was a romantic move to a location which held a special place in their hearts. Approaching their 25th wedding anniversary, they were moving to the town where they had got engaged all those years before. But Sara Dobson tells me that at one car boot sale Tina had confided in her that she didn't want to move to Youghal. 'She had family in Fermoy. If she moved to Youghal she didn't know anybody there.'

CAR BOOT SUNDAYS

In May 2016, having spent close to 20 years in Fermoy, the couple moved into 3 Grattan Street, Youghal. Not one family member or friend visited them at their new home in the 10 months before Tina vanished. The two social outlets Tina had were the visits to the local swimming pool – when she would be driven by Richard – and the trips to car boot sales – where she would also be driven by Richard.

———

As Tina travels in the car with Richard to the car boot sale in Carrigtwohill this last Sunday of her life, it is a particularly poignant time. The following day, 20 March 2017, will be the 20th anniversary of her grandmother Florence's passing. Tina was heartbroken when Florence died.

It is already getting busy when Richard and Tina arrive at Carrigtwohill GAA club and set up a stall in the third line of cars in the field. A short distance across the road is the local garda station. It will be another four years before a cold-case review of Tina's disappearance will discreetly get underway in that building.

Here, in the field at Carrigtwohill, Tina has her last interactions with people other than Richard. Those who encounter Tina this day will remember her, saying how she was always chatty, always interested in distinctive clothes people were wearing or selling. People remember Tina as glamorous and colourful.

Tina sits in the front passenger seat of the parked car with the door open, saying hello to passersby, as Richard works the stall at the boot of the car. Tina files her nails and then goes looking at what is on offer around the field. Richard later tells gardaí Tina bought a small make-up set and a mini hair-dryer that, when folded over, was smaller than your fist.

One fellow stallholder, John Keohane, chats with Tina about a beautiful jacket she is wearing. Tina is very proud of her look. John jokes that Tina must be meeting someone that night. Tina tells John, 'I have one man, one man only, and I love him so much.' She also says she'd never do anything to hurt Richard. The phrasing is strikingly similar to what she has said to Sara Dobson on other occasions. It is like a mantra Tina has adopted over time. Or, if she is trapped in a controlling relationship, has she been instructed by Richard to express love for him when in public?

Just before 1.40 p.m. the couple pack up the car and head home. They arrive at Grattan Street half an hour later and go inside. Tina will never leave the house alive again.

―――

Richard expands on various stories after Tina's disappearance. He will initially tell gardaí that on the journey home to Youghal the couple discussed ordinary things, like whether to get food from the Roma Grill or Apache Pizza for dinner. Later, when Tina's body is recovered and Richard is arrested for a second time, he will claim Tina attacked him on the journey home, knocking his glasses off. He will tell detectives a story of being assaulted by Tina on many occasions, but ultimately decline the opportunity to give such direct evidence at his own murder trial.

At around 6 p.m. that Sunday, 19 March 2017, Richard leaves the house to go to Apache Pizza. There is a special meal-deal offer of two pizzas, drinks and a side for €22. He buys a Cajun chicken pizza and another with chicken, mushrooms and sweetcorn, along with chips, a garlic dip and two Cokes. He brings the food home. Richard will later say that he and Tina sat in the front room and ate the Cajun pizza and that he put the other pizza in the fridge to have the next day. He will claim he ran a bath for Tina at 9 p.m., one of their nightly rituals.

The next time Richard leaves the house is 11 o'clock the following morning when, shortly after killing his wife, he goes to the post office with the two dogs to collect the couple's dole money. With Tina lying dead on the floor of their home, Richard's elaborate cover-up has already begun.

2.

Where, When, How

Only Richard Satchwell really knows where, when and how he killed Tina. When her body is located in October 2023, and Richard is under arrest and in an interview room at Cobh garda station, he says she died on top of him in the hallway of their home on the morning of 20 March 2017. His story is that Tina flew at him with a chisel and was trying to stab him, and that he fell backwards onto the ground. He claims Tina continued trying to hit him with the chisel in her right hand and that he used the belt from the dressing gown Tina was wearing to hold her off. He says he used his outstretched arms to hold the belt at the front of her neck as she flailed above him. He maintains Tina's death occurred as he tried to protect himself.

Ultimately a jury will not believe his story of self-defence. Nor will they believe the crime was one of manslaughter. The jury of seven women and five men form a unanimous view, having heard all the evidence in the case, that Tina's death was murder.

But while the crime of murder is proven, the precise details of the crime are never established. We will never know if Tina was strangled manually or with a ligature. We don't know if she was suffocated. We don't know if she was struck on the head with an object, or was pushed and hit her head, suffering a fatal injury. It's less likely Tina was stabbed because no blood was found at the house when the property was subjected to a special chemical test during a garda search three months after Tina disappeared.

———

When Tina's body is examined in late October 2023 by Assistant State Pathologist Dr Margot Bolster, she is unable to establish a cause of death, but she can determine that Tina's hyoid bone has not been damaged. The hyoid bone supports the tongue and is known as 'the floating bone'. It is the only bone in the human body not connected to any others, instead being attached to ligaments, muscle and cartilage. The bone is very fragile but is usually only damaged during manual strangulation. It doesn't always fracture during such attacks but is more likely than not to be damaged when thumbs are pressed violently against it when a person is strangled. The hyoid bone is less likely to fracture during ligature strangulation, as the pressure on a victim's neck with something like a belt or a rope is not focused primarily on the hyoid. All that can be deduced from the fact that Tina's hyoid was intact is that, if strangulation was the cause of death, it was perhaps more likely a ligature was used.

By the time Tina's body is examined at Cork University Hospital – six and a half years after her death – some of her body has become skeletonised. Many of her ribs are visible where skin has disappeared. All her vital organs – her heart, lungs, brain, liver and kidneys – have dissolved and decomposed. By successfully hiding Tina's body for so long, Richard Satchwell has ensured the cause of her death will never be established by science.

One thing that can be determined is that Tina has no fractures to any of her bones. Almost all of Tina's bones are present, except for some toe bones that have disintegrated as her body lay beneath the concrete of her home. She has no fractures to her arms, legs or ribs, and her skull – although detached from the rest of her body due to decomposition – shows no signs of violent trauma. If Tina was struck, to stun her during the lead-up to an attack or during the course of an attack, it is not possible to establish this. Also, her finger bones show no sign of fracture. If she tried to defend herself from any attack there is no evidence of this.

Richard's only account of Tina's death claims she died in the hallway of their home, but detectives have long considered if she might have died in another part of the house. Was she killed in one of the bedrooms upstairs or in the bathroom? Richard is a strong man and over six feet tall. Tina was petite, about 5 feet 4 inches. If he murdered Tina in one of the upstairs rooms, Richard could have carried her body downstairs afterwards. When her body was found, the belt of her dressing gown was in a strange position, wrapped tightly around her upper body. It extended over the left side of Tina's neck and under her right shoulder and arm and was knotted at the front of her chest. This might suggest the belt was used to help drag Tina's body some distance, which could also fit in with Richard's account of dragging his wife's body at various times over a number of days. He said he brought her body out to the back garden and put her in a chest freezer for a number of days, then later dragged her back into the kitchen, and then into the hallway, before burying her under the stairs.

So much of the narrative of what happened to Tina has been given by the killer, but he has given different stories at different times, and trying to distinguish truth from fiction is impossible. Long before Tina's body was found, and when I interviewed Richard in the front sitting room of the house in November 2017, he said when Tina came downstairs on the morning she disappeared he was doing plastering work at the bottom of the stairs. But Richard later told gardaí that when Tina woke up that morning he was out the back working on plumbing in an outside sink. Which story is true, or is either one true?

Richard's web of lies contains multiple conflicting stories. Soon after Tina disappears he is telling various people different stories, different accounts. He doesn't have just one false narrative, he has a few. Within a week of murdering his wife he tells gardaí she had left their home and taken €26,000 in cash with her, but he is separately telling people at a car boot sale that Tina has gone to England at short notice as she had become very sick due to damp in the walls of their home.

The one thing that is certain is that Richard killed Tina at

3 Grattan Street sometime after the couple returned from the car boot sale at Carrigtwohill. The most commonly considered scenario is that the killing happened the next morning – that's what Richard says in his only account of Tina's death, which he gives to gardaí after her body is found. It's possible Richard murdered Tina on the Sunday afternoon or evening, but he says the altercation that led to her death happened on the Monday morning. But based on all his lies, how can he possibly be believed?

———

On the morning of Monday, 20 March, as Tina lies dead close to him in the house, Richard composes a text and an email, both of which are designed to cover his tracks. The two messages relate to monkeys and suggest Tina was going to leave Richard because of the failure to acquire Terry and Thelma, the marmoset monkeys.

At 10.42 a.m. that Monday he sends an email to an entity calling itself an international monkey rescue organisation, saying, 'I've put an awful lot of work into this and my wife is saying she will leave me over this.' Over previous weeks and months Richard has indeed sent several thousand euro to international bank accounts at the behest of an organisation which claimed it could provide him with the two monkeys. Richard has slowly come to realise he has likely been scammed. Now he's going to use that scam to try and pull the wool over the eyes of gardaí.

Four minutes after sending the email, Richard sends a text

to his designated contact with the so-called monkey rescue organisation. Richard knows this man only as Mr James, and the text reads: 'I am in a mess right now because my wife has said she is leaving me over this so please let the organisation know.'

In very close proximity to the time of the killing, Richard is being clever and conniving, beginning the big lie that Tina had simply left the marital home, abandoning him, walking out on their marriage. The text message is only located during the garda investigation in October 2023, when specialist software is used to access Richard's Samsung phone, while the email is discovered on a laptop during the cold-case review in late 2021. Both messages indicate a depth to Richard's cunning and premeditation. He never directs gardaí to find either message, never tells them they are there. Detectives find the messages themselves.

Next on his list for the cover-up is a trip to the post office. At 11.12 a.m., and with Tina dead on the floor, Richard takes Ruby and Heidi to collect both his and Tina's dole. Richard has Tina listed as a 'dependent adult' with the Department of Social Protection, so he is permitted to collect her dole money as well as his own. Just like Richard makes the tea and Richard does the driving, Richard collects the dole. The claiming of Tina's social welfare payment on this day implied she was still alive and well.

Richard is acting normal, walking the two-minute journey to the post office, arriving at 11.14 a.m. CCTV captures the entire two-minute visit to the post office. Richard is wearing a multicoloured jumper and walks inside the premises with the two dogs. Only years later, after Tina's body is found, will Richard tell gardaí he 'got out of dirty clothes to look normal before going to the post office'.

On the footage Richard walks to the postal counter nearest the camera and the top of his head is visible for a few moments. He then leaves with the dole money. A woman who stood behind him in the queue has by now gone to the next counter, so Richard has to walk around her to exit the building.

There is nothing out of the ordinary in his body language, in his gait, in his interaction at the post office. Having collected Tina's dole money would later help Richard spin the yarn that she was still alive and that when he returned to the house she asked him to go to Dungarvan for some shopping.

In reality, Tina was dead, dressed in blue-and-red tartan-square pyjamas and a lilac dressing gown, her body lying on the living-room floor. Richard would ultimately say that on the morning of the killing, and after he returned from the post office, he had sat with Tina's body and pulled her into his arms.

So much mystery remains about what transpired within the walls of 3 Grattan Street in the hours, weeks, months and years after Richard killed his wife. The only narrative is Richard's, and that narrative changed often, but some truths were eventually established by gardaí.

———

During the cold-case review in 2021, newly appointed incident-room co-ordinator Detective Garda Dave Kelleher discovered a Gmail address, richard.richardsatchwell.satch@gmail.com, attached to the phone Richard had carried in March 2017. Richard had another email address – rickiesat@live.ie – which he normally used, including for his subsequent email contact with me, but the discovery of his Gmail address would prove particularly important to the garda cold-case review. Detective Kelleher found that at some stage Richard had – perhaps unwittingly – consented to Google's recording the phone's location whenever the Gmail account was active on the device. The detective went to Google's dedicated law enforcement portal to learn more, and found there were 25,000 GPS co-ordinates in the phone attached to the Gmail address.

The discovery was a huge boost to the cold-case investigation. The phone was like a digital diary, showing where the handset – and by extension Richard – had been at specific moments in the week he said Tina had simply left home and gone missing. Richard Satchwell told lie after lie, weaving different narratives at different times, all designed to continue the one big lie – that Tina had left of her own accord – but his own phone would help unravel truth from fiction.

Google's GPS tracker indicated that after returning from the post office to 3 Grattan Street on Monday, 20 March 2017, Richard remained in the house with Tina's body from 11.20 a.m. until 12.49 p.m. He then drove to Aldi in Dungarvan, stopping along the way at Grange Church, arriving there at 1.08 p.m. Richard maintained for the six years from 2017 until 2023 that he stopped at the church to light a candle at Tina's request for her grandmother Florence, to mark the 20th anniversary of her death. He said he also lit a candle for Pearl the parrot, who had died just months before Tina vanished. Richard was able to provide the extra information that there was a push-button switch to light the candles rather than a flame. Such trivial factual details were important to a man trying to convince people of a narrative. 'It was a push-button memorial candle stand' – truth; 'I lit a candle for Florence as Tina had asked me' – lie. It was only after Tina's body was found that Richard told detectives that he actually stopped at the church that day to light a candle for Tina, having killed her in their home earlier that day.

―――

Richard continues on to Aldi from the church, arriving in Dungarvan at 1.20 p.m. For years Richard would say that he went to Dungarvan because there was no Aldi supermarket in Youghal at the time, and Tina loved the cod and haddock from Aldi. He would say that, on that fateful day, he bought tins of sardines and some packets of cod and that he also got birdseed from a pet shop in Dungarvan. He would maintain that he arrived home to Youghal at around midday or 12.15 p.m. In fact his phone's digital diary indicated that he didn't arrive home to Grattan Street until 2.47 p.m. In the meantime he had returned to Youghal, but he drove to the strand overlooking the sea and spent 40 minutes there, from 2 p.m. until 2.40 p.m. After his arrest Richard would say he drove there to try and think. That location had been a favourite spot of Tina's – it was where he'd proposed all those years before.

From very early on in the investigation gardaí have the CCTV from Aldi in Dungarvan. Garda Seán Killigrew obtains the footage, which is then viewed by officers on many occasions. The camera doesn't lie: Richard enters Aldi at 1.20 p.m. – you see him coming into the store and, given the way the camera is positioned, you see a less clear image of him leaving less than two minutes later. If he had indeed purchased cod and sardines, it was a very quick purchase. But based on the CCTV imagery Richard didn't appear to be carrying such items: he seemed to just have a bottle in his hand. Officers ponder what such inaccurate information from Richard, about buying fish, could mean. Also the timings are off. For six years Richard maintained he had been to Aldi and returned to Youghal much earlier in the day than the CCTV footage clearly showed. Gardaí wondered what this might actually mean.

———

Richard has a phrase – it is like a mantra that he says to me on multiple occasions – 'we would always have ...' Several times when I ask Richard a specific question about what he did on 19 or 20 March 2017, he begins his answer with 'we would always have ...' This allows him to be vague in his response, not answering the question directly but keeping to the generalities of routine – taking a little bit of information from one past experience and marrying it with a different experience to create a third, and false, experience.

It was true to say he drove to Aldi in Dungarvan on the day Tina disappeared. It was true to say Tina loved the fish in Aldi – sure, hadn't he made such a trip many times before for her – and this was one of the main reasons he might make a journey to Dungarvan. Only Richard knew it was incorrect to say Tina had asked him to go to Dungarvan at all that day. His journey to the Waterford town was simply so he could arrive back at the house and 'discover' that, while he was away doing the shopping she'd 'asked him to get', Tina had 'upped and left'.

On the day Tina is murdered her phone receives a text message from the Medina Medical GP centre in Fermoy. The message is actually for Richard, to remind him of an upcoming doctor's appointment that coming Friday. The office had tried to contact Richard, but when they couldn't reach him they sent a text to Tina's phone instead. Very few people had Tina's mobile phone number. Richard is planning to create a story that Tina has left home without her keys and phone. It is natural that he'll be asked by her family if he checked her phone for clues to her disappearance. He sees the text reminder for his doctor's appointment later in week. It is still only Monday, and Richard needs to think. Where is he going to hide Tina's body? And if he goes to the doctor on Friday in Fermoy, won't he have to check with Tina's family to ask if they had seen her? To fail to do so would look suspicious. If he keeps the appointment with his doctor, Richard now has until Friday to create a false narrative in his mind, one he can repeat to family and gardaí.

After returning to the house at 2.47 p.m. that Monday, Richard remains in the property with Tina's body until the following morning, when he leaves the house for a short walk, spending nine minutes walking close to Grattan Street between 9.32 a.m. and 9.41 a.m. Perhaps he needs fresh air; perhaps he needs to get away from Tina's body for a few minutes, unable to accept what he has done.

Richard will ultimately state that he lay beside Tina's body on the first night after he murdered her. He will claim that on Tuesday morning – the day after he killed her – he lifted her up onto the couch. This is the same couch on which I will sit with Richard eight months later, conducting a lengthy television interview.

Richard does not leave the property again that Tuesday after returning at 9.41 a.m., and he does not leave the house at all the following day. He will later say he cried continuously, and the two dogs licked his tears. The dogs are also sniffing and licking Tina's body and Richard is finding the situation very distressing. On the Thursday Richard leaves the house for only six minutes, walking to the post office just after 2.30 p.m. and arriving back home before 2.40 p.m.

At some stage, he takes Tina's body from the couch and puts her in the chest freezer in the shed. The couple had brought the chest freezer from Fermoy but never plugged it in in Youghal. The way the kitchen extension is built, it is impossible for anyone in nearby properties to see the pathway between the kitchen and the back shed. Richard has complete freedom to carry or drag Tina's body around their property. Richard will ultimately tell gardaí: 'I laid her in the freezer … Away from the dogs … The dogs kept going over to her … I was robotic, working on automatic … Freezer was in the shed outside … Took her from the couch … She was heavy … Like trying to lift a ten-tonne bag of coal … Freezer was middle sized … It was horrible, she just slipped in.'

On Friday, 24 March, Richard leaves 3 Grattan Street for a significant journey to Fermoy. He is planning to keep the doctor's appointment, and he is going to visit family and gardaí too. He is going to say how he had returned from Dungarvan the previous Monday and Tina was gone, that she had left her house keys, she hadn't taken her phone and she hadn't left a note. Richard will say he thought she had gone back to Fermoy.

3.

Fermoy

Just after 4 p.m. on Friday afternoon, while Tina's body lies inside the chest freezer in Youghal, Richard arrives at Medina Medical on the southside of the river Blackwater in Fermoy for his appointment to get the results of a blood test monitoring his long-standing high cholesterol. He knows it may be unavoidable to talk about Tina. He and Tina almost always attend the GP in Fermoy together – they have been doing it for decades. Richard has a plan: he is going to say Tina left him – she had 'upped and left', as he will put it. She hasn't taken her phone or her keys, but she is gone from Youghal. Richard will say he felt she had left to get 'her head straight'. She'd been 'a bit upset of late', he will claim.

Richard leaves the GP practice 40 minutes later, having been told he has a Vitamin B deficiency, and having told the doctor that Tina has left him. He goes to Tina's original family home at St Bernard's Place on the northside of town, where her uncle Frank Dingivan still lives. This is Richard's first interaction with Tina's family since he murdered her four days before. With Tina lying dead in Youghal, Richard asks Frank if he has seen his wife in recent days. Frank says he hasn't. They had all last seen each other over a month ago, when Richard and Tina had dropped in to see Frank as they returned from Portarlington with their new parrot, Valentine.

Up until Tina was almost a teenager she believed Frank was her brother. But shortly before Tina made her confirmation she discovered that Frank's mother, Florence, was not in fact her mother, but her grandmother, and Mary – Frank's sister – was actually Tina's mother. Tina has a sister, Lorraine, and a brother, Shane. Another brother, Tom, had tragically died in 2012. Mary still lives in Fermoy, as do many other family members.

Richard is now trying to position Fermoy as the focus of future enquiries about Tina's whereabouts. This is Tina's hometown. This is where he and she had lived for over 20 years. This is where Tina has friends, though not close friends, as Richard didn't like Tina having those. He always believed he was enough for her. But Tina knows people in Fermoy, and it is natural that, if she had indeed left Youghal – where she didn't know anybody – she might have returned to Fermoy.

Richard says goodbye to Frank and drives to Tina's aunt Florence, who lives at St Mary's Crescent on the southside of Fermoy. Richard arrives there at 5.55 p.m. and asks Florence the same question he had asked Frank. Has she seen Tina? She isn't back home in Youghal, and he didn't know where she was. He has assumed she was with family in Fermoy.

When Florence tells him she hasn't seen Tina, Richard feigns surprise and upset. As he keeps up the pretence over the next six years, he will claim 'it was like having 20 tonnes of bricks fall on you' when he realised Tina wasn't in Fermoy.

Next, Richard goes to the gardaí. Forty kilometres from where he had murdered his wife, and where her body right then lay crumpled inside a chest freezer, Richard enters Fermoy garda station at O'Neill Crowley Quay, close to the main bridge in the town.

———

Richard knows his name is on file with gardaí. He has a number of criminal convictions from over a decade ago, all for non-violent crimes, and he is on the radar of some gardaí because of his odd behaviour in 2015, which resulted in the ASBO. But Richard needs to speak with gardaí, and he needs to do it before any other family members might. He needs to control the narrative.

Garda Conor Gately is on duty when Richard enters the station at 6.15 p.m. At a height of 6 feet 2 inches, Richard is an imposing figure, but he has an ability to carry himself lightly, with rounded shoulders and his head down. He approaches the public counter, saying he wants to let gardaí know that his wife has left their home. He doesn't want to report her missing, doesn't want any fuss, as she probably just wanted to get away to get her head straight. Richard tells Garda Gately that Tina has left the marital home in Youghal because of a 'deterioration in their relationship'.

Garda Gately notes that Richard is 'matter-of-fact' and 'not over emotive'. Richard behaves in the manner a spouse might if a relationship was ending and their partner had left abruptly but in a manner of their own choosing. Richard says he's not overly concerned, and while he doesn't want to report Tina as missing, he tells Garda Gately he just thought gardaí should know, as he had checked with family members and they hadn't seen Tina either. He says he last saw her the previous Monday, and she had gone when he arrived back from getting some shopping. He is calling into Fermoy station as he thought she would be in Fermoy, the town where she knows people. He and Tina have only been living in Youghal for 10 months, he tells the garda. They had lived in Fermoy for 20 years.

Richard leaves Fermoy garda station after three-quarters of an hour. He has now reported that his wife is no longer living with him in Youghal, but he hasn't filed a missing person report. He feels he has got the balance right: he has raised the fact that she is unaccounted for, but he hasn't raised the alarm to a larger degree.

Conor Gately opens up the garda PULSE computer system that records all notable interactions with members of the public. He is unable to open a missing person case as Richard has not formally reported his wife as missing. But Richard has brought something to his attention that he feels needs to be followed up on: he is stating that his wife isn't at her home address and she is unaccounted for. The garda navigates to a non-crime section on the system headlined 'Attention and Complaints' and inputs detail of his interaction with Richard, information his garda colleagues in Youghal garda station will later act upon.

Meanwhile, Richard arrives home to Grattan Street at 7.40 p.m. He has now alerted both Tina's family and gardaí that she is 'gone' from the house. By travelling 40 kilometres to Fermoy he may have diverted attention towards there rather than Youghal. Tina is still in the unplugged freezer in the back shed. Richard is tired and hasn't yet decided what to do. He needs a better hiding place, a more permanent spot. But he also has another appointment tomorrow, and he needs to make that trip so that he can keep his licence for driving large trucks. Although currently claiming the dole, Richard has plans to resume his career as a long-distance truck driver around Ireland.

That night, inside the house in Youghal, Richard picks up his laptop and at 9.08 p.m. – less than three hours after notifying gardaí that his wife has left their marital home – he does an internet search for 'quicklime'. The results bring up a YouTube video entitled 'Quicklime and Water Reaction', which Richard accesses and plays twice. The video is 90 seconds long and shows a powdery substance inside a large metal bowl, which in turn is inside a blue basin. The video illustrates the chemical reaction caused when water is added to the powder, showing the material crackling and, within 30 seconds, particles spitting out of the basin violently towards the camera. Text appears on screen advising viewers to 'always use face protection, gloves and apron'. Uses of quicklime include as an odour suppressant and to aid in the decomposition of bodies. Ultimately Richard does not acquire any quicklime. He will allow Tina's body to decompose naturally in her secret grave – once he finally gets around to burying her.

4.

Ballincollig

Richard gets up early on Saturday. His head is likely full of thoughts. When he had lifted Tina's body into the freezer a few days ago, she had fallen in heavily. Yesterday he had told gardaí Tina was gone from the house. He had spun a yarn that would buy him time.

Today is the driver's course he has had in his diary, a competency test he has to do to keep his licence as a truck driver. Richard knows he will pass with flying colours. He is an expert trucker with 20 years' experience. He already has the certificate of professional competence (CPC) card, which is due to run till 7 June 2020, but the Road Safety Authority requires drivers to do one day's training every year to keep this card valid. Richard hasn't been working recently, but now with Tina dead he will have lots of time to kill, and he wants to get back trucking.

Richard hasn't always had respect for the rules of the road. On the day after New Year's Day, 2001, he had encountered a routine garda checkpoint on the northside of Fermoy. The officer was stopping vehicles and checking for tax and insurance. Richard was caught with a doctored tax disc. He had actually cut part of a tax disc from another car that was off the road and stuck it to the out-of-date disc in his 91C car. At that time, Richard was working around Fermoy as a window fitter. He was also stealing small items from shops, petty theft, and had been caught a few times.

An eagle-eyed garda had spotted the bump on the disc, and a closer examination confirmed it was in fact fake. 'Name and address,' the garda had requested. 'Richard Satchwell, Liam McGearailt Place, Fermoy,' the softly spoken English driver of the vehicle had replied. It all led to a court appearance in Fermoy District Court at the end of November 2001, when Richard was given seven days in jail for larceny and fraudulent use of a tax disc. He was also disqualified from driving for a year. He had come up against Judge Michael Patwell in the District Court, a formidable man he would meet again two years later in the same courtroom when Richard was eventually brought to justice for being a 'dole cheat' – claiming €3,161 in benefits from October 2000 until February 2001 while also working and not declaring his income.

Richard sets off early from Grattan Street on Saturday, 25 March 2017. It is now five days since he has murdered Tina, and nobody, other than him, knows her body is in the freezer. The truck-driving competency course is on the far side of Cork city, in Ballincollig.

As he pulls the door shut at 7.40 a.m. and gets into his Nissan Primera, no one in the vicinity has any idea of the horrific scene contained within the Satchwell home. Tina's body, clothed in her pyjamas and dressing gown, barefoot and lifeless, is dumped in the couple's freezer. The murder scene is quiet, but for the occasional sounds of Valentine the parrot and the pitter-patter of Ruby's and Heidi's paws.

Richard's journey to Ballincollig takes him on the N25 west towards Cork city. This is the road he and Tina travelled less than a week before, as they attended the car boot sale in Carrigtwohill. Now Richard drives alone, just his thoughts for company.

The drive to Ballincollig takes less than an hour. He knows this part of County Cork, but he would usually be going to the Blarney car boot sale, and Tina would be with him. No more of that. Tina won't be going anymore. Richard will go to a car boot sale soon to keep up appearances and will make up an excuse when people ask where Tina is. There is one on tomorrow in Castletownroche, out past Fermoy, on the road to Mallow. That will give him an opportunity to call to more family members in Fermoy afterwards and check if Tina has been in contact with them.

———

Richard pulls into the car park of the Oriel Hotel in Ballincollig just before 8.30 a.m. He is in good time for the truck driver's competency course. He pays attention during the morning part. He is easily going to keep his CPC card, which will allow him to get working again. He has the driving skills, and now he has time to think only of himself.

During the lunch break, Richard decides against eating in the hotel. It is a comfortable location, with casual dining and a pool and gym, but he wants to get away, to walk on his own. He doesn't want to get involved in conversation with other motorists on the course. He walks into Ballincollig's main street and crosses over the road to a row of shops. Beside a menswear store he spots Drumstix Diner, which offers a good variety of fast food. You can sit in or get a takeaway. Richard sits inside the premises for half an hour and eats his lunch, alone with his thoughts, while, almost 60 kilometres away, Tina's body lies inside a freezer.

Richard goes back for the two-hour afternoon segment of the driving course and is duly marked down as having completed his required full day attendance. He says goodbye and heads back to Youghal, arriving just before 5 p.m. He pulls the front door shut. An hour after entering the house he sends a text to his father. Richard doesn't usually keep in touch with his family in Coalville in Leicestershire, but this contact is part of his web of lies. 'Hi Dad,' he texts, 'hope you are well and good. Tina left and took all our savings … Hope she gets in touch. Love, Richard.'

Richard thinks about the next day. Tomorrow is another car boot Sunday, his first without Tina. He'll go and set up a stall in Castletownroche as normal, then call to more of Tina's family in Fermoy to check if they've seen her, and then he will return home to begin digging her grave under the stairs.

5.

The Grave

When Richard and Tina moved into the tall, narrow house at 3 Grattan Street in May 2016, no one had lived there for the previous 12 years. It is an old house, close to the pier in Youghal. The foundations of the house contain the natural sand and seashells of the environment, mixed with stone. Richard will later say that, as they explored the house after moving in, it was Tina who spotted that under the stairs was compacted hard soil and sand rather than concrete.

―――

The bottom of the stairs is actually part of the dining room. When I walked into the house in November 2017 – eight months after Tina vanished – I was struck by the fact that the stairs were straight ahead of me as I entered the hallway from the front door, but that within four steps along the hallway, and before I reached the bottom step of the stairs, the room opened up to my right and I was in an open-plan dining room. It made sense that the stairs were actually part of a room, as space was so tight in the property, and the dining room was the biggest room in the house. Including the stairs, this room is less than 14 feet wide and 12 feet long.

Before he digs Tina's grave, Richard has gone, as planned, to the car boot sale in Castletownroche. He was up particularly early that Sunday morning, leaving Youghal at 5.38 a.m. and arriving at Castletownroche an hour later. Just a week prior, Tina had been with him at the car boot sale in Carrigtwohill. Now she is nowhere to be seen. Richard tells people at the car boot sale that Tina isn't well. Over the following weeks and months he will elaborate on that story, saying Tina has gone for treatment in a specialist hospital in England for a chest infection caused by damp in the walls of their home. 'No one had lived in the house for 12 years before we'd bought it, and there was damp and mould in the property,' he will say. It is one of many stories he will tell in order to account for Tina's disappearance.

After leaving the Castletownroche car boot sale at 1.10 p.m., he drives to Fermoy, stopping first at Tina's old family home at St Bernard's Place and then visiting another relative at the Meadows estate across the river on the southside of town. Everyone Richard meets that day tells him they haven't seen Tina, and he returns to St Bernard's Place, where he spends over an hour expressing his growing concern for where she might be, before returning to Youghal just after 3 p.m. He doesn't leave the house again that day. He has work to do, digging a grave.

THE GRAVE

Richard gets a shovel and begins digging out under the stairs. He digs and he digs. He brings Tina's body in from the chest freezer and lays her out on the kitchen floor. He digs a large hole, transferring much of the soil he removes to a location out the back door. He will later say his knuckles began to bleed as he dug over a period of hours. He will be unable to remember how long it took to dig the grave, just that it was bright when he started and dark when he finished.

Richard digs a hole that is almost six-foot long and three-foot wide. He digs down to a depth of 84 centimetres, or almost three feet. The base of the grave isn't level, nor are the sides even. Richard simply digs as large a hole as he can. The work is time-consuming, a lot for one person, but is made somewhat easier by the fact that the sandy soil is diggable.

Richard already has the tools for this job. He has long been doing renovations on the home, so naturally he has a shovel, and he also has cement, which he has bought from Flavins hardware store, just two doors up the street. Any sounds of digging, mixing cement or shovelling soil and stones will be natural in a house where renovation work is already underway.

———

Richard lays Tina's body out on black plastic that he normally puts on the ground at the car boot sales. Usually the large sheeting would be the base where the couple display shoes, clothes and trinkets. Now the sheeting covers Tina's body.

Within the sheeting Tina is covered by a bedsheet and

beneath that she wears her pyjamas and dressing gown. Her wallet is in the pocket of her dressing gown. Richard will later tell gardaí Tina left the house without her phone but had definitely taken her wallet.

One matter never solved is what happened to Tina's wedding ring. Richard will maintain, even during the subsequent murder trial, that the ring was in a pocket of Tina's dressing gown when he buried her. The ring is not found when her remains are recovered six and half years after. The ring is not in the dressing gown, it is not within the sheeting and it is not in the empty grave when it is completely excavated by authorities in 2023. Another small piece of jewellery – Tina's belly-button ring – is recovered from where her body lay, but her wedding ring is nowhere to be found. Detectives later wonder if Tina had removed her ring as she was planning to leave the relationship, or if Richard secretly kept the ring and hid it somewhere. In a number of interviews when he was pleading for his missing wife to return, Richard recounted how Tina chose to bury her first wedding ring with her grandmother Florence, who Richard said had never had her own wedding ring, in 1997. Richard then had to get Tina a second wedding ring, and that is the one that is never located.

Richard drags and carries Tina's body to the hole under the stairs. After the grave is discovered by gardaí many years later, Richard will tell Detective Dave Noonan that before he filled in the grave he went to the shop to buy flowers to put in with Tina. He will claim he wanted to get roses – Richard has long had a tattoo of a rose on his right arm, with Tina's name within the design, and he often refers to Tina as his 'Irish rose'. However, Sunday, 26 March 2017 was Mother's Day, and by the time he went looking for flowers there were very few to be found anywhere. He will say he got tulips instead of roses – the GPS tracking of his phone does indeed indicate a journey to Tesco in Youghal on Monday, 27 March, just after 10.50 a.m. which might substantiate this claim of buying flowers, but after so many years, no footage of this journey remains.

In his confession to Detective Noonan in October 2023, Richard claims he was seeking to be respectful in his secret burial of his wife's body. 'Tina in the plastic ... I laid her down in the hole in my arms ... I didn't drop her into the hole ... I wasn't disrespectful.' During this part of his confession Richard cries, and when handed a roll of toilet paper to use as tissue, he blows his nose loudly. He doesn't speak in full sentences, but rather a stream of thoughts. 'Sandy stuff and the next thing I remember – cement ... I was working automatically ... Blindly ... I was sat there with wet cement under me ... I heard Ruby bark ... Black plastic into the hole and then placed Tina inside ... I didn't get her dirty ... I put the wedding ring in the pocket of her robe ... Didn't buy the cement especially ... I started filling the hole and the next thing I knew I was sitting there with it done.'

Despite Richard's claims of being respectful of Tina's body, he buries her face down. She isn't lying on her back with her hands linked together as an undertaker might prepare a body for a wake and burial. Tina is put lying on her stomach, with her legs bent at the knees and pushed up towards the rest of her body. The belt of her dressing gown is wrapped around her upper body in a fashion that suggested it had been used to drag her. Richard puts a stone slab over Tina's head as he backfills the grave with some of the soil he had dug out earlier. Then he mixes some concrete and pours it on top to level off the floor.

On Tuesday, 28 March, with the concrete still wet in the house, Richard drives to Killarney, leaving Youghal at 11.10 a.m. He has already told other members of Tina's family that he is going to County Kerry to check if Tina is with an aunt who lives there. He has even asked one of Tina's nieces, Sarah Howard, if she would like to go with him to Kerry, but Sarah has texted him from Fermoy to say that she is working. Sarah was very close to Tina and is already very concerned about her missing aunt. 'I knew when Richard said that Tina was gone but she hadn't taken the dogs with her that something just wasn't right,' she later tells me.

Richard arrives home to Youghal just after 3 p.m. and texts Sarah: 'Just back from Killarney – they said they don't know anything.'

Over the following weeks Richard will exhibit strange behaviour, which Sarah will witness. She is the family member Richard is most in contact with in the aftermath of Tina's disappearance. The moment Sarah heard from other family members that Tina was missing, she had phoned Richard and he had said he and Tina had an argument and she had left home. Richard also claimed Tina had thrown a cup at him. Sarah and Tina have been very close for years, sharing a love of fashion and style. They know each other well, and Sarah has never seen Tina being violent. Sarah is deeply worried about her aunt's disappearance and over the coming weeks and months ensures she keeps in contact with Richard, seeking information.

On Friday, 31 March 2017, Richard Satchwell posts an ad on the DoneDeal website: 'Large chest freezer free to take away, working perfect just needs a clean only, giving away because I need the space.'

Less than a week after the chest freezer contained Tina's murdered body, Richard is trying to get rid of it. In a particularly callous act he also offers the chest freezer to Sarah, texting her 'Sarah do [sic] want big chest freezer?' Sarah does not respond to this text, which she finds strange for a number of reasons. With Tina missing, it's odd that Richard is finding time to think about a chest freezer. But also, he is offering it for free, and that isn't like Richard. He is a haggler, a 'Del Boy' type, who wouldn't give something away for nothing.

Once when Sarah's children had been at a car boot sale and saw items they liked at Richard's stand – nail varnish and a CD – he had charged his young relatives 50 cent each, rather than give them the goods for free.

Sometime in April or May 2017, someone comes to Grattan Street and takes away the chest freezer, oblivious that it has recently contained the body of a woman who now lies buried under concrete beneath the stairs of her home. The freezer is never located, and the new owner is never identified.

In the weeks after murdering Tina, Richard gets a new job driving a delivery truck for a tyre distributor. The work brings him on journeys well beyond County Cork, and Richard likes being out of the house. Over the following weeks he attends a number of car boot sales, selling many of Tina's items. He encounters a number of people who had come to know the couple from car boot events around County Cork. All are concerned when Richard tells them Tina is now in hospital in England and it's unlikely she'll be able to return to car boot sales again. She is being treated for a severe infection, he claims, brought about by damp in the walls in Youghal.

It is intriguing that Richard decides to tell the people at car boot sales one story about Tina, but tells her family and gardaí – and eventually members of the media – a different story entirely. Long before Tina's body is found, Richard will say he lied to the people at car boot sales as he wanted to protect Tina's privacy, and the truth of the matter was she had left home, simply walked out of the house, and if and when she returned, he hadn't wanted people to know their private business. His explanation sounded plausible, but it was simply another elaborate lie.

On 10 April, Richard texts Sarah to tell her about his new job – and to spread more lies. 'No news but I had to get a job and they needed some paperwork,' he writes. 'Discovered birth cert and marriage cert gone. Trying to keep everything ticking over until she gets in touch, don't know what else to do.'

Sarah is troubled by Richard's story and continues to ask around if anyone has seen Tina. Her concern is added to when, towards the end of April, Richard texts her to say he has won two tickets for *Purple Rain*, a musical tribute to the late musician Prince, which is due to take place at the Cork Opera House the following month. Richard wants to know if Sarah would like the tickets. It is another bizarre move by Richard. Sarah and the rest of her family are concerned about Tina, as her disappearance is completely out of character, but Richard has time to be thinking about a concert. Sarah doesn't accept the tickets, just like she hadn't accepted the chest freezer.

Throughout April 2017, Richard continues going to car boot sales and selling Tina's belongings. He tells people he needs to make money to pay for the house repairs which are needed if Tina is going to be able to return from England to live in Youghal. One car boot enthusiast, Linda Hennessy, had come to know Tina well – they would often chat about handbags. She is at a car boot sale in Rathcormac in early April and sees Richard alone at his stand. When she asks him if Tina was 'running around buying stuff', he puts his head down and says Tina is 'very sick and in hospital'. Richard elaborates that Tina had got an infection through 'dry rot', and Linda asks Richard, 'How come you didn't get it?' He looks down at the ground again. Growing more curious, Linda asks Richard if he is going over to Tina in the UK. Richard replies he would need to get passports for the two dogs.

Another regular car boot sale attendee is Julie Crowley who, along with her mother Mary, got to know Tina in late 2016 at an event in Doneraile. Tina had admired a pair of Doc Martens that Julie was wearing, and Julie had bought a River Island waistcoat from Richard and Tina. In mid-April 2017, Julie and Mary meet Richard at another car boot sale, where he says Tina has a respiratory illness and is in hospital. Richard tells the Crowleys that a doctor had told Tina she had gone to him 'just in time'. Richard says mould in their house was the problem and that Tina has told him to continue selling at events without her. Julie buys a pair of knee-length Doc Martens from Richard that have a rose pattern on them. The Crowleys encounter Richard again at a car boot sale on the May bank holiday weekend of 2017, where Julie buys a pair of tan-coloured boots for €30.

Sara Dobson, who sold Ruby to Tina and Richard, also encounters Richard at a car boot sale in the wake of Tina's disappearance. Sara has long had concerns about Tina and Richard's relationship and believes Richard is a controlling man. Sara has long felt uncomfortable in his presence. Richard tells Sara the story about Tina being sick in England.

'It was very strange,' Sara later tells me. 'He was selling Tina's things, the likes of her Juicy Couture handbags and her boots and things like that. There was no way she was ever selling her Juicy Couture bags, and he said, "Oh well, we need the money because we've got to raise that kind of money for the walls." It didn't make sense as I know she wouldn't have sold those.'

Sara also finds it strange that Tina has reportedly gone to England without Ruby. Tina dotes on the chihuahua – they are rarely apart. Now, as Sara encounters Richard at the car boot sale without Tina, Ruby is standing beside him.

'Ruby kept jumping up at me,' recalled Sara, 'and he was stood on the lead so she couldn't get away from him because he was dealing with other customers. I asked him could I take the dog for a walk around because he'd been there since six or seven in the morning. He said no, but I insisted on taking the dog anyway. I had her about an hour, took her back and the dog refused point blank to go back to him. I had to lift the dog up and physically hand her to him. And she still tried to get away from him.'

About six weeks after murdering Tina, Richard stops going to car boot sales altogether. He also begins to neglect the two dogs and the parrot. With Richard not taking the dogs out for regular walks, both Ruby and Heidi begin urinating and defecating around the house, and Richard stops cleaning the bird cage where Valentine is leaving her droppings. Richard sleeps in the same bedsheets that he and Tina had used, and he never changes them. By contrast, he does maintain some personal hygiene – this is particularly important for him because of his new job driving a truck. Richard has a public life he is trying to continue where, outwardly, he is apparently functioning, but he also has a private life where, behind closed doors, he sits on a stool inside the ever-dirtying house and talks to Tina's body beneath the stairs.

Sometime in April or May 2017, Richard builds a red-brick wall and an adjoining cubbyhole door to block up the side of under the stairs. He can still access the grave area if he wants to, but it is now covered from view as he walks around the dining room. At some point he gets under the stairs and puts down a length of old linoleum on top of the fresh concrete.

Richard is living with a secret, and he is maintaining his charade. But gardaí will shortly come knocking on his door, and Richard will soon be thrust into the glare of the media.

6.

The First Search

On Tuesday, 2 May 2017, Garda Thomas Keane knocks on the door of 3 Grattan Street. It is now just over five weeks since Richard Satchwell called to Fermoy garda station to alert officers that his wife had left the family home. Although Richard had not wanted to make a formal missing person report, Garda Conor Gately had still recorded his interaction with Richard on the PULSE computer system, under the 'Attention and Complaints' section. As good standard garda practice, Garda Keane is following up on that interaction, to see if Tina has returned to her home or has made contact with Richard or anyone else.

Garda Keane's call to the house is unexpected. Richard doesn't invite the officer inside, but instead speaks to him at the front door, telling the garda there has been no sign of Tina, no news since he called to Fermoy station on 24 March. He repeats that he has no concerns for Tina's safety and that he feels she will be home sooner rather than later.

Richard is advised that there is more gardaí could do to try and establish where Tina might be, and he is invited to make a formal missing person report and to come down to Youghal garda station to make a statement. Garda Keane departs and Richard closes the door.

Richard now changes tack. Tina isn't coming home, he knows that, but the focus is turning towards him and how he might be able to help find her. He needs to figure out what to say. Garda Keane's arrival at his front door is bringing the case in a new direction. While he had elected to call to Fermoy station five weeks before, now gardaí were calling to his front door, the door of the very house where he has buried his wife's body. He needs to divert attention again.

On Thursday, 11 May 2017, nine days after Garda Keane's call to the house, Richard formally reports Tina as a missing person. He calls to Youghal garda station and outlines to Garda James Butler how Tina had asked him to go to Aldi in Dungarvan on 20 March, and when he returned from there he discovered she was gone. She had left her keys behind – they were on the floor in the hall; and she had left her phone behind – it was on a table in the kitchen. He had checked around the house and found that two suitcases were missing. They were part of a set they had got from SuperValu with coupons some years before. He knows what they looked like, and he's certain they are gone, he tells the garda.

Furthermore, Richard claims €26,000 is missing. He says

THE FIRST SEARCH

Tina has taken cash from the house, money they had saved up from selling their old house in Fermoy, some small lottery wins and the proceeds of some sales at car boot events. Richard tells gardaí that when he saw the money was missing, 'I felt like the ground opened up beneath me'.

Richard also tells gardaí about a previous conviction in Ireland for stealing a cheque book from an employer over 20 years before. He says he had got into 'financial and legal trouble' and had returned to the UK for a year, before he returned to Ireland to face up to his crime.

Gardaí begin to study the missing person report and look at the timeframe involved. Every adult has the right to go missing if they wish. It is not a crime to walk out of your life and create a new one. But some gardaí already have a feeling about Tina's case. They are concerned that Richard had waited four days to alert gardaí that she was gone, and officers also find it strange that he travelled over to Fermoy to report that she had left their home. Detectives are also intrigued that Richard hadn't originally wanted to formally report his wife as missing. The more detail Richard gives to officers, now having finally made a missing person report – seven weeks after Tina was last seen – the more gardaí are concerned. That concern is heightened when Richard begins to tell a story of domestic abuse.

Three days after Richard formally reports his wife as missing, he returns to the garda station in Youghal to give another statement. He is keen to be seen to offer all assistance required of him, and so, on Sunday, 14 May 2017, Garda Aidan Dardis takes another lengthy statement from Richard Satchwell. Richard outlines a lengthy tale of domestic violence that he claims he has suffered. He says Tina assaulted him on many occasions over many years. Richard claims that the week before she had gone missing she had 'got angry out of nowhere, saying, "I wasted 28 years with you, I compromised myself with you."'

Richard tells Garda Dardis that Tina 'wore the trousers' in their relationship, and he says he was 'a bit of a walkover'. He claims Tina had 'some undiagnosed psychiatric condition' and would be violent towards him. He maintains he would 'never lay a hand' on Tina. He says Tina 'isn't a bad person and I don't want to paint her like that'. He just wants to know Tina 'is safe and sound'. He tells the garda he doesn't think Tina is a danger to herself, as she is 'too vain and in love with herself to hurt herself'.

Richard's claims of domestic violence – even if ultimately untrue – quickly elevate Tina's disappearance as a significant missing person case in the minds of gardaí. Detectives know there is more to it than meets the eye, but figuring out exactly what will be the challenge. Officers are already checking CCTV around Youghal to establish if Tina did indeed walk out of her life. Sensitivity is also required in such a case, as Tina, if she did leave the marital home, may not want her husband to know where she is.

A number of gardaí begin to analyse the case. With Richard claiming violent incidents had occurred in 3 Grattan Street –

THE FIRST SEARCH

albeit that he was the alleged victim – officers need to establish what might have actually transpired within the property.

Each time he leaves Youghal garda station, Richard feels empowered. He has now reported Tina as missing, and gardaí are assuring him they will do all they can to find her. They are checking with ports and airports and sending her details to all garda stations, and even to police forces in England and further afield through Interpol. On 16 May, Richard texts Tina's niece Sarah with an update, showing her he is in contact with gardaí. 'Sarah, just got called to gardaí,' he texts. 'They found a "Tina Satchwell" but it's not our Tina.'

Richard is satisfied with how things are panning out. The further away that gardaí look for Tina, the less likely they are to find her. He has told officers about her family in England, as well as Fermoy. Richard is trying to appear helpful to officers, telling them it was possible Tina might have got to England, but helpfully adding there was no way she would have flown, as she was afraid of flying, so she would only have travelled by ferry.

Throughout the last two weeks of May 2017 gardaí carry out extensive enquiries to try and find Tina. In a trawl for CCTV footage from almost two months before, they find footage from the post office in Youghal for 20 March and also from

Aldi in Dungarvan. The images clearly show Richard's timings are off in terms of when he says he went to collect the dole and when he had been in Dungarvan, but detectives know such inaccuracies can be common when people make statements weeks after an event.

Gardaí check with all local taxi drivers to see if any of them collected Tina on the Monday she vanished. Officers also check with bus operators, but no one has seen Tina. Enquiries are hampered by the fact that parts of Youghal are not covered by CCTV, including the part of Grattan Street where Richard and Tina live. While the credit union across the road from the couple's house has a number of cameras, they are trained on the windows and entrance to the credit union, rather than the rest of the street.

In the two weeks after Richard formally reports Tina missing, gardaí discuss the case at length and, based on the information they have now assembled, decide they need to get into 3 Grattan Street. There is no indication yet that Tina has been murdered – she is still officially a missing person. But gardaí are forming an opinion that something criminal may have happened in the house.

On Friday, 2 June, heading into the bank holiday weekend, Sergeant John Sharkey goes to Youghal District Court and applies to Judge Terence Finn for a search warrant for the Satchwell home. Based on all the information gardaí provide, Judge Finn agrees the threshold has been reached to grant a search warrant in relation to a suspected crime of assault causing harm. Gardaí will be looking for any signs of blood on household surfaces or any other signs of a struggle. They'll be looking for broken items inside the house or in the back garden, anything indicating evidence of violence.

Crucially, Tina is still designated a missing person, and the belief, just over a fortnight into what is now an official missing person investigation, is that she might still be alive somewhere. There is nothing at this stage to prove otherwise. The scheduled search of 3 Grattan Street will not be an invasive search involving excavation or tearing down walls. Such a search of the property will not take place until October 2023, and only after Tina Satchwell's disappearance has been re-categorised as a murder investigation, when all other valid lines of enquiry have been exhausted.

Over the bank holiday weekend of June 2017 gardaí make arrangements for a significant search of the property. They contact Forensic Science Ireland and arrange for blood-pattern scientific expert Dr Edward Connolly to travel by train to Cork the following Wednesday. Dr Connolly is experienced in using chemicals to search for traces of blood or blood spatter which can be invisible to the human eye. An officer will meet him in Cork and bring him to Youghal to establish if any suspicious traces of blood are to be found inside 3 Grattan Street.

No cadaver dog – specialised in detecting the scent of dead human bodies – is arranged to be brought. The subsequent murder trial will lead to much discussion about the fact that An Garda Síochána doesn't have its own cadaver dog, instead borrowing one on occasion from other police forces. In non-criminal cases gardaí also sometimes use cadaver dogs kept by Civil Defence and other volunteer organisations.

Cadaver dogs can detect any part of a body, from a single tooth to flesh and bone. The very best cadaver dogs can detect body parts both on land and in water. It is not until the second search of 3 Grattan Street, in 2023, that a cadaver dog is brought into the property and soon shows interest in an area around the bottom of the stairs.

Early on the morning of Wednesday, 7 June 2017, a team of gardaí arrive unannounced at the Satchwell home. They knock loudly, declaring themselves as members of An Garda Síochána, but there is no answer.

Richard had left very early that morning. Ever since getting his new job, he is spending a lot of time away from the house, driving a truck, delivering tyres across the country. He likes being on the road, as it means he doesn't have to spend so much time in the house. When he is at home he sits on a stool next to where Tina is buried and tells her about his adventures travelling around Ireland.

Sergeant John Sharkey has Richard's mobile number, so he rings him and Richard answers. The officer tells Richard they have a warrant to search his home as part of their enquiries into Tina's disappearance. Richard tells Sergeant Sharkey he was on the road early and isn't in Youghal. When the garda asks if Richard could return to open the front door, he replies that he is 'upcountry, in Abbeyfeale', and won't be back until later. Sergeant Sharkey tells Richard the team will have to gain access, and gardaí arrange for a locksmith to come and

THE FIRST SEARCH

allow garda entry to the front door of number 3 Grattan Street.

Garda Cathal Whelan, a crime scene photographer, is the first garda into the house. The photos the officer takes on 7 June 2017 will be of significant benefit to the cold-case review undertaken in 2021. Garda Whelan's photographs show an untidy, unkempt house, with dog faeces on the floor throughout and unwashed dishes in the kitchen sink.

The photos show how the front door leads to the stairs, which are within a dining room, which is the middle room downstairs. Within this room is a set of double doors which leads to a sitting room towards the front of the house, and there's a small kitchen at the back of the property.

There is a small storage space under the stairs with access via a latticed door, which is to the right of a newly built brick wall that covers the rest of the access to under the stairs. Out the back of the house there is an outside toilet and a shed, which houses a washing machine and tools. There is a wheelie bin out the back which is full of stones.

Sections of the house show some home-improvement works. Gardaí know the house was bought the previous year as a 'doer-upper', and general building materials are evident in parts of the property. The stairs itself is made of new untreated, unvarnished wood. The wall to the side is unpainted and composed of new plasterboard. The first floor contains a master bedroom, which is untidy. There is no wallpaper on the walls and there are a lot of DIY tools in it. On the second floor Garda Whelan photographs a room full of clothes. The officer estimates there are hundreds of items in this room.

Further up the stairs, in the attic conversion, the garda sees one room which contains shoes and handbags and another which contains a sunbed.

Garda Dinny Barry is another member of the 10-strong search team. His job is to identify any electronic devices within the house which might be of assistance in garda enquiries. He finds two laptops, which he labels DB 6 and DB 8 (DB for his own initials), and he removes them from the house and diligently hands them over to be held as part of the garda investigation. Four years later, an analysis of one of those laptops will uncover details of a Google search for 'quicklime' on the night Richard had first made contact with gardaí, claiming his wife had left their home. The delay in accessing this information is not explained at the subsequent murder trial.

―――

During the 12 hours gardaí spend searching inside 3 Grattan Street, Richard does not return to the property. Officers walk throughout the house looking for any clue which might indicate what happened to Tina. The warrant is specifically for a search for any evidence of assault causing harm, but gardaí do not find any evidence of a crime.

In the evening, as the search is coming to an end, Dr Edward Connolly from Forensic Science Ireland arrives to conduct a test for blood spatter. He has brought a blood testing kit known as Bluestar. He arranges with gardaí for all lights to be turned off, and he slowly and methodically sprays the Bluestar

THE FIRST SEARCH

material throughout the house. If the material comes into contact with any blood spatter or blood clean-up, it will turn luminous blue for a number of minutes. Dr Connolly carries out the test everywhere in the house, including the stairs, stairwells and hallway. No suspicious traces of blood are found.

On the evening of 7 June 2017 gardaí pull the door shut on 3 Grattan Street, having completed a search without finding any trace of Tina, nor any evidence of a crime. Richard goes to Youghal garda station to pick up a fresh key to his front door, after the locksmith had helped gardaí gain entry. Richard makes sure that a copy of the key is left at the garda station in case Tina ever returns and he isn't home at the time.

Richard feels much more emboldened after the garda search failed to find Tina. The following day he is invited to attend Midleton garda station to continue assisting gardaí with their enquiries, and he dutifully attends at 7 p.m. He meets with Detective Sergeant Daniel Holland and Sergeant Tom O'Halloran. It is made clear to Richard that he is not under arrest and his discussion with them is entirely voluntary. Richard says he is happy to assist, and he repeats that Tina had assaulted him on a number of occasions. He tells the officers he would never react, but would drive off and 'have a good cry'. He claims that on two occasions he has been knocked unconscious by Tina. He says the €26,000 he claims Tina had stolen was kept in a tin box and the cash was to be used to buy a central heating system.

Gardaí note that Richard is easy to talk to, but at times will veer off in conversation. He shows what seems to be genuine emotion and says he is available to assist gardaí going forward.

Richard receives a setback when Sarah texts him on 20 June asking him not to call to her house again. Sarah explains that her children are getting upset as they are wondering where Tina is and why she isn't with Richard. But Richard still keeps in contact with Sarah by phone, letting her know on 30 June that he is planning to set up a website – tsatchwell.wordpress.com – to help find Tina. The website never materialises.

For Sarah and Tina's sister, Lorraine, and her mother, Mary, and all the wider family, the results of the garda search of 3 Grattan Street make them wonder if Tina has indeed actually gone away. With no sign of any suspicious activity detected in the house, Tina's loved ones are perplexed. Some of them have long had concerns about Tina's relationship with Richard – they never liked the way he spoke to her or about her. He was known to describe Tina as his 'trophy wife' and it never sat well with family members. They felt that Richard had managed to isolate Tina, but now some wonder if she has, in fact, managed to escape from her controlling husband.

Richard's manipulation continues throughout the summer of 2017. In early July Richard asks Sarah to accompany him on what will be an upsetting visit. The coastguards in Youghal have recovered women's clothing from the sea, and they want Richard to see if he can identify the clothes as Tina's or discount them. On 3 July he texts Sarah, 'they want me to identify clothes tomorrow and I don't want to do it on my own, clothes the coastguard found'. He later views the clothes and says they are not Tina's. Richard continues his charade that Tina is alive, out there somewhere, and will come home at some stage by sending Sarah a birthday card in August 2017 signed 'Tina and Richard'.

———

Feeling more and more empowered, Richard begins to engage with media about the case. News about the garda search of his home is beginning to spread. Journalist Ann Mooney of *The Irish Sun* is the first to call to Richard's door. She interviews him in the front room of the property, and Richard poses for a photograph. The *Irish Independent* also gets a photograph of Richard inside the house, with journalist Catherine Devine and photographer Kyran O'Brien travelling from Dublin to Youghal, where they film a video interview with Richard at the pier, then photograph him inside the house at the walk-in wardrobes which contain many of Tina's clothes, some of which still have tags attached.

The video recorded outside the house by Kyran O'Brien shows Richard wearing glasses, sporting a goatee and casually dressed in a Le Coq Sportif top, with a clip-on Bluetooth earpiece attached to his right ear. He is calm, speaks softly and is very much in control. He states Tina 'took clothes, money ... But I haven't got a clue what she took in the lines of clothes because she's got so many clothes. It's like a department store up there.'

This video is the first time Richard is asked on camera about being a suspect. When Catherine Devine asks him directly if gardaí have ever treated him as a suspect, Richard answers, 'I've not been cautioned or anything like that, but it got back to me through members of the family that they were asking what I thought was unfair questions about – did the family think I could harm my wife and I actually came here back down to the barracks here in Youghal and I made a complaint about it ... I wouldn't lift a finger to my wife.'

Richard also speaks about the recent search of the house, saying: 'I didn't know they were going to search it. I got the phone call telling me that they was [sic] going to search it. I've actually given the gardaí a key so they can enter the house whenever they want. You see I've told nothing but the truth, I've got nothing to hide. So I've got no problem with them entering the house when they want.'

RTÉ's southern editor Paschal Sheehy and cameraman Martin Hartnett are also in 3 Grattan Street at the end of June 2017, but they decide not to film inside. Martin slips in dog faeces in the hallway and almost falls to the ground. Paschal and Martin invite Richard across the road to the Old Pier, where he does an interview marking 14 weeks to the day since Tina disappeared. The interview is filmed to coincide with an appeal to be broadcast on *Crimecall* later that night. Separate interviews have been filmed with Sarah and an aunt of Tina's, Margaret Maher. As part of the significant appeal, Detective Sergeant Seán Leahy will be in the studio in Donnybrook with *Crimecall* presenter Keelin Shanley to ask the public for help with the case.

Richard will also come to be interviewed on a number of occasions by TV3's southern correspondent Paul Byrne, who will famously ask Richard if he would take a lie detector test – Richard says he would, although he never does. But the fact that neither RTÉ News nor TV3 News ever filmed inside 3 Grattan Street makes my subsequent lengthy interview with Richard, recorded inside the property, unique. The hours I spend inside the house in November 2017 will also include filming many of Tina's personal belongings in the very places they had rested since she disappeared. Only time will tell just how significant all this filming actually will be when it is played before a jury at the Central Criminal Court.

7.

Making Contact

It is 15 November 2017 – 34 weeks since Tina disappeared – when I first make contact with Richard Satchwell. I have many thoughts as I ring him on his 085 phone. One is that I could well be phoning a killer. I have repeatedly watched Richard's appearance on *Crimecall* on 26 June and I am very troubled by it. His demeanour is completely different in that appeal to other television interviews he has done. On *Crimecall* he appears distraught, sobbing, but in the other interviews he has struck me as slightly removed or even defiant.

Throughout the summer and autumn I have spent hours watching Richard's interviews on news bulletins on RTÉ and TV3 News, which he gave in June and July. I am trying to see what I can learn, not only by what Richard is saying, but also by the manner in which he is saying it. It is normal for anyone to be upset while making an appeal for a missing loved one to return home, but the emotion Richard exhibits on *Crimecall*, staring straight at the camera – as if looking directly at Tina – jars completely with his demeanour in his other television interviews. Having interviewed dozens of families of missing people, I have never encountered anyone displaying the varying emotions Richard was exhibiting at different times.

On the same day the *Crimecall* appeal is broadcast, Richard stands on the Old Pier in Youghal and, in the interview with RTÉ's Paschal Sheehy, turns to face the camera, as if speaking directly to Tina – 'Tina, the parrot's got lovely. The dogs are missing you.' He seems more matter-of-fact, not terribly upset. During this interview Richard speaks about the impact of Tina's disappearance on him. 'I'm getting more and more worried. I'm finding it more difficult to sleep with worry. I'm struggling to eat, and I just know someone out there has to know something.'

In the *Crimecall* appeal the emotion on display is completely different. 'Tina, come home, there's nobody mad at you,' Richard says while taking off his glasses, wiping his teary eyes and looking directly at the camera. 'My arms are open. It's killing me, Tina, love.' During July and August, at my desk in RTÉ, I replay the *Crimecall* segment a number of times, trying to figure out what is really going on with this case. Richard seems genuinely upset, his eyes are moist, but there are no tears falling down his cheeks. He is shaking with emotion; he is troubled. I can't figure it out, but I know the *Crimecall* appeal is different to the others, where Richard seems defiant while also approachable, steady while also vulnerable. Richard's personality is a conundrum – he seems a complicated character, whom I very much want to meet and interview.

Another thought I have, as I dial his number this Wednesday afternoon in November, is that Richard might be completely innocent. Based on his media performances, I feel he could be a good fall-guy for someone else – perhaps a serial killer – who might have caused Tina harm and is quite happy to let suspicion fall on Richard.

I want to allow Richard to tell his story and not pass judgement before he does. Every time I think that he might be the person responsible for Tina's disappearance, I remind myself not to jump to conclusions, and I chide myself for not keeping an open mind.

It is *Prime Time* researcher Paulette O'Connor who first suggests I do a lengthy report about Tina's case. 'Well, Barry, what did you make of *Crimecall*?' Paulette asks as we chat in the office towards the end of June 2017. She is the acting deputy editor of the programme at the time. As Paulette speaks with me, the programme editor, Donogh Diamond, comes along the corridor, and he is also intrigued by the case of the missing woman in Youghal and the husband now making multiple media appeals.

'It's definitely a story we should cover if it continues long-term,' I say. I know, from experience of other cases, that following the *Crimecall* appeal a number of leads will be given to gardaí by members of the public that will have to be followed up. That may mean further reporting by the RTÉ newsroom, and if that happens it will limit the opportunity for *Prime Time* to do anything significantly different. 'I'll keep an eye on it,' I tell Donogh and Paulette, which they know means I'll keep a very close eye on it. Given my huge professional interest in missing persons cases, especially having written five true-crime books, the editors in RTÉ know that, if I am given time and space, I can bring something very different to the reporting of the case of missing woman Tina Satchwell. I am already in touch with a number of sources about the case, and I know there is a lot of suspicion about Richard and his movements in the week his wife disappeared.

I wait throughout the summer of 2017 to see if there might be a breakthrough in the case. I know gardaí will be following up on the many tips from the public that will result from the publicity the case is receiving. I am not surprised to hear in August 2017 that a full day of extensive searching, both on land and in the water, is taking place in Youghal. Garda divers comb the waters of the Old Pier near Richard and Tina's home, and Superintendent Eamon O'Neill does media interviews, outlining the extent of searches following up leads that have come to light in the wake of the *Crimecall* and other media appeals. The superintendent reiterates his request to the public for assistance in finding Tina.

With the search in August 2017 failing to find Tina, or establish any credible lead, I know the time is right to look into doing a longer, more extensive report on what is now becoming a cold case.

Now, towards the end of 2017, I want to dedicate my time to the case of Tina Satchwell. Despite all the garda activity, there has been no breakthrough, and in October I contact Inspector Conor O'Murchú in the Garda Press Office asking for assistance in contacting members of Tina's family to see if they will do interviews. I could easily have made contact without garda help, but I have long believed that, when a case is subject to garda investigation, the proper way to reach out to families is via a garda liaison. And so, on Wednesday, 15 November, Detective Inspector Brian Goulding rings me from Midleton station and tells me that, with their permission, he is giving me phone numbers for Richard Satchwell, Tina's niece Sarah Howard and Tina's aunt Margaret Maher. I thank Brian, saying I will ring all three that afternoon.

———

As I dial Richard's number, I know I need to be clear that I can only commit to doing a lengthy report about Tina's disappearance if I can film inside their house. After 14 years working in RTÉ, I know what works visually and editorially. *Prime Time* is coming late to this story and needs a good reason to justify putting in the resources now on a report that will take the team and me at least a month to film and edit.

Having watched all the media coverage of the case during the summer of 2017 I know that two newspapers have managed to take photographs of Richard inside the property, but both RTÉ and TV3 have not filmed inside the house. That's the one element missing in the reporting. Tina was last seen inside her home: that's where Richard says she waved him off as he headed to Aldi in Dungarvan on 20 March. That's where she left her keys and phone. That's where all her belongings are, and there's a parrot and two dogs there too. So many elements of her life are in that house. As I wait for Richard to answer the phone, my mind is very clear – I need to get into that house. Only filming inside the property will allow me to bring something different to my reporting on the case and ensure my report is lengthy and detailed – hopefully, in turn, leading to information being passed on to gardaí.

I have heard Richard is being selective about who in the media he will speak with. Although he first spoke with two newspapers in June 2017, over time he has come to criticise other newspaper coverage of his wife's disappearance and is now referring to many print journalists in a disparaging way. He has engaged with radio stations in Cork, speaking on 96FM and Red FM, and he seems to like that such interviews are live: he can control what he says, and he can ensure what he says isn't edited. He doesn't have similar control with television appearances, but he is apparently happy with the way the pre-recorded TV interviews were edited. Richard seems particularly comfortable with Paul Byrne of TV3 News, who pulled no punches in putting to Richard that some people were speculating that he had caused harm to Tina. But Paul also allowed Richard space to answer the question, and Richard seemed to like that.

I know that if ever I get to interview Richard he has already been asked 'the hard questions', and my unique way of telling a fresh version of the story will be to make Richard as comfortable as possible to allow him to say as much as possible. If he agrees to do an interview with me, I plan to seek to meet him a number of times in different locations, and so build layers of the story over time.

I am standing on a street in Ranelagh looking at the leaves of a large tree as I wait for Richard to answer. I could have been anywhere, but I remember exactly where I was. Within moments of getting his number I have dialled it. I have studied this man so much in his interviews, and I'm now about to speak directly with him.

After a few rings, Richard answers his phone, saying hello. I say hello back and identify myself, saying gardaí have given me his number. He tells me he has been expecting my call, after a detective contacted him earlier. The line sounds busy, with background traffic noise, as if Richard is travelling or standing by a roadside.

He sounds friendly, and I quickly get to the point, making my pitch in one go. I look at the leaves in front of me, and I tell Richard I am sorry for his situation and for all of Tina's loved ones and that I am very interested in doing a lengthy report for *Prime Time*. To do that, I feel I need to film inside his house, to show Tina's environment, and to interview him inside the property. If he can do that, I can guarantee I will do a significant report that might assist the ongoing appeal. I take a breath. 'Is that something you feel you'd be able to do?' I wince slightly as I ask the question, suddenly nervous that, after all my effort and research, Richard could simply say no and that will be that.

Richard waits less than half a second before responding with one word: 'Yes' comes the reply. I clench my left fist in a gesture of success.

As I stand on the street in Dublin 6, asking Richard if I can bring a television camera into his home, it never dawns on me that Tina might be buried within the property. I haven't thought too much about it, but given the garda search earlier in the year, the one fleeting thought I've had is that inside 3 Grattan Street is the one place Tina is not to be found. I am not trying to trap Richard or trick him – I still have no idea whether or not he has any secrets – but I feel that filming inside the house would allow viewers a more considered insight into who Tina is and also, importantly, who Richard is.

I ask Richard if the following Tuesday might suit to do an interview. 'I'm off on Mondays, but I could meet you Tuesday evening,' Richard tells me. 'I'm at work at the minute, actually. I'd be home from work about four thirty or five o'clock on Tuesday.' I know then and there that Richard will do an interview no matter what – even if something happens to change the date and time. I feel from his voice that he'd already been considering whether to speak with me at all, and he has decided I am someone he can trust. I have a feeling he has looked me up and knows what I do.

I tell him I am going to ring Sarah and Margaret as well

to see if I can meet them on a different day in Fermoy. Richard says that is fine. I have no idea that Tina's family have become increasingly concerned at aspects of Richard's behaviour, with some suspecting he is hiding secrets.

The phone call is quick, but it sets the tone for a future relationship between us. The conversation is friendly, not confrontational. I am straight with Richard, and he seems to be a straight talker too. We will never be friends, but we will become close acquaintances, and we are on first-name terms from that first phone conversation. Soon after I hang up I send him a text: 'Hi Richard, good speaking with you. I'll check in with you over the weekend to see if you [sic] free to meet next Tuesday afternoon/evening. Best wishes, Barry Cummins, RTÉ.'

I immediately contact my editor, Donogh Diamond, to say Richard has agreed to an interview and that it will be in his home in Youghal. Donogh is delighted and says that, if all works out, he's planning for me to broadcast a lengthy report on the case before Christmas. I feel that is very doable and ask for a producer to be assigned immediately. Donogh says Kevin Burns is free and I immediately get in contact with him. Kevin and I have worked together for six years, and know each other well. We have recently worked on a documentary marking the 40th anniversary of the disappearance of six-year-old Mary Boyle who vanished near Cashelard in Donegal. I know Kevin will have a good way with Richard, will be conversational and will have an eye for what to film inside the house.

On Sunday, 19 November, I ring Richard again. It is a

quick conversation but he confirms he'll be free to meet at his home the following Tuesday. I tell him we will be driving from Dublin and would aim to be in the town for around half past four and will check in with him to see when is good to call to the house.

Meanwhile, Kevin arranges that Shirley Bradshaw will be our camera crew for the interview. Shirley has only recently joined *Prime Time*. In subsequent years we will work closely together, travelling to Moldova and Spain to film lengthy reports about other stories. We will come to know each other's cues very well. But our first time working together will be inside 3 Grattan Street in Youghal. I am unwittingly about to bring Kevin and Shirley inside a property that holds chilling secrets.

On Tuesday, 21 November, I ring Richard after 4.30 p.m. but the phone rings out. I am not too worried. I trust my instinct, and I trust the phone conversations we have had over recent days. I know Richard will meet us as arranged, I am convinced. I am in a coffee shop in Youghal with Kevin and Shirley, having a brief meeting about the job we are about to do. 'We should be in no rush to leave the house,' I say. 'No other TV crew has filmed inside. I haven't met Richard, but I've spoken with him on the phone and he's happy for us to visit the house. Let's take our time there so we film everything we need.'

At 5.07 p.m. my phone buzzes with a text – it's Richard: 'Hi back in Youghal.' We gather up our equipment – camera, tripod, microphones, lights – and head for the house. There is a nervous energy about what's to come. I have heard the house may be unpleasant to visit, but nothing can prepare us for what we are about to encounter. And I could never have imagined, approaching 3 Grattan Street on this dark November evening, that what we are about to film will one day be played as part of a prosecution case leading to the interviewee being convicted of murder.

8.
On the Couch

Richard opens the front door and I shake his hand. Kevin and Shirley are right behind me, and Richard invites us into the house. We walk by him into the narrow hallway so he can close the door behind us. He gestures for us to walk on further down the hallway towards the stairs, where we turn to our right before we reach the bottom step. We are in the dining room but it is completely full of clutter, and it is dark. 'You can go on into the sitting room,' says Richard, telling us to turn to our right and walk through the double doors to what is the front room of the house. The curious geography of the property has meant that, to get to the sitting room, we have walked down the hallway and into the dining room to then turn almost 180 degrees. As we enter the sitting room, we have unknowingly walked less than three feet from where Tina is buried beneath the stairs.

I hear the parrot before I see her. It is just a gentle squawk, but I feel Valentine is letting us know she is there. She is in a cage in a corner beside the front window. The curtains are pulled over, the ceiling light on, but it's a low-watt bulb, and it still feels like the room is very dark. 'Ruby and Heidi are in the kitchen,' Richard says, telling us the dogs won't disturb us as we film in the sitting room. We are less than a minute in the house and it is clear to Kevin, Shirley and me that the only location to film an interview will be the sitting room. It is cramped, but the dining room is even more so, and the floor is full of general house clutter. We are also mindful that Richard has guided us to the sitting room, so it seems this is where he feels comfortable.

Kevin and Shirley put down the camera, tripod and lights and quickly discuss what will work best regarding the camera position in the room; meanwhile I chat with Richard. We are all standing in a tight space, and there are two conversations going on. I thank Richard again for his time, and I repeat what I'd said on the phone – that my plan is to do a report that will be much longer than the news appeals that have been broadcast on RTÉ and TV3. Richard nods. He hasn't said much since we've arrived, but he seems comfortable with our presence.

It is only after a few minutes that I notice the smell. It's actually a mixture of smells, but among them is faeces – I assume dog faeces. I can't see any, but it is definitely somewhere in the house. It's now an all-consuming smell. I begin to breathe through my mouth rather than my nose – a trick I learned long ago when faced with challenging smells.

I find myself looking at Richard's hands. His fingernails are cut short, but I see layers of dirt under his nails, and his hands seemed blackened. I know he works delivering tyres so the dirtied hands make sense. 'I'm only in a short time from work,' he says as Valentine squawks, and Richard glances over at the parrot. 'We only got her in the February,' he says, gesturing at the bird cage.

'Would you like a cup of tea?' he asks. Normally I would say yes to such an offer – having a cup of tea is always a good ice-breaker. From the first day I started work in RTÉ, 14 years before, I have been taught two lessons by cameramen who've spent careers working on the road: always consider having a cup of tea if it's offered, and never pass up an opportunity to use a toilet. But given the smell in Richard's home, and the general sense of untidiness, I quickly decide that accepting my host's hospitality shouldn't extend to tea. 'No, thank you, Richard, we had a cup up the road just before we arrived to you,' I say – which is true.

Aspects of Tina's life are evident in the room. The only photo hanging up is a single portrait-style photo of her. There are bottles of nail varnish on the shelf to my left and ladies' clothes – a jacket and pair of jeans – hanging on the back of a door. I wonder if Tina chose the multicoloured cushions on the dusty black couch beside us.

It takes just a few minutes to set up the room for a sit-down interview. There is only one option for filming, based on the cramped conditions. Both Richard and I will sit on the couch, and Shirley will focus the camera directly on Richard. Once the interview is finished, Kevin will have to step out of the room, to near the stairs, to let Shirley swing the camera in a different way to film myself and Richard looking through the many photos of Tina he has in a briefcase by the side of the couch.

Kevin and Shirley suggest that Richard sit on the section of couch nearest the window, and I sit to his left. This will mean that, for the duration of the interview, I am unwittingly the closest person to Tina's body.

Richard and I sit down and get comfortable, or as comfortable as I can be, breathing through my mouth to withstand the dusty, smelly conditions. As I sit with Richard I notice how tall and strong he is. He doesn't flex his muscles or hold himself tall – he carries himself in a slightly stooped way, and as he sits on the couch his shoulders are slouched, which masks his true strength. Only occasionally, when he gestures at Valentine or towards Tina's clothes hanging on the door, do I see his strong muscles show beneath his short-sleeved collared T-shirt.

I suddenly notice how cold it is in the house. We have walked from a November evening into a house that seems chillier than outdoors. There is no heating on. I am dressed in a suit, shirt and tie, and, as I look at Richard's bare lower arms, I wonder is he not cold. Over the next two hours, the room will warm up with the heat of four bodies breathing the same dirty air.

'Count to 10, please,' says Shirley, once the microphones have been clipped to Richard and myself. She wants to check the sound levels so myself and Richard need to do a sound check. For a moment Richard looks like a deer in headlights as the light of the camera focuses on him. He begins to count 'one, two, three', and Shirley says thank you, and I give a 'one, two, three', and Shirley indicates that the levels are good. For many lengthy interviews, we would have a sound operator with us to ensure the sound levels are perfect throughout. However, I'm glad we don't have an extra body with us tonight, as there simply wouldn't be any space to fit them. Kevin is arched behind Shirley at an angle meaning he won't be able to move once the interview starts. It's the only place to stand.

We have turned off the light in the sitting room, only using the camera light, to avoid a shine appearing on Richard's glasses, but Shirley has to change a setting on the camera. She needs the room light back on for a moment and Kevin has to lean over me to switch it on and off. It is a very tight squeeze to have four people and a parrot in this room, but it is the only remotely adequate room for filming in, and so, with Richard and myself sitting beside each other, so close that our knees occasionally touch, we begin.

As I compose my thoughts, I look at Richard as he looks back at me. He is wearing thick glasses but behind the lenses his eyes are wide, his pupils dilated. He only seems to blink very occasionally, certainly much less than me. He seems very calm, accepting of our presence. I'll start by asking him about how he met Tina, I think to myself. What age were they both? When and where did they meet?

———

I haven't even completed my first question when Kevin coughs. I'm not surprised at the sudden interruption, as the room is incredibly dusty, and I stifled a sneeze myself soon after sitting down. The house feels as if the windows haven't been opened in a long time. Two flies are buzzing around the couch area, but I'm not too bothered by them – they only occasionally seemed to fly past my face and Richard's. Kevin gives another loud cough to clear his throat. 'Excuse me, sorry about that,' he says, as he stands right behind Shirley.

And then we film an interview that will last 43 minutes. It is the most surreal interview I have ever conducted. I don't have questions written down – it is all spontaneous on my end. That's how I have always conducted interviews. I always have a list of questions in my mind, but I listen carefully to the answers given, and that way I can change direction during the interview if need be. First rule of interviewing: always listen to your interviewee, and not just to what is being said, but to what is not being said.

I have no idea I am sitting on the couch where Tina's body lay eight months before. The interview I conduct there will one day help convince a jury that Tina Satchwell's death was not an accident as her husband will ultimately claim. His demeanour, his answers to my questions, his lies in this and my other interviews with him, will eventually help convince a jury that Richard orchestrated a calculated and callous cover-up of his wife's murder.

9.

Cat and Mouse

'Her grandmother had moved next door to my brother, and I seen [sic] her, and, before I even met her, I told my brother I was going to marry her.' Richard smiles as he looks me straight in the eye, answering my first question. I have brought his mind back to 1989.

Richard was 22 years old when he met 17-year-old Tina Dingivan in March of that year. The moment he saw her he made a pledge to himself that he would marry the Irish teenager just arrived in the Leicestershire town of Coalville. It was the stuff of romance novels, love at first sight – for Richard anyway.

I probe for more detail. When a person goes missing, every aspect of their life is parsed and analysed. I want to know as much as possible about Tina, and I want to know everything about her relationship with Richard. Valentine squawks softly in the corner, and Richard holds my gaze. The start of his relationship with Tina is obviously a happy memory for him, so I continue focusing on the past. 'Tell me a little bit about your early years,' I ask.

'When I met her it was a friendship at first.' Richard is

now gazing off slightly to his right, caught in memories. 'And over a spell of time we got close – after about 12 weeks I moved over here with her.' Twelve weeks, I think to myself. That was quick. Tina was still 17 when she moved back to Fermoy with Richard. Within three months of meeting for the first time, Richard and Tina were a couple and living together. The way Richard tells the story, it was a whirlwind romance.

But as I sit on the couple's couch I am troubled. Although there were only five years between them, Tina was still a child when she met Richard; he was an adult. There was a power imbalance from the start. But a durable relationship can perhaps start like that, I think. I am still breathing through my mouth and occasionally gripping my toes together to deal with the smell in the house. Focus, I say to myself. Focus, listen to Richard, listen to every word.

'Where did you live at the start?' I ask, leaning my right arm on a cream-coloured cushion.

'Well, in the early days it was extremely hard to get work over here,' Richard replies. I notice he is now only occasionally looking at me, preferring to focus on a spot on the floor in front of him. We are sitting so close together that I need to move my right leg slightly so I'm not resting it against his left knee.

'We got married in Oldham on Tina's 20th birthday.' Richard smiles as he says that line. 'Tina had a sister living in Oldham, so we went to Oldham. Her grandmother was originally from Rochdale – that's why she had come to England in the first place. Eventually we moved back to Fermoy, and I've spent 29 years of my life over here.'

I change tack with my next question, bringing the discussion directly to 2017. 'Tell me about what was going on in your life and Tina's life early this year.' Valentine squawks, and I gesture towards her. 'You got a new bird this year. What was going on in your lives?'

Richard takes the question smoothly – he's not thrown by my moving so quickly from one decade to another. 'Well, we moved here last year, and even though the house is still a mess, it was a whole lot worse back then.' I figure he is referring to the refurbishments he has been doing. Parts of the house are visibly a work in progress. Apart from the unpleasant smell, the dust and lack of fresh air, this cluttered house shows potential. It's a house that's been neglected ever since Tina vanished, I presume.

'We both love Youghal – that's why we decided to come here.' Richard is speaking about Tina in the present tense, I notice. 'Tina had been upset for a little while,' he adds. I am thrown for a moment by Richard's speech pattern. I can clearly follow his soft, slow English midlands accent, but it's some of the words he uses that capture my thoughts. He says 'lickle' rather than 'little'. Later he will say 'pacific' rather than 'specific'. His verbal hiccups are disarming. How could someone who says 'lickle' cause harm to anyone? I think. In my next breath I remind myself to keep focused, stop analysing, let him talk, let him guide me.

'In January this year Pearl, our other parrot, died, and she was like a child, and we both took it very bad.' The couple had Pearl for three years and doted on her. Then they found another parrot for sale in an online advert on Valentine's Day and drove to Portarlington to buy her. 'Tina decided we'd call her Valentine,' Richard says, smiling directly at me. His next line brings me right to the day Tina disappeared. 'Unfortunately, we only had her a couple of weeks before Tina got up and left.'

Five minutes into the interview and Richard has told me the first of many lies that he will tell that night. It will be another six years before I know that Tina did not get up and leave her home – in fact, she never left the house.

I bring the conversation directly to the car boot sale in Carrigtwohill that the couple attended the day before Tina disappeared. I notice Richard is listening carefully and using his upper right teeth to bite down softly on his lower lip. 'I used to sell and Tina used to buy,' he says, when I ask what they did at the car boot sales. He gestures with his left hand past my head to my right. 'That stuff up there is the last stuff she bought the day before she went.'

'What's up there?' I ask, craning my head to look at clothes on a yellow hanger that have a film of dust on them, as they rest on the back of a wooden door.

'That's a jacket and dress. She hung them up there when she come [sic] back, and I've never moved it.' As Richard looks at the clothes, he is also looking in the direction where Tina's body is buried. On the far side of the door is the stairs, beneath which lies the truth.

I bring the focus back to the house. 'What were your plans for this particular house?'

'To be honest with you, the main thing we thought about was doing it up and selling it – we picked it up really cheap.

That was the main idea, but that kind of stalled with her being gone.'

'I want to ask you about your last conversation with Tina.' I'm moving the discussion directly to 20 March. 'What are your memories, what happened that day?' I've left the question open-ended.

'Not a lot really, to be honest,' replies Richard, giving a slightly ironic half-grunt. That's the second time he's said 'to be honest', I note. It *can* just be a catchphrase, but during my career interviewing people, I've long wondered about some of those who say 'to be honest' – are they actually being honest at all?

'I got up and I was actually plastering the stairs there, and she came down.' In that one sentence, I have been told something no one else has been told. Years later Richard will tell gardaí he was out in the shed when Tina got up that fateful day, but he has just told me he was at the stairs, plastering. It is only after Tina's body is discovered that I will wonder if this comment, which Richard makes to me during our first interview, is the closest anyone has ever got to the truth. Tina was buried under the stairs, and Richard told only me and no one else about working at the stairs the day Tina disappeared. Was he actually there when the murderous confrontation occurred? Or is this another of his many lies?

On and on we chat, Richard doing most of the talking, me occasionally seeking more detail. 'She came down at around ten past nine, and I always made her a cup of tea and a bit of breakfast – it could be cereal, it could be toast.' That generality again, I think. 'I always made her a cup of tea and breakfast,' but did you on the 20th? I wonder.

Richard then tells me his last conversation with Tina was in the very room in which we are sitting. It feels poignant being in this room, as Richard points towards the corner where Valentine's cage now sits, saying that is the corner where Tina was sitting on a chair when she asked him to go to Dungarvan to get some food. He describes coming home from that trip, and finding Tina's keys on the floor in the hall. 'The two dogs were in this room here,' he says matter-of-factly. 'Originally I thought she'd be upstairs on the sunbed or something, but she wasn't.'

Richard continues his lies, adding to his story to further distract from the truth. 'I did another look around, and I spotted the box that we kept the money in was open and the money gone.' Richard is claiming that Tina took €26,000 in cash when she had left the house. I repeat what he has said, to confirm I've heard it correctly. 'Yes, it was in a specific hiding place,' he says, glancing over to a corner in the room. I immediately wonder if that is where the tin was hidden, but by thinking that, I am doing what he is intending. I'm wondering about a tin box, and I'm wondering about the cash. In reality, no such money existed – there was no large bundle of cash. A garda forensic accountant would later testify in court that the couple didn't have the means to have amassed such money.

Years later I will come to believe that Richard was actually a very clever liar. Say Tina took money and give a specific amount. Don't say she took €25,000, say it was €26,000. That's more believable. It was a similar embellished lie to the one he had created about Tina taking two suitcases when she left the house. Add in the detail that the two suitcases had been part of a three-piece set they had collected years ago with coupons from SuperValu – that sounded believable. The truth was Richard and Tina had indeed saved up coupons to get the suitcase set, but the lie was that Tina had left the house with two of them. Two suitcases never left the house on 20 March, and of course neither did Tina, but embellishments help a liar to keep a story going.

'She had been saying that one day I might be on my own, and things like that, but this was totally out of the blue, because the day before, she was telling people at the car boot sale that she loved me and that she'd never do anything to hurt me.' Richard is revealing a lot in that one sentence as we sit close together. It is hard to unpick the details. He is saying Tina previously indicated she might one day leave him – whether she ever said this or not, Richard making this comment continues the lie that Tina had actually left him. And her reported declaration of love for Richard at the car boot sale is strange – even if she had said such a thing it sounds odd, and it makes me wonder if it was said under duress.

―――

Shirley begins to zoom the camera lens in on Richard as I continue asking questions. It's our first time working together but Shirley is reading the room, realising that Richard is giving in-depth detail about the circumstances of Tina's reported disappearance. She has been focusing on Richard from mid-chest upwards, but now she brings the camera closer, focusing closer on Richard's face. 'She could be laughing and joking one minute, and the next she could be crying, it could be like a switch,' Richard says, clicking his fingers to illustrate how he says Tina's mood might change suddenly.

'Was there any particular reason for this?' I immediately ask.

'I have my own ideas, but that's between me and her,' Richard answers. 'And it is external to the relationship.'

Richard is a clever liar, claiming to be a trusted keeper of his wife's secrets. He would never betray her confidence. And of course a man who would not betray his wife's confidence would never have killed her.

I move things back to the car boot sale the day before Tina disappeared. 'Do you have strong memories of that day?' I ask. I know this is the last time anyone other than Richard saw Tina. Did something happen on that day? I wonder to myself.

'To be honest with you, every moment is in my head, from the day we first met, right up to the last time I saw her.'

'Where was she, that last time you saw her, where was she?' I ask firmly but politely. He's already answered this, but I want to see if his detail changes in any way – but it doesn't.

Richard turns to his right and points toward the front window and towards Valentine. 'She was in a chair where the parrot cage is now. That's the last place she was sitting.'

I keep pressing. 'Do you have any idea what happened that day?'

Richard doesn't pause with his reply. 'My best fear [*sic*] is she got up, obviously felt she needed a break, to get her thoughts together, to get her head straight, and I do believe that she'll come back, and if not come back, get in contact just as suddenly as what [sic] she left.'

I move on smoothly to ask Richard about why he waited four days to report Tina missing. He describes how he had the doctor's appointment in Fermoy on that fourth day, and he thought Tina might have been with family in Fermoy, but when they told him they hadn't see her, 'literally within five minutes of being told that, I was in the garda barracks in Fermoy'.

I ask about Tina's state of mind. Could Tina have had thoughts of harming herself?

Richard raises his head to look me straight in the eye, his pupils still large. 'She, in my opinion, she's too much in love with herself to harm herself.' Richard keeps my gaze after saying this.

What a strange thing to say, I think. What is really going on here?

As Richard eyeballs me, I ask if someone might have attacked Tina. I couch it in a way which acknowledges I understand his view that Tina left of her own accord, saying, 'There may be someone who has caused harm to her, do you think about that?'

Richard says he has thought about that possibility for some time. 'But then, there's nothing to say either way. I know Tina as a person, she isn't a pushover, and to be honest, if someone tried attacking her she'd pick up the nearest thing and whack them with it.' Again Richard is staring at me and holding my gaze as he delivers that last line, and he then looks down slightly and gives a small swallow. I know a swallow like that shows an uncontrolled reaction. I don't know exactly what has caused it, but I know Richard is uncomfortable about something.

I move on to the issue of searches. This house has been searched, I acknowledge to Richard. Gardaí spent a full day here looking for any sign of what might have happened to Tina. 'Did you understand the need for that, the need to search from where last seen?' I ask. Although clumsily worded, I have no idea this question is so relevant. I'm assuming that, if any harm had come to Tina in the house, that garda search would have found evidence. While I'm thinking Richard's story about his wife's disappearance is more than a little unusual, it never enters my head that Tina might still be within the property in which I am now sitting.

And there, sitting on his couch, with his wife's body hidden just a few feet away, Richard brazenly answers my question about the first garda search of his home.

Looking off to his right at a spot on the ground, he takes a few seconds to compose his thoughts. Then he turns his head slightly back towards me and says, 'At the time I was put off by it, I'll be honest. But then they have to prove or be satisfied that no harm came to her in this house.' He delivers the lines calmly, and he continues, 'At the time my head was here, there and everywhere. And if I was to tell you I'm alright now, I'm better than I was back then, well, I'd be lying. I probably think a little bit straighter than what I did back then, but it still goes round in your head.'

It would only be after Richard was charged with murder that I would re-analyse his words about the garda search of June 2017. He must have been so worried that the officers were going to find Tina's body, and then when the search ended without success, he became emboldened, empowered. When he says on camera to me that his head was 'here, there and everywhere', only now do I fully understand what he's saying. As he sits with me on the couch in November 2017 he must feel that, because gardaí previously failed to locate Tina's body, she will never be found, and he will have her all to himself once the media interest dies down.

On and on Richard speaks to me on the couch, telling me lies, telling me some truths, and mixing facts with elements of fiction. The more he speaks, the more I realise Tina had been almost completely isolated in Youghal. Even when she joined the local swimming pool, Richard would drive her there and wait for her to come out. Only when Tina was in the pool, did she have space, I think. Only when she was under the water, did she have peace and time to herself.

Towards the end of the interview Richard tells me that he became reclusive after Tina disappeared; he would only leave the house to get food from the Roma Grill takeaway. Referring to Tina, he says, 'It's hard to say anything bad, because to me everything was good.' That's another strange thing to say, I think. Richard adds another lie to his mountain of untruths. 'I live in hope that she walks in that door and we spend the rest of us [sic] lives together.' I say thank you to Richard and ask Kevin if there is anything I have forgotten to ask. Only later will I learn that Shirley takes this opportunity to focus the camera on Richard's hands, filming up close his dirty fingers. Years later, after Richard is convicted of murder, I will show this image in a special television report and refer to 'the hands that murdered Tina'.

Kevin suggests getting more detail about the suitcases Richard says Tina took with her. It is a good call, as during the subsequent answer from Richard he suggests a journalist might have deliberately planted a suitcase at the Tesco shopping centre car park in Youghal that looked like one Tina was said to have taken. This is important in terms of getting a feel for Richard's sense of reality. He says a journalist tried to get an interview with him on the day the suitcase was found, and he feels there's a link. In reality, of course, no journalist planted any such suitcase – it had simply been dumped there the previous August – and it had nothing to do with Tina's disappearance, because of course Tina had never left her house with a suitcase.

I have one last question as we sit on the couch. Was there anyone who might have given Tina assistance to leave? As I'm speaking, Richard's nose begins to run, and he runs his right hand and arm, from his thumb up to near his elbow, against his nose to wipe it clean. That's the hand I'll shake as I leave later, I think.

'It would have to be someone she trusted. She was reared in Fermoy, she had friends in Fermoy. Yeah, it is a possibility that someone gave her hand [sic].'

Just as Richard finishes his answer Shirley says the disc is about to run out. We have been filming for almost 45 minutes. It is time to change the disc, and the sit-down interview has naturally come to an end. Valentine squawks, and I squeeze my toes and think quickly. The interview has been powerful, and I really want to stand up and get some fresh air. But I stay sitting and breathing through my mouth. There is more work to do right here on the couch. I want to film the photographs Richard has indicated he has in a nearby briefcase, and we definitely want to film the parrot – if that is okay with Richard? He says that's fine, and he stays sitting beside me. Shirley and Kevin agree that we'll film the photos first. Shirley adjusts two lights she has brought with her to focus more light on the images of Tina which Richard wants to show us. Richard opens up the purple-coloured leather case. We are only halfway through our visit inside 3 Grattan Street.

10.

The Photos

As Kevin and Shirley shift position to begin filming the photographs, I stay rigid on the couch. There isn't any space to move around, and I want to keep focus on the photographs. Richard has a treasure trove of images, all stored within the briefcase he's now lifting onto his knees and opening up beside me.

I make chit-chat, gathering as much information as I can. I ask about the specific location where he proposed to Tina, telling him I am planning to film some footage in that area to help tell that part of their backstory. 'It's near the car park for the pitch and putt club, up on the bank overlooking the sea.' Richard raises his hand to indicate the proposal spot is high above the water. By this stage I'm holding the first of many photos of Tina that Richard will hand me. Shirley is to my left looking through the lens of her camera and Kevin is to her left – they are both just a few feet away from where Tina's body lies buried.

As Richard shows me each image I'm struck that many of them are posed. Richard was the photographer, capturing his wife on camera. In so many pictures Tina is by herself, sometimes

THE PHOTOS

with hand on hip or holding a bag. She is always well dressed and always smiling.

I study each image intently, taking in every element while I can. Tina is photogenic, comfortable with the camera. Richard adds detail for each photo he hands me. 'That's outside the front of the house in Fermoy – we lived 19 years in total in Fermoy,' he says as I look at one image of Tina posing with sunglasses on her head, holding a flower-motif bag in her right hand and dressed in an orange and grey matching top and trousers.

Richard is smiling as he describes each photo. I am happy to let him be the narrator. I'm also happy to let him select which photographs to show. I am a guest in his house, and he is looking at images of his missing wife, I remind myself. I am learning a lot. Let him lead.

Richard leans in towards me to point out certain details in some of the photos. Valentine has stopped squawking. I glance over to her cage and the parrot is looking back at me, just standing still, looking. If that parrot could talk, what would it say? I wonder.

We go back in time with the photographs. Richard shows me one of Tina in Oldham when she was learning to drive. She's behind the wheel of a car and Richard is taking the picture from in front of the bonnet. Tina is laughing, she seems happy. He shows me another taken in Rochdale, also from the early 90s. Tina had brown curly hair when she got married, which over the years became blonde, long and straight.

'Just hand each one a little bit slower, Richard,' says Kevin, so Shirley will have time to focus on each image. Richard is happy to oblige – he seems very comfortable with our presence and eager to assist. By filming the photographs we are also filming 'a sequence' which will ultimately be shown in our report. We are recording not just the photographs, but also Richard showing me the photographs, handing them to me one by one. Every image he hands me I take carefully, holding the sides, not wanting to put any finger smudges on them. These are treasured memories I am being invited to view, and I make sure to be careful doing so.

In one image I notice Tina is wearing a belly-button ring. Little do I know that ring lies with her body so close to where I am sitting.

'In every photo there's different fashion, a different outfit.' Richard smiles as the briefcase resting on both his legs knocks against my knee. He takes another image and says, 'And this is Tina on our wedding morning, holding the puppy I got her the week before.' I study this image, wondering what she was thinking at the time. She is not smiling, but is cuddling a small brown dog. Tina is sitting on a carpeted floor looking at the camera. She is wearing a white dress, tights and a white necklace. She looks directly at the camera as she cradles the puppy. Where could you be, Tina? I wonder. Where have you gone?

'Just turn the photo towards me,' Shirley says.

'That's Tina's 20th birthday, and the day we got married,' says Richard, smiling as he speaks.

The next photograph is particularly poignant, but it will be many years later before I realise just how significant it is.

THE PHOTOS

It's a photo of Tina with Ruby and Heidi and the couple's first parrot, Pearl. Tina is sitting on a couch with the two dogs and the parrot is in her cage beside her. 'This photo was taken last Christmas Day in this house,' Richard says matter-of-factly. I look more closely at the image and realise that Richard and I are sitting on the very same couch. It's a black two-seater, and I also recognise the cream cushions with purple dots either side of Tina.

I notice the image isn't of where Richard and I are now sitting. 'Where was this photo taken, Richard?'

'It was in that room in there,' he says, gesturing past me to the dining room where the stairs are. It will be years later that I realise the photo was taken in the same room where Richard would dig out a grave and bury his wife's body.

'You've loads of very nice photographs,' I say, genuinely glad that we are being permitted to film all these images of Tina.

'I never stopped taking them,' replies Richard. 'I've got discs with thousands and thousands.'

As I'm chatting with Richard, I hear Kevin quietly asking Shirley to film Richard as he passes the photos to me. Kevin has noticed the emotion that seems to show when Richard is talking about specific memories of Tina. He occasionally seems lost in them.

As Richard hands me yet another photo, I again say they are lovely. It seems important to acknowledge the life of the person in them, to compliment the photos. 'They've all got a story,' says Richard.

I am resisting the urge to take any photos from the briefcase, but rather am waiting for Richard to select more and hand them to me. My slow approach is allowing Shirley time to adjust the camera and get footage from various angles, which is proving difficult due to the limited space, but she is managing well. The time I'm taking with each photo also shows Richard my genuine interest in learning as much as I can about Tina and their relationship. He takes out three more photos, and this time he's in them too. They are all images of Richard and Tina in much younger years. One is of the couple snuggling together on a sofa, taken a year after they started going out. Another from around the same time shows Tina sitting on Richard's knee and they are both laughing. The third is taken in a restaurant while on a trip to Sligo around that time too. In all three images the couple look happy.

Shirley asks Richard to pull down the top of the briefcase slightly to avoid a shadow creeping across my face, and she asks me to sit back a little to enable a better angle for filming. It's all very surreal. We are in no rush to leave – we want to capture everything that Richard will permit us to film, and he seems very comfortable with us. He also seems to know the dates of every photo he shows me. 'That's taken along the river Blackwater in Fermoy in 1994, and that one is Paddy's Day 2011.'

Richard shows me another image – and it catches my eye because it's so unlike the other images. It's a group photograph and shows Tina in a white chef's uniform. She is standing with a man and woman wearing mayoral chains. Richard tells me it's from a time Tina was working at the English Market food hall in Cork city and the lord mayor was posing for

THE PHOTOS

photos with workers. I ask for more detail and Richard tells me Tina had been doing a cookery course. The image intrigues me as it shows Tina in a work environment, and she looks so happy. What happened that Tina stopped working? I wonder.

Valentine is beginning to make noise again in the corner as I ask Richard if he knows what clothes Tina might have taken with her in March, a question I neglected to ask during the interview. Richard refers to the photo he posed for with the *Irish Independent* earlier in the year and says that shows all the clothes Tina had: 'The amount of stuff she has upstairs, you'd never be able to pick out what she took and what she didn't take.' Strange choice of words, I think to myself, analysing that phrase 'the amount of stuff she has'.

'Are the clothes still upstairs?' asks Kevin. He's thinking what I'm thinking – we would very much like to film Tina's clothes, to show more of the life of this missing woman. 'Yes, but they're not to go in a photo,' replies Richard. 'Because last time I showed all those, I was getting calls asking why I didn't get her psychiatric help.' Richard stumbles over the word *psychiatric*, swallowing it and saying something closer to 'psychiakric'. Kevin asks Richard to repeat himself as he didn't understand the first time. Richard repeats the line and adds that people were suggesting Tina needed psychiatric help because so many of the clothes still had tags on them.

I don't know much about fashion, but I've heard that people can wear an outfit once and keep the tags on, so as to return the item or sell it on 'as new'. It doesn't strike me as strange that clothes might still have tags on, especially if Richard and

Tina were involved in selling at car boot sales. But once again Richard has introduced the idea that Tina might have psychiatric issues and that might be why she disappeared. Another complete distraction.

11.

The Shrine

In the sitting room, Shirley films the denim dress and black coat hanging on the door behind the couch. These are the items Richard says Tina bought at the car boot sale in Carrigtwohill on 19 March. 'Things like that still make you feel like she's here,' Richard says with a rueful half-laugh. I look at the items and wonder where their owner is. As I stand up and stretch my back, I'm conscious I have spent close to 90 minutes in the one spot, listening to every word Richard says, trying to think if there's anything else I should be asking.

Kevin is looking at a shelf beside Valentine's cage and he asks Richard about various items, which all seem to have relevance to Tina. There is a thick layer of dust over everything, but it's clear that the items are important for us to film if Richard agrees. He says it's fine. The only thing he's rejected during our visit is the request to film Tina's clothes upstairs. He is in control; he decides what we can film and what we can't.

'I'm still buying her stuff, even though she's not here,' Richard says, as we look around the room. 'These are the things that people don't hear about,' he adds. As Kevin directs

Shirley on filming ornamental birds he has spotted on shelves above the couch, I'm chatting with Richard about how I appreciate it must be difficult that, when a person goes missing, people like me come asking questions and looking to film as much as possible. This seems to bring Richard to a pet hate of his – some members of the press. 'I think there should be some governing body or something for the press,' he says. 'They should at least have to print it the way it's said.' It's clear he is insinuating he's been misquoted somewhere. What he's really doing is muddying the waters even more. By criticising journalists Richard is appearing to be a victim, when in fact he is something very different. He continues, 'I've only spoke [sic] to two members of the press, but people think I've spoken to every newspaper. I haven't.'

Kevin asks Richard if we could film a sequence of Richard telling me about how Valentine came to live with him and Tina. Richard says that is okay. After occasionally hearing Valentine squawking during the earlier interview, now she is going to be filmed herself. As Shirley adjusts the camera and changes position, Richard and I discuss the scarcity of CCTV cameras in Youghal, and he tells me there was no report of Tina being sighted on the small number of cameras that are actually working in the town. 'Some people have cameras but they are not working, they are dummies,' he tells me. That's such a shame, I think. A modern town in a modern country without adequate security cameras to capture a missing woman's last movements.

Just before we film Valentine, Kevin reaches in to remove a can of cleaning spray on a cramped shelf beside the bird cage. It's been some time since that spray was used, I think to myself. Shirley zooms in on Valentine's face, showing her green-blue head with yellow fur beneath her eyes.

'The bird has gone quiet,' says Shirley, as Valentine looks at the camera with her head half-cocked to her right.

'She won't be quiet if I walk out that door,' laughs Richard.

Shirley has now turned the lens to the wall beside the bird cage. A single photo is hanging on the wall: it's a portrait-type image of Tina. Next the camera focuses on a bottle of cava – with the label 'Tesco Finest' – which rests on a glistening red ornamental woman's high-heeled shoe.

Kevin arranges for Richard and me to walk into shot – whereby we are off to the right near the couch, out of vision, and then walk towards the bird cage, so that Richard can start talking about Valentine. Richard is happy to do this.

We walk into frame and Richard describes how Tina and he drove to Portarlington on Valentine's Day to buy Valentine after Pearl had died. 'They are both Amazons,' Richard says, looking into the cage. 'This one has a blue head, but the other one had a yellow head. The other one died on 17 January.'

'You were both very upset,' I say, standing next to Richard, as we look in at Valentine.

'It was like mourning a human being,' Richard replies. 'We were both very upset, we cried for weeks. We even got an autopsy done and everything on her.'

The interaction feels very strange. Richard seems genuinely upset thinking about the parrot that died – I can hear it in his voice. I am listening to him but looking at the bird droppings all over the bottom of the cage. I wonder can he see the dirtiness of it, or is he in a different world, or does he just not care anymore. Is it that he cannot function properly without Tina? I really don't know what to think. Richard is courteous and friendly to me, Kevin and Shirley. Apart from the smell and the dust, Richard is a good host.

Kevin asks Richard to tell me about the cava and the portrait photo. Richard takes a step forward and says, 'This is a bottle of cava that I got last year for our 25th wedding anniversary, and she never opened it. I don't drink, I'm a teetotaller, and Tina would only drink on special occasions.'

Richard reaches up to touch the photo and a little bit of sticky tape falls away from the back of the frame as he speaks. 'And this photo we had done up in Tallaght, up at Covergirl. It was actually took [sic] professionally. And that was back in 2005.'

Shirley asks Richard to repeat the sequence again, so she can pan up from the cava to the photo. This kind of filming is important in order to get enough imagery for a lengthy report, but it can also be awkward to ask someone to repeat their actions and words a few times, especially when it's someone whose loved one is missing. But Richard is more than happy to repeat his movements and words for us. He seems relaxed and is being very helpful.

As I stand beside Richard and we both look up at the photo on the wall, I quietly take in his height. He's well over six foot, and he is fit. I notice the bottom of a rose tattoo creeping out from his sleeve on his upper right arm – his arms are strong. He seems to mask his towering figure and strength, partly with his posture, but also with his soft voice, never getting animated, always of a low timbre; it all helps to make him less imposing than he could actually be.

There are several bird ornaments on a shelf. Shirley has filmed similar ornaments in other parts of the room already. 'One thing you could do is tell us about the fascination with birds,' Kevin says to Richard.

'There's loads of them – why so many of them?' I chime in, almost at the same time, adding, 'Also I see there are bottles of nail varnish, so we can chat about that too.'

Richard is happy with our requests and immediately begins talking. 'All the birds are because she loves birds.' He points to one in the middle of the shelf and says that is the first one they ever bought, and they got it at Mitchelstown market in 2013.

Richard then speaks about the various small clocks on the shelf. 'These clocks are actually things that I am buying, because before she left, she went mad into the cut glass. Anything I think she'll like I buy it. It's there for her for when she comes back.'

On numerous occasions during our visit Richard is barefaced lying to us. He has just said 'before she left', when in fact she never left. And he's saying he's buying things for when she comes back. Only he knows Tina is never coming back.

We turn our attention to six bottles of nail varnish – two are red, one is purple glitter, the others are lighter shades. 'The nail polishes, she would have used them on the Saturday night to get ready for the car boot sale. And pretty much I haven't had much motivation to move anything. In a way it's a comfort just having them there.'

A small cut-glass clock in the centre of the shelf shows 7.20 p.m. We have been in the house almost two hours now. I'm getting a dull headache from the lack of fresh air. Kevin gives another cough – everything on the shelf is covered in dust, so when Richard touches anything it releases dust particles towards us all. Kevin coughs a second time. 'Excuse me, sorry,' he says.

The way I'm positioned behind Richard, I cannot see his face as he looks at the shelf. He repeats the line about buying the cut-glass clocks, so they are there for Tina when she comes home. He swallows hard as he says this – the same swallow I noticed during the interview. It's a sign of something, an upset he won't speak about.

Kevin is looking at everything on the shelf and is struck by the exact same thought as me. Time seems to have stood still inside the house. As Kevin directs the filming of the last part of this sequence, he tells Richard, 'Just explain what you are doing here: it's almost like a shrine, you're not changing things and you're buying things in the hope she'll come back.'

I add, 'Richard, as we look at this mantelpiece it tells a story. What's going on here?'

Richard's jaw begins to shake ever so slightly. His voice wavers – just a tiny bit. I only recognise the change in demeanour because I've spent the last two hours in his company, but this is definitely the most emotional he has been. 'Well,' he begins, looking at the mantelpiece. 'It's part of Tina. The nail polishes she used, the birds is [sic] stuff she loves. The cut glass is stuff I'm buying when I see it, because it's stuff that I know she'll like. In a way it's a comfort thing.'

THE SHRINE

Richard is now turning his head away from me and away from the camera. He is swallowing harder.

I feel I need to probe more. 'How do you feel when you look at the mantelpiece?'

'Sad,' replies Richard. He pauses then says, 'Because it's synonymous of my life before she left.' He turns further away from me – only Valentine can now see Richard's face fully. I know he's upset. He's not crying, but looking at the shrine, and talking about the shrine, has affected him.

That is the end of our filming in the sitting room. 'Thank you, Richard,' I say. After a second or two he turns back towards us; he has regained his composure. 'You're welcome to look at the other rooms, but there'll be no photos,' he says. We turn off the camera lights and turn back on the main light. Valentine squawks loudly, as if she's upset we are finishing our filming. 'Alright, you noisy bugger,' Richard says to Valentine. I'm immediately struck by the phrase. Given the poignancy of what we've been filming, and Richard's demeanour just seconds ago, it seems a strange thing for him to say. But so much of the evening has been strange.

As Shirley disassembles the portable lights in the sitting room, Richard leads the way for Kevin and me to walk upstairs. We walk out of the sitting room through the double doors into the dining room. Much of this room is full of clutter, and there is a table and large cabinet against one wall. We take two steps to the left and we are at the bottom of the stairs.

We walk up the winding stairs, which rises three floors. There are twelve steps, then a very small landing and then three more steps and we are on the first floor. We continue on up, following Richard's lead: there are nine steps to the next landing and then a further three steps and we are on the second floor. This is where Richard shows us the walk-in wardrobe. The air feels lighter, fresher up here. There might be a window open somewhere, but I can't see it. Richard stands proudly inside the door of the walk-in wardrobe. He has switched on the light and we can see rack upon rack of ladies' clothes hanging up, dozens of jackets and dresses. There are also many shelves, with neatly folded jumpers, sweaters and trousers. It strikes me that, although there is dust visible in the air, this room is much cleaner than the others I've seen in the house.

The room is genuinely impressive and is somewhat of a surprise, having spent two hours downstairs in a cramped sitting room. Richard has already told us we cannot film the walk-in wardrobe. But now, as he is showing us the room, I double check with him. 'You don't want us to film anything here, Richard, is that right?' He confirms that he doesn't. He seems a little apologetic about it. I say it's okay – I don't want to push, and I already have other filming ideas.

Next he wants to show us the sunbed room. This is one floor up, at the top of the house. There's also a room up there with bags and shoes. We hover in the doorways of both rooms, looking into them. I thank Richard for showing them to us. It is definitely helpful to have seen the rooms, even if we are not permitted to film them.

As we walk back downstairs – again walking directly above

where Tina's body lies – I ask Richard if he would come with me on a different day to the spot where he proposed to Tina. I want to spend more time with Richard, and I'm struck by the idea of doing a car journey with him. I suggest that I'd very much like if he showed me around Youghal, pointing out areas of importance in making a public appeal for help in finding Tina. He says he's happy to do that, and it'll just depend on when he's working. In that moment I know he will do it – he's not going to change his mind or fob me off. What he likes is the power to choose when and where to do things. He'll let me know when he's free over the next few days. He is comfortable with me, and I am comfortable with him. I do find him a strange man, but the more time I spend with him, the more I am learning. I don't yet know that the more time I spend with him, the more he will lie to me, spinning me a false story that will ultimately help convict him of murder.

———

In the hallway, Shirley, Kevin and I say goodbye to Richard. Shirley and Kevin are carrying the camera and lights and don't have a hand free. I do, and I shake Richard's hand, the one I'm conscious he used to wipe snot away earlier. It doesn't matter – I'll wash my hand later. Richard has a warm hand, with hard coarse skin, and a firm handshake.

'Thanks, Richard, talk to you soon.' And then we are gone from 3 Grattan Street. I will never set foot inside the door again, but my work that night will, one day, be part of Richard's undoing.

Shirley, Kevin and I take in the fresh Youghal sea air. This has been a baptism of fire for Shirley, and a night that we will remember forever. But we are not finished working just yet. 'Let's go to Apache Grill,' suggests Kevin. 'We can get some footage of it and some food too.' We are famished. An intense two and a half hours inside Richard and Tina's home has taken its toll on us. We walk up Grattan Street, then turn left up the oddly named Meat Shambles Lane and onto Main Street. In the dark evening, Shirley films the exterior of the takeaway, then we order some food to eat back at our cars.

Just as we have collected our order, Richard walks in. It's the strangest feeling to see him there after the time we have spent in his house. He is coming to get his late dinner too. 'Just getting the food before we head back to Dublin,' I say, stating the obvious, but it seems natural. Richard smiles at me and holds the door open, and we say goodbye. 'I'll see you soon again, Richard,' I say.

'Okay,' he replies, and he turns to the counter to order his food.

Years later, when I hear Richard's claim that he had a stool for sitting and talking to Tina in her grave under the stairs, I wonder if he sat there that night after getting his takeaway. Did he talk to Tina about the visit by RTÉ to the house? Did he tell her how he'd shown us around upstairs, and had given us an interview, and was going to meet us again soon? Did he tell her we were oblivious to her true plight? Did he tell her that no one would ever find her, that he, and only he, had her now, and she'd always be his?

12.

Mics, Camera, Car Journey

Almost three weeks after I first met Richard, I knock on his front door again. This occasion is also by arrangement. Today is the day we are going to drive around Youghal and film our journey.

Sunday, 10 December, is the day Richard has chosen. He has been busy with work for the past fortnight. He's told me that driving and staying active is what is keeping him going.

The planned car trip around Youghal will tick a number of boxes for me. It will allow me to learn more about Tina and what her life was like in the 10 months she had been living in the town prior to her disappearance. Importantly, filming inside a car will also allow for another intimate interview with Richard. The physical nature of such an encounter is important. I have already watched him do a face-to-face interview with Paul Byrne on TV3 where he'd been directly asked if he had caused harm to his wife. I need to do something different with my report, and I feel that myself and Richard sitting side by side, looking ahead out a car window, is a good way to ask him sensitive questions.

Richard had understood when I told him, during our first

meeting, that my report about Tina would not be broadcast for a number of weeks. I still intend the report to be broadcast before Christmas. Richard understands the difference between what I am seeking to do and what other reporters have already done – I am looking to do a long report which will be as informative as possible, with various layers of Tina's story being profiled. I have the luxury of spending a number of weeks researching and filming. The more straightforward appeals on news bulletins, which had already been broadcast months before, have not led to any breakthrough in the case. Because the case has hit a wall, I have the opportunity to commit the resources of RTÉ *Prime Time* to do a detailed report.

By the time I return to Richard Satchwell's door on 10 December, I have also been inside Midleton garda station, filming a case conference about Tina's disappearance. Although Youghal is the closest garda station to Tina's home, Midleton is the largest station in the district and is where the investigation is based. I interview Detective Inspector Brian Goulding, who outlines the extent of garda enquiries, at home and abroad, to try to find Tina. He tells me 200 lines of enquiry are still being followed up; he speaks of how there are only a small number of CCTV cameras in Youghal and there is still no credible sighting of a woman matching Tina's description in the town on 20 March. As I film inside Midleton station, it is clear the team of officers are busy dealing with the 'jobs' attached to Tina's case file – possible leads which need to be followed up.

I have also made contact with Tina's aunt Margaret and her niece Sarah Howard. I arrange an interview with Sarah in Fermoy, and she speaks movingly and with great dignity about her missing aunt. When I ask her what she feels might have happened to Tina, Sarah replies that she just doesn't know. 'It's puzzling – it's a complete mystery,' she says. Sarah tells me of Tina's love of fashion and how she is loved by many people. By the time I meet Sarah she has private concerns about Richard's behaviour, but we don't discuss that during our interview.

I have felt it important to speak with Tina's family to get a sense of what might be really going on. Having spent two and a half hours with Richard inside 3 Grattan Street, the thought has struck me, more than once, that perhaps Tina simply decided to leave him. She had every right to walk out of her life with Richard, and she might have had very good reason. But the more I speak with gardaí, and with Sarah and other members of Tina's family, the clearer it is that no one helped Tina to escape from Richard, and if she had left by herself she would almost certainly have been found by now, due to the intense media attention the case has garnered. It is becoming increasingly likely that something sinister has happened to Tina, but does Richard have the answers?

As we drive from Dublin on Sunday, 10 December, Kevin and I plan to be in Youghal by midday, but the weather is poor, and we are delayed. I have sent Richard a text the day before, checking if 12 o'clock suits for us to meet, and he has replied 'Yes that's good'. Richard and I are now in regular text contact. I have told him I have interviewed a garda about the case and that I've met with Sarah to do an interview. Likewise, I have told Detective Inspector Brian Goulding and Sarah Howard that I have spent a considerable amount of time inside 3 Grattan Street, and that I intend to do more filming with Richard.

On the journey down Kevin and I discuss what we've filmed so far and what we hope to achieve today. Our plan is simply to let it happen – to adapt to wherever Richard brings me on the car journey and to guide the interview according to whatever he might say. We both realise, from that first evening's lengthy filming inside the house, that the more time we spent with Richard, the more he said and the more information we got. Kevin and I are now in that perfect zone for a reporter and producer working on a difficult and complex report – we are almost finishing each other's sentences, completely in tune with how we will tell this sad and intriguing story.

Our cameraman this day is Nick Dolan, a vastly experienced operator, who has worked in *Prime Time* for years. I filmed with Nick in the United States many years before, as we followed the trail of 'Jihad Jane' – an American woman who had travelled to Ireland to join a terrorist plot to murder a Swedish cartoonist. Nick knows my reporting style and the unique stories that I like to cover, and today in Youghal will be no different. He has set off early from Dublin in his van to be in position for this day's work.

I mention to Kevin on the journey down that I'm due to travel to Wales the next day on a different story. It will be a quick-turnaround report relating to the body of an Irish person being finally identified after almost a quarter of a century, and I'll be travelling with cameraman Aidan McGuinness. I am operating on adrenaline, driving all the way to Youghal for filming with Richard and planning to be in Wales on a completely different story the following day. This is the kind of mad-dash journalism I thrive on.

―――

Kevin and I are almost an hour late when we finally reach Youghal. I park my Volkswagen Passat next to Nick's car, down past the credit union, and walk to Richard's house. Heavy rain bounces off the footpath on Grattan Street as I arrive.

I hear a shuffling sound inside the house and Richard comes to the door. We say hello and I shake hands with him again. Despite the rain, Richard doesn't invite me to stand in the hallway. He disappears inside for a few seconds, then is suddenly back at the front door. He pulls it shut and walks with me up to the right, towards my car. He is wearing a lumber jacket, heavy work trousers and runners; I'm wearing a long coat over my suit. The rain hits our faces as we walk the short distance to my car.

'Thanks again for your time today, Richard,' I say.

'It's no problem, I'm off work today,' he replies.

I also thank him again for doing such a lengthy interview

almost three weeks before. We cross the road near the Old Pier. The rain is easing slightly as I introduce Richard once again to Kevin and for the first time to Nick, who is busy fixing a suction camera to the window on the driver's side of my car.

This is going to be a two-camera shoot – the camera stuck to the inside of my window will capture both me in the driver's seat and Richard in the front passenger seat. Nick will be behind me, in the back of the car, holding a much larger camera and will film Richard's side profile and any areas of interest that Richard points out as we drive around Youghal.

On the journey down, Kevin and I have come up with a loose plan. Kevin will drive Nick's van, following my car as I drive Richard wherever he directs me. Kevin won't know what we are discussing during the car interview, but we have spent the two-hour drive from Dublin going over the areas I should focus on with Richard.

We have talked about the possibility of Richard suggesting we do the filming in his car, with him driving. But there are health and safety concerns that mean we cannot consider this as an option. I've only met Richard once, and although I haven't felt threatened by him, I need to consider that he might in fact be a violent man, a volatile individual who might seek to cause injury to Nick and me as we travel with him. I want to be the driver so I can control the vehicle, and I want to use my Passat – I'm confident driving my own family car, which I've had for a decade, and where I know I can counter any sudden movements from Richard.

Kevin and I have agreed that we can explain to Richard

that my car is particularly wide in the back to allow space for a cameraman to operate, and we have it all cleared out and prepared. However, despite us spending considerable time chatting about all of this, Richard never suggests travelling in his car; he is quite happy to sit into the front passenger seat of my Volkswagen.

As we arrive at the vehicle, Richard and I quickly get in out of the rain while Nick makes final adjustments to the cameras, and Kevin gets into Nick's van beside us.

The rain is beating heavily on the windscreen and the condensation is growing on the windows. We are not going to be able to film very much out the windows today, but we will get lots of material inside the vehicle as we drive around Youghal. Richard and I have arranged that I will drive up to where he proposed to Tina, and we'll stop off en route for him to show me 'a favourite spot of Tina's', near the lighthouse, where she would spend a lot of time sitting on a bench, overlooking the sea.

Before I reverse out of my parking space to begin the journey I show Richard the camera to my right, which is trained on both of us, and he can see Nick sitting in the back seat. Richard seems very comfortable with us, and I notice he is freshly shaven and seems more together than the first time we met. He seems keen to do the journey and the filming – and so am I.

In the strange way of making television, Richard ends up holding a large furry microphone, which Nick hands to him in the front seat, asking him to hold it down below his waistline, in his right hand, so it's out of shot.

Richard seems comfortable with the mic. Nick, ever a professional, is treating Richard with the same respect as any interviewee, addressing him by first name and getting him involved in what we are doing. Filming for a television report can be an awkward thing to do, but just like Shirley in the house, Nick in my car is making Richard feel comfortable with the mechanics of it, so the unnaturalness of what we are doing soon comes to feel natural.

The rain is now hitting the car heavily, the windscreen wipers are going full speed and I have the air conditioning on to clear the windows. It is all very atmospheric and, I am privately thinking, potentially disarming for Richard. We are doing filming that no one else has managed to achieve with him.

Nick hands Richard a small clapperboard, about the size of his hand. The clapperboard has an important function – to synchronise the suctioned camera on the window with the sound being recorded onto the camera Nick is holding on the back seat, something which is crucial for when the report will be compiled in an edit suite. As I sit strapped into the driver's seat I am wearing a small microphone, and Richard beside me, also wearing his seat-belt, is holding the boom mic.

'Other camera is on?' asks Nick.

I check that the red light of the camera to my right, suctioned onto the window, is showing. 'Other camera is running, Nick,' I reply.

MICS, CAMERA, CAR JOURNEY

'Okay, clapperboard please, Richard,' says Nick, inviting Richard to close the clapperboard, which makes a short firm sound when depressed. It adds both a sense of distraction and importance to what we are doing.

Richard depresses it, and I slowly begin driving. Before I'm in third gear I pull back into the side of the road, as Nick needs to readjust his camera and the rear-view mirror to hide his reflection from what is being recorded. He asks Richard to depress the clapperboard again, which he does much more forcefully this time. We are off on our journey, and I am about to learn a lot more about my front-seat passenger.

13.

Up to the Lighthouse

We pull out into traffic on the one-way system of Market Square, an extension of Grattan Street. My mind is suddenly consumed by various thoughts. This is the way Tina would have travelled if she got into a vehicle to leave her old life behind. Where did she go, why did she go, or did she have a choice about going at all? Did Richard force her into a vehicle, did he entice her into their car on some false pretext, or was Tina abducted by a random stranger? Or is it actually possible that she arranged to flee, to escape the life she and Richard had shared? From my time spent filming with Richard in 3 Grattan Street I got the sense that life inside the house was a claustrophobic world; he was a constant presence in his wife's life. Had she tried to get away from that? Had she been successful?

I force myself to focus, to snap out of my thoughts. I need to listen to Richard. I need him to guide me, both in terms of where I should drive and what we should discuss. He is in control here.

The sound of the windscreen wipers is loud and irritating. I'm frustrated by the wet weather, I want to be able to get out and walk with Richard if needs be. Perhaps he would like to walk and talk, as well as drive and talk. But the weather is atrocious, so we are going to be stuck in the car. However, as I continue the journey, I will come to realise that the claustrophobic setting inside the car is actually a good ambience for filming.

As we drive further up Market Square, hardly anyone is out walking, as it is so wet. I negotiate a sharp corner, turning right, and Richard helps me by craning his neck to the left, telling me we are clear, and I proceed slowly. On we drive, up along O'Brien Place with the coast immediately to our left. We continue onto Lighthouse Road, and I begin the interview by asking Richard why Youghal was so special to him and Tina.

'Tina always liked it from when we first met. So we'd always come here on a regular basis. Back then we didn't have a car, we used to hitch-hike. Over the years when we'd have a car we'd be down every week.'

Richard's voice is clear; he is in control, directing me where to go. He is relaxed, and in his first answer I've learned of the couple's links to Youghal going back over a quarter of a century. This bodes well for a talkative car journey. Approaching a fork in the road I ask for Richard's assistance – 'Do I stay in this left lane, Richard?' He confirms that I should.

'So you're saying, Richard, that although most of your life in Ireland was in Fermoy with Tina, that Youghal is also an important part?' I ask, with my eyes on the road ahead.

'I'd say Youghal was a major part. Because we were sorry that we didn't buy here instead of Fermoy,' Richard replies.

'Fermoy is where Tina is originally from?' I know the answer already but I want Richard to talk more about Fermoy. I am increasingly puzzled as to why he had not reported Tina missing in Youghal, but rather had gone all the way to Fermoy to do it. But I feel if I ask him that specific question right now it will create a barrier. I've already asked him about it during the first interview in the house.

'Yes, Tina's from Fermoy,' Richard answers as he looks out the front window. 'She has family there, but this is where she always wanted to come.'

The windscreen wipers are moving at full speed, and I've again moved into third gear as we drive along. 'And why, Richard? I mean it's a lovely spot, but why were you attracted to Youghal?'

'Well, I think Tina always loved the beach,' he answers. 'Tina's one of these lucky people that only have to look at the sun to get a colour.' I move from third to fourth gear. He's talking about Tina in the present tense, I think to myself.

'Just turn slightly towards Barry, please, Richard,' asks Nick from the back, wanting a better side profile of my interviewee, and Richard complies happily. He seems relaxed and willing to do whatever is asked. I'll pull in soon for a little bit, I think. I'll give it another minute or two of driving.

'Richard, how has it been for you since Tina went missing?' I ask. 'You're still in your home and Tina's home, in Youghal. You've stayed here, you walk the dogs here and this is your home. What's it like being in Youghal at the moment with Tina missing?'

If only I'd known at that moment the significance of that

question. 'You are still in your home ... What's it like?' But I've no idea of the secrets buried within the house, or buried within Richard.

'It's lonely, very lonely,' replies Richard. 'Because I built my life around her. So when that's gone, you know, you've got nothing.'

I notice Richard's answer seems quite final. The life built around Tina is 'gone', he now has 'nothing'. Just a minute earlier he was describing Tina in the present tense and now, in the next breath, there seems to be finality. My mind is racing – maybe I'm overthinking things. I turn off the windscreen wipers for a bit, as the rain is easing slightly.

'And, Richard, I know you're working, you're driving for work, you're busy a lot of the time. But when you're not working, what are you doing?' This is a personal question, but I feel that showing the impact of Tina's absence on Richard is important.

'Well, a lot of the time I sit down like a zombie. Sometimes I motivate myself to do a bit of work on the house 'cause there's still a lot of work needs doing on it. I take the dogs out 'cause you can't neglect the pets. It's things like that you have to try and use to keep yourself some bit motivated.'

As we continue driving with the coast to our left, I notice that Richard has never mentioned having any friends – he seems very much alone. I feel I am filling a void: we are not friends, but we seem to chat easily with each other. He is talkative, telling me new information, but I believe there is more – I believe he is holding back. Time to pull in, I think to myself.

A few hundred yards from Youghal lighthouse, I pull in on the left, high above the water's edge. The normally scenic coastline is hard to see because of the dull wet sky. I put on the handbrake and keep the engine running. The air conditioning is still on, the windows de-misting.

'I'm just going to pull in here for a minute. The number of appeals you've done, and you're doing this appeal as well, does it take its toll? The constant media attention is important, but what do you feel about the media?'

Richard looks out the window straight ahead. That's the way we are chatting, occasionally turning towards each other, but mostly looking out the window, just the way I'd planned it with Kevin earlier: Richard and I like two men at a bar or sitting on a wall, shooting the breeze.

'As regards doing stuff like this I think it's good,' Richard says. 'But I think the way the papers do stuff, to be honest with you, I myself find it misleading.' I notice Richard is again using the phrase 'to be honest' – are you actually being honest, though, I wonder.

'Turn a little bit more towards Barry, please, Richard, once again, thank you.' Nick's voice comes from behind me.

Richard complies as I ask, 'In terms of some of the reporting that's going on, what's upsetting you?'

'The way the press twist everything.' Richard is again referring to the print media – he doesn't seem to like 'the press'. 'It's like the way I did the report there with Paul Byrne on our anniversary.'

I know the interview Richard is talking about – a solid straight-shooting interview the TV3 southern correspondent had conducted with Richard the previous month. Paul Byrne had directly asked Richard what he said to people who wondered if he had something to do with his wife's disappearance.

I have been planning to go down this conversation route with Richard, but he has now gone there himself. This is good, I think. I don't react, I just listen, I want him to continue speaking. I can't see the logic in Richard's dislike of print journalists, and I know he is also being selective in which broadcast journalists he will speak with. It is becoming clear that he really only seems to like speaking with Paul Byrne and myself. His selection of the two of us as his 'trusted' media people is intriguing, as we have different interviewing styles. Paul is more direct – as a journalist for a news programme, he has to be. I, on the other hand, as an investigative reporter, can take my time, often circling the subject, getting them to relax and slowly divulge as much information as possible – I have the luxury of taking weeks before I will broadcast a report.

I stop the windscreen wipers, as the rain is a little easier and we are parked up. Richard continues talking about the newspaper coverage which followed his interview with TV3 the previous month. 'It then comes up in the press, like, "I deny anything to do with my wife's death". As far as I'm concerned, my wife is out there somewhere, and one day she is going to come back. I do not believe she is dead.' I turn off the air conditioning for a moment as I listen to every word

Richard says. He is back speaking about Tina in the present tense, I notice. And he's also just acknowledged that he has become part of the story.

As he speaks about 'the press', I sense that Richard is getting slightly angry. 'You believe Tina is still out there somewhere and can be found?' I ask him, feeling this is the most animated he has been.

'I honestly, truly, believe that,' he replies.

I wait a beat, then come back with a question I've held off asking him until I feel the time is right.

'What's your message directly to Tina then?' I want to see if Richard will do it, but eight words into his answer, he stops speaking to Tina directly, and slips back to speaking generally.

'I just want you to get in touch. I want her to get in touch, let people know that she's alright. If she needs time on her own, fair enough. There's nobody going to hold grudges or anything like that. I mean, she knows me well enough that I won't.'

I am fascinated by this response. I asked Richard very specifically what his direct message to Tina was. I prefaced the question by acknowledging his clearly expressed view that Tina is still alive. But despite my making the situation as conducive as possible for a direct appeal to be made to his wife, Richard isn't able to speak to her apart from saying, 'I just want you to get in touch.'

Something is off about all of this, but I don't know exactly what. I have a lot more questions to ask.

'Do you think there are people out there who have information?'

His answer to this is clear: he is blaming someone somewhere for what has happened. 'I believe there is somebody or somebodies [sic] out there that actually does know where she is, because she didn't get up and leave without some kind of help from somebody,' Richard says, looking out the front window into the middle distance. I feel there is ever-growing anger in his voice now.

I look out at the dark sky, and I let a few moments of silence pass as I reflect on my passenger's comments. Richard is very different today to the first day I met him. He is more animated, more angry, but I feel he's trying not to show his anger.

I glance at the man sitting right beside me, a long-distance lorry driver. I know that if he has killed his wife he may have hidden her body anywhere in County Cork, or further afield. But he is also showing signs of stress and seems very alone. He is speaking about Tina in the present tense, yet doesn't seem able to speak directly to her. Something feels wrong about it all, but I can't put my finger on it.

'What kind of emotions are you feeling at the moment, so many months after Tina has gone missing?' I'm looking out the front window but talking to my left, where Richard is sitting. There is little or no eye contact, but our conversation is intimate. I press more, adding, 'The reason we're doing this interview is that there is no big lead, and the fear is that months become something longer. What are you feeling at the moment?'

'I live in a state of hope,' answers Richard. 'I just hope that one day she'll knock at the door as suddenly as what [*sic*] she left, or ring a member of the family, ring me or ring the gardaí. I live in hope from day to day.'

Time to move gear again, I decide. I know that gardaí fear Tina has been the victim of violence. 'While I know you think Tina "upped and left", even having done that, if that's what happened, she may have come to harm thereafter. Have you contemplated that?' I ask.

Richard takes the question but again brings it back to a belief that Tina is alive. 'Well, naturally after so long, them [*sic*] thoughts do creep in and you're just hoping, wishing that she's somewhere and she's well and safe and she's got loyal friends around her somewhere that's not willing to leave her whereabouts be known [*sic*] for the time being.'

I think of Tina's niece Sarah in Fermoy – if anyone knew that Tina was in hiding it would be Sarah. But Sarah does not know where Tina is and she is extremely concerned for her. Still, I don't want to challenge Richard's views completely; I am trying to gauge his thoughts and tease them out further. I'm asking hard questions in a soft way. Richard is a guest in my car, just like I had been a guest in his house.

Time to shake it up again, I decide, and I move into first gear and go to pull out to drive further up Lighthouse Road. Nick interjects again: the large microphone in Richard's right hand has slowly crept up during our chat. Nick asks him to swap it to his left hand to make it less obvious in the shot, and Richard complies. This interruption from Nick is welcome; it gives me a second or two to think.

I'm now convinced that Richard has secrets. I can read it in his body language, and I can hear it in his voice. But I have

UP TO THE LIGHTHOUSE

to be careful how I probe. We all have secrets, I think. We all have bits of our lives we don't want to discuss, especially on national television. Having secrets doesn't mean someone is a killer. But what is really going on here?

As I move from second to third gear and we drive towards the lighthouse I look at the clock. It's only lunchtime but I have my exterior car lights on. The sky is dark grey, pools of water are gathered along parts of the road, and the rain continues to fall. 'This part of Youghal is important to you. Tell me about it, Richard,' I ask gently.

'This is a favourite spot of Tina's,' he says as we approach the lighthouse. 'Tina would walk up here, sit on the third bench in, overlooking the water, with a small flask of tea that I'd make before she left. And she'd sit there listening to music on her headphones. And she'd walk along towards the strand with Ruby and she'd ring me to let me know she was on her way back so I could have a sandwich or something ready for her. And then every evening we'd bring Ruby ourselves together and we'd walk up and stand overlooking the water at the railing, and then we'd sit down and cuddle in for a bit, talking.'

There is so much to digest in what Richard has just said. I am struck that, within this happy memory of Tina, are descriptions of things that Richard would do for her. He made the flask of tea, he made the sandwiches. And the description of cuddling on a bench is striking, and also strange. It reminds me of 'puppy love', the first throes of a loving relationship.

How many men in their fifties would describe cuddling with their wives? I wonder. Stop being judgemental, I chide myself, gripping the steering wheel. Richard is making a public appeal, and he has chosen to speak with you. Be respectful.

———

We continue driving past the lighthouse to the location where Richard proposed to Tina 28 years before. We have much more to talk about. I have asked to see this particular place, and Richard has readily said yes.

I have no idea the location we are travelling to is also part of Richard's cover-up, his callousness, his control.

Swish, swish go the windscreen wipers, and we drive further up Lighthouse Road towards Front Strand, overlooking Youghal Beach.

14.

Proposal Spot

Visibility is pretty bad as we drive towards Front Strand. The wipers are going full speed and, at another fork in the road, Richard tells me to keep right to stay on the main road, which rises high leaving Youghal.

I check my back mirror and see Kevin is following close behind in Nick's van. Nick is directly behind my seat, his camera trained on Richard in the front, and occasionally getting reaction shots of me in the mirror. More than once I have demisted the windows, the breath of three men often quickly fogging the windows on this journey.

I ask Richard if members of the public have recognised him as a result of the many appeals he has made for information about Tina's disappearance. In other circumstances it might seem like a strange question, but as we drive along in difficult weather conditions, both of us looking at the road straight ahead, the unusual environment makes such questions easier to ask.

'Especially with me being out on the road, I get a lot of people wish [sic] me well, and ask if there's any news,' Richard replies.

'And what do you say to them?' I ask.

'Same thing I say to anybody – I wish,' he replies with an ironic grunt.

'Just turn to Barry a bit more, Richard, thanks,' Nick asks, and Richard turns so that more of his profile is visible on camera. Richard is a very amenable interviewee, following any requests Nick makes in terms of how he sits and what way he faces. Nick is doing a great job in the back, filming in a tight space with a large camera propped on his shoulder. I am driving as slowly as I can, trying not to go past third gear – the driving conditions are now so bad outside.

'This spot here means so much to us. You'll be able to pull into a car park just up here on the right,' Richard says, using his right hand to point over to a tarmacadamed area which is empty of any other cars this afternoon. I pull into a parking spot and press the brake button, leaving the engine running. I see Kevin stop Nick's van close by, and he stays in the vehicle. He knows to keep back and let the rhythm of the interview continue – if we are having any issues I will alert him.

I know from my previous meeting with Richard that this location is very special to both him and Tina, and he reminds me of that as I park up. 'It means so much up here that when Pearl died we brought up her leftover seed and we spread it up here for the birds. And we sat over the road for two hours, just watching them.'

What Richard doesn't say, as he sits just a foot away from me in my car, is that birdseed isn't the only thing he has spread in this location. This is also the location where he drove by himself in the aftermath of burying Tina's body. Over the course of a number of nights, this is where he brought bags full of soil that he had unearthed while digging the large hole in which he had placed Tina's body. Under cover of darkness Richard repeatedly emptied the bag, just like he had previously emptied the birdseed when Tina was with him. He scattered the soil at this spot where he proposed to Tina decades before.

―――

'This area is what they call Mountpleasant,' Richard says. He's lost that little bit of anger that I sensed earlier. 'And I actually proposed to Tina on the prow of that hill, overlooking the ocean. That was in October 1989.' Richard uses his right hand to point to his left at a point on the cliff that looks down at sand dunes and a scenic expansive beach.

This is a very nice part of Youghal. A pitch and putt course is nearby, and a caravan park is just a little further on. A panoramic view of Youghal town is normally visible, but not on this wet day.

I decide to keep Richard thinking of the past, a time when he and Tina began their relationship. I stop the windscreen wipers and ask, 'You were saying before, Richard, that when you first saw Tina you knew you were going to be together?'

Richard's speech is quick as he gets out the next sentence. 'I know people say that it all don't [sic] exist, but I knew before I even spoke with her that I wanted to spend the rest of my life with her.'

I think of a 17-year-old Tina and her limited life experience.

For half of that young life she thought her grandmother Florence was her mother. Tina was extremely close to her grandmother, so much so that she had followed her over from Fermoy to Coalville in Leicester in 1989. Tina had never been in a relationship before, and then Richard Satchwell spotted her.

'I actually seen [sic] her a couple of days before I spoke to her,' he says, looking out at the spot where he proposed. This is a new detail. I didn't know that he didn't speak to Tina for a few days after spotting her in Coalville. Was he working up the courage to speak with her? Why wait to chat up the woman or girl of your dreams? I chide myself for letting my mind wander. Keep quiet, keep focused and let Richard talk.

Richard continues his recollection of how Tina was living next door to his brother and had called into the house to say hello when Richard happened along. 'She was actually in my brother's house, and that's how we got speaking first time.'

Just as I'm thinking how Richard was 22 when he met Tina, how he was a young man and she was a girl, not a woman, he answers my unspoken thought about what her family thought of his interest in Tina. 'She's not a trusting type of person, she wouldn't trust anyone straight away, and anytime we did go anywhere together, we either had her mother with us or a sister that was living over there at the time. And it was probably three months before we went out together on our own.' I notice that Richard is using the present tense again for Tina – 'she's not a trusting type of person'.

I move the conversation to present day and an issue I'd broached in the first interview. 'You were saying before,

Richard, that there was something on Tina's mind or troubling her?' I immediately sense that Richard is going to say more about this – he's beginning to talk almost before I've finished the question.

'Tina's one of these people that wouldn't go to the doctor unless absolutely necessary. I'm the same, my mother was the same. My opinion was, and still is, that she knew she was depressed – one thing she always said was that she didn't want to end up on antidepressants. And I personally think she went away for a while to sort her own feelings out. I went away for a while – I went away for a year myself.'

If I wasn't sitting down I might have fallen over. Richard went away for a year? He left Tina? My mind is spinning, but I don't react, I just listen, and I look out the front window of the car. This is a bolt out of the blue. A man who, up to now, has spoken about being so completely devoted to a woman he first met when she was a teenager is now telling me he left her for a year? What is going on?

'I went away for a year myself when I got down. And I came back after a year. But the difference is I was in touch with Tina. Tina knew, so that's the difference between the two.'

My mind races. Did he go away due to mental health issues? Did he have depression? I want to know more, but I'm walking a fine line. Richard is an interviewee and entitled to some degree of privacy. I'm only interested in information which might help find Tina, yet I feel Richard has more to say.

'When you went away, you were married at that stage?' I ask.

'Yes, we'd been married 10 years at that stage.'

That'd be around 2001 or so, I think to myself. 'And Tina was in the house in Fermoy?'

'Yes,' Richard replies.

'And you were elsewhere?' I clumsily ask, but Richard gives me the detail I am seeking.

'I was in the UK,' he responds.

It will be years later that I learn Richard spent that year in England by himself because he had fled Ireland after being caught claiming the dole while also working. He owed significant moneys to the State, and he went to England for a year, but then decided to return to Ireland and face the music, plead guilty and resume his life with Tina after being sentenced to a short jail term for social welfare fraud.

We have now been in the car for over 45 minutes, and I need to finish the interview soon. The air is stale, and I can't open the windows without rain coming in. Richard has given me a lot of new information. I get the sense that I could meet him countless more times and get new information every time. This filming today has been very beneficial – I have learned a lot, and it will greatly assist in compiling a comprehensive report. I have a few more questions, though, and Richard seems to have more to say. He is now speaking spontaneously, without any questions being asked by me. He tells me Tina and himself used to have long chats.

'I know that leading up to her going, the frequency of our long conversations had altered somewhat,' he says, turning more towards me but still looking out the front window. 'The bit I don't get is why she didn't turn around and say I'm struggling. A couple of times I did broach the subject with her, but she'd just go within herself and that'd be the end of the conversation.'

Richard continues speaking about Tina and the time they spent together. 'Relatively much [*sic*] we'd spend every waking hour together. Even when I was driving for work she'd be in the passenger seat with me.'

I want to bring this chat back to Tina and what might have happened to her. I think of the dogs – Richard told me earlier that he has left them in the house today. 'Are the dogs missing Tina, are they wondering where she is?' In one way it's a silly question to ask, but I feel that anyone with a pet will understand the love Tina had for her dogs and the animals had for her. It might strike a nerve in a public appeal.

'When she first went away they'd be lying outside the room I converted into a wardrobe for her.' Again, I notice how Richard is inserting himself into an answer. So often, he's telling me what he has done for Tina. I feel he's making sure to tell me it was him who made the walk-in wardrobe. Maybe it's just his way, I think. He continues: 'If I'm doing work on the house and I move something that's got her scent on it, their tails wag, and it's just totally heartbreaking.' His voice seems to waver as he says this; he seems upset, but holding it inside.

I'm almost finished, but I decide to give Richard another chance to speak directly to Tina. 'I've asked you this already, Richard, but it's the most important question. What is your message to Tina?'

This time he seems better able to speak to a woman he maintains is alive somewhere. 'Just get in touch, let me know where you are, and if you don't want to let me know where you are, let me know you are alright. That's all I want to know, that's all the family wants to know.'

I stay silent in case he wants to add anything, but after a second or two it's clear he is finished speaking directly to Tina. Years later, his calculated, conniving answer to me, as we sit in my car at this place, will be played to a jury who will decide he is guilty of murder.

I pull out of the car park and, as we head back towards Youghal, Richard directs me to drive past the leisure centre where Tina had begun swimming in the weeks before she vanished. Richard recounts how he would drive her up to the pool and then he'd walk the dogs while Tina swam, and he'd be waiting for her when she came out. Her only personal space, time to herself, was when she was underwater, I think.

I steer the conversation back to media coverage of Tina's disappearance. Richard again takes a swipe at 'the press'. 'I don't think they are helping,' he says. 'If they can't print what is said, then don't print nothing [sic].'

'And that interview with TV3 you mentioned earlier,' I say, 'you're saying some print media reports after that interview were twisted in some way?'

'Well, it did become twisted,' Richard replies, visibly keen to answer. 'Because I never once denied having anything to do with my wife's death. Because in my opinion she is not dead. Yes, Paul Byrne asked me straight out – did I kill my wife – and I've never laid a finger on her. I couldn't. I'm just not that type of person anyway.'

I run Richard's last answer through my mind. He is being categoric, saying he has never laid a finger on Tina; he's acknowledging a question that has been previously asked of him, if he killed Tina; and he is stating clearly that he believes she is still alive. There is nowhere else to go with this interview – for now, we are done.

'You're okay this side,' says Richard, checking traffic to his left as we drive on back to the Old Pier, close to 3 Grattan Street. The rain has stopped, and I smile ruefully to myself – it would stop raining now, wouldn't it, just as we finish up. But I already know that the filming in the car has recorded powerful material. It has shown a more talkative Richard, a man who has revealed a lot more about his own past life and who seems to change between speaking about Tina in the present and past tenses.

———

I stop the car close to a bus stop on Lighthouse Road, and Nick steps out onto the footpath. It's a welcome stretch of the legs for Nick, who has by now been filming Richard inside the car for over an hour. Nick sets the camera on his shoulder as I drive off with Richard and do a U-turn a short distance up the road. We drive back down past Nick so we can get an establishing shot, showing Richard and myself in the car driving along. Six years later this will be the exact spot where Detective Garda Dave Kelleher will formally arrest Richard for the murder of Tina, and Richard will never be a free man again.

As I sit alone in the car with Richard while we film the establishing footage, I am struck by his height once again. I don't feel threatened by him, but I do have a strange feeling, one I cannot figure out. We make chit-chat as we do the driving shot, and Richard tells me he will give the dogs a walk once I drop him back. 'Could we film you walking the dogs, please, Richard? It'd be the last thing we'd do today – only if it suits?' I ask.

'That's no problem,' he replies.

'I meant to ask you, Richard, do you have any video footage of Tina that we could show in our report?' I have intentionally waited until now to ask this. I have wanted to build up the best rapport possible first.

'I think I have something on my phone,' Richard answers. 'There are videos, but the gardaí have the laptops with those videos. I'll look on my phone later.'

We pick up Nick and go back to the Old Pier, and as Richard returns to his house to get Ruby and Heidi, I give Kevin a quick update, which I sum up as 'we have more than enough material to go to air with a report now'. We agree we'll chat it through on the drive home and that we'll make a pitch to our editors to get a report broadcast within the next two weeks, before *Prime Time* goes off air for the Christmas break.

Richard arrives back with the dogs. Ruby is in a bright

pink coat, with a fur trim on the hood, and Heidi is wearing a light purple coat. Richard holds both of their leads in his left hand as he walks just a foot from the water's edge at the pier, with me to his right. We walk towards the camera, again making chit-chat, discussing Youghal and how scenic it is.

Then we say goodbye to Richard and pack up our equipment. I tell Richard I hope to have the report on air very soon, and I'll be in touch. He again says he'll look for video footage of Tina. I shake his hand, and I wish him well. I find myself saying goodbye to the dogs too and thanking them for being filmed. It's been that kind of day.

When I get home to Dublin that night I tell my wife, Grace, that I had Richard in our car that day and that the filming went well. Grace is well used to me doing unorthodox things in pursuit of my work – it's not the first time I've had interviewees in our family car. But this is the first time I've had someone like Richard Satchwell. Grace says it's good to hear that the filming was a success, and in the next breath tells me to make sure I get the car valeted. Time will prove that Grace is a particularly discerning woman.

15.

Into Christmas

Early next morning, Monday, 11 December, Kevin and I tell our editors about the previous day's filming. We know we have a powerful programme to put on air, but we quickly realise we will struggle to find a time slot – political issues and other important stories are already scheduled for broadcast on the upcoming *Prime Time* programmes, and we estimate we have almost a complete half-hour documentary from our time in Youghal. Our editor, Donogh Diamond, tells us it's looking more likely our report will have to hold until January. I'm disappointed, but I understand, and I don't yet know it, but the delay will allow for even more filming with Richard, where he will reveal more of his angry side.

After chatting with Donogh I immediately head from Donnybrook for the ferry; cameraman Aidan McGuinness and I are en route to Holyhead. Days earlier I'd received a call from police in Wales to alert me that the body of an Irish woman who had been buried unidentified in Wales for 23 years was finally being exhumed so she could be returned to her family in Ireland. Pauline Finlay was last seen walking her dog on a beach in County Wicklow in 1994. It was only decades later, during a cold-case review, that DNA comparisons confirmed the body buried in a cemetery near Anglesey in Wales was Pauline's.

This will be a quick-turnaround report for broadcast on *Prime Time* – a 'belt and braces' dash over to Wales and back to Dublin to get a report on air within 36 hours. My working life is a constant juggle of different stories.

On the way to the ferry I text Richard to say thank you again for his time the previous day. I also text him my email address so he can send on any videos of Tina he might locate.

I text a contact and tell them that, as well as filming in Richard and Tina's home, I've now also had Richard in my car, and we are very much on first-name terms. So much of my investigative work is based on anonymous sources, people who trust that I will never betray their confidence, never reveal their identity. For months I have been seeking information on Richard Satchwell, and quietly learning about his life in Youghal, and previously Fermoy. This contact believes Richard to be a manipulator, seeking to play various people against each other, including journalists. My contact has a firm suspicion that Richard knows more than he's letting on. 'Keep him talking' is the short answer I get back.

Shortly after driving off the ferry in Holyhead at 5.15 p.m. I get a text from Richard. 'Hi Barry, could you please let me know if the video is allright [*sic*] Richard.' I check my inbox but there's nothing there. 'Hi Richard. Just checking – I haven't got any email yet. Barry,' I respond. 'It's come back 5 times as undeliverable,' Richard quickly replies. 'Could you try cumminsb@yahoo.com,' I text back, knowing that RTÉ firewalls can sometimes block emails arriving into the system.

An email finally makes it through from Richard at 8 p.m., as I'm checking in at a bed and breakfast in west Wales. From rickiesat@live.ie he has sent me a video where you can hear Tina's voice. He writes the accompanying message to me all in capital letters, the first of many such messages he'll send me: HI BARRY HERE IS VIDEO TINA SAYS MORE THAN I REMEMBER THANKS RICHARD.

I immediately download the accompanying video. I can only see Tina for a second or two, as the video is actually one Richard has taken on his phone of their parrot Pearl. But for a few seconds, and just a few words, I can hear Tina. 'Heidi has distracted her,' Tina says in a clear Cork accent, as Pearl looks away from the camera. A few seconds later I hear Tina once more. 'What you got, Pearl?' she calls across the room at the parrot. Tina is out of vision, but her voice is distinct.

I find this video quite moving. I watch it a number of times, and I listen to Tina's voice again and again. It's now just a day since Richard sat in my car, and I've been thinking about him a lot, and now, with Tina's voice playing on my phone, I try to figure out what's going on. If Richard has actually caused harm to Tina, why would he send me a video of her? Is it possible he is simply a sad lonely man who doesn't know where his wife has gone?

I text Richard to confirm I have the video. I think texting is a little more personal than email, but I decide to keep the message brief. He seems to like directness. 'Thanks Richard. That's great to have. Talk soon. Barry.'

INTO CHRISTMAS

I need to get ready for my next day's filming in a cemetery in Wales, but I find myself again watching the video of Tina and studying every frame. She only appears for a second or two, sitting in a chair to the side of a fireplace. A glass table is in the foreground and there is various clutter. Pearl is playing in her cage with a plastic toy, and she is showing off, clinging to the cage with her claws and walking up the bars. The video is less than three minutes long. I listen to Tina's voice again.

Where are you, Tina? I wonder. Where are you?

A few days after I arrive back from Wales, Donogh Diamond confirms there isn't enough room in the programme schedule before Christmas 2017 to broadcast a lengthy report on Tina Satchwell. I have known this decision was very likely, and I understand. I adopt a 'glass half full' approach. I know that if we can hold the report until January it will reach a large audience, much larger than might watch television in the run-up to Christmas.

On the morning of Monday, 18 December, I ring Richard on his 085 number to tell him the report will be delayed, and I am worried that he will be annoyed. I would well understand if he was. His wife is missing, and every second counts.

'Hello,' Richard says, answering after a few rings.

'Hi, Richard, it's Barry.'

'Hi, Barry,' he replies, almost before I've finished saying my name. It makes me think he has my number saved and knew it was me ringing. It sounds quiet in the background on his end, no sound of traffic, or indeed the dogs. He must be in the house, I think.

I get to the point quickly, explaining that the report will not be broadcast until January, but that I am confident a very large number of people will watch it because of all the material we had filmed. 'I'm sorry it's not being shown immediately, but I know this will reach a lot of people, and hopefully get a breakthrough.' I close my eyes and wince slightly as I say this. I genuinely believe the final report will be impactful, but I am nervous about his reaction to news of this delay.

'That's alright, I understand,' he says. I breathe a quiet sigh of relief, but am somewhat surprised that he isn't expressing disappointment. He seems emotionless, quite matter-of-fact.

I move the conversation on to certain photos of Tina we had discussed during our car journey together the week before. Richard had told me about a sequence of three images he had taken of Tina walking the dogs in Youghal on Christmas Day 2016. He had been keen to send them to me and, during this phone call, says he'll do it today. I feel more relaxed now that he's becoming a little more animated. I honestly feel bad that the report is going to be delayed for a number of weeks, but with Richard saying he'll send me more photos, I know he is still keen to help with my research.

I tell Richard I'll be thinking about him and I'll be thinking about Tina over the Christmas period, and I'll be in touch as soon as I know when the report will be shown. And to myself, I'm thinking how, just days earlier, Kevin Burns had suggested we might want to film a short segment with Richard in Fermoy in the new year. Such filming would bring the report right up to date and give a new-year feel to the story. It would also allow us a third session of filming with Richard, and this time in the town where he and Tina had lived for two decades. As I bring our telephone conversation to an end, I tell Richard I might want to meet him briefly in the new year for some final filming if that's okay. He says that's fine, as long as he's not working.

A short time later an email lands from Richard. Unlike previous correspondence, this one is not in capital letters. 'Here are the photos you asked for' is the message accompanying three photos of Tina which were all taken in quick succession – in the images Tina holds Ruby by a lead in her right hand, her left hand is on her hip, and she is standing on a footpath, wearing a beige top and leggings and a woollen dress over them. She smiles at the camera, with the sand and sea in the distance behind her.

Just as I'm looking at the photos, a text arrives from Richard – 'Please could you check your emails, Richard.' He's obviously keen to ensure I have received these images; they are important to him. I reflect that, as we approach Christmas, Richard is thinking of last Christmas Day and the time he spent with Tina. 'Hi Richard, got those three photos. Thank you very much, Barry,' I reply.

Years later I will wonder if, over the Christmas period in 2017, Richard spent much time sitting on his stool and speaking to Tina's body under the stairs? Did he think about those photographs he had sent me, images of a happy Christmas Day 12 months before? Did he look at the concrete which covered Tina's body and tell her he was making media appeals, and that RTÉ were going to do a big report, and that he was helping the reporter by doing lots of interviews and giving photos? Did he reflect on the garda search of the couple's home earlier in the year which had failed to find Tina? Did Richard tell Tina that no one would ever find her now? Did he feel he would never be caught? Is that why he felt he could let me get so close?

16.

The Bridge

It is the second week of the new year when I meet Richard for our third interview. It's just over three weeks since I phoned him to say the report wouldn't be broadcast until early in 2018. In those three weeks I have kept in touch by email and text, wishing him well and saying I was thinking of Tina. I am genuine in my good wishes, but I also feel it important to keep in contact. Richard seems to be completely alone; I had got the sense, when I met Sarah Howard the previous month, that Tina's family in Fermoy are not in close contact with Richard. It is dawning on me that I am probably the person he is most in touch with – both in person and on the phone – over December 2017 and early January 2018.

On Monday, 8 January, I send Richard a text shortly after midday – 'Hi Richard, are you free to meet in Fermoy on either Wednesday or Friday of this week? Best wishes, Barry.' I wait for a reply all afternoon, but none comes. This is the first time in all my dealings with Richard that I feel worried he might stop speaking with me. With the many previous texts, he had always responded quite quickly.

I don't want to ring him – I want to wait for a reply to

the text. I dislike the practice of someone ringing to say, 'Did you get my text?' – it seems very pushy, and I don't want to do that with Richard. I decide to send an email, so he can see I am keen to meet soon but am letting him consider the options for when to meet. 'Hi Richard, How are things?' I write. 'Are you free on either Wednesday or Friday of this week to meet in Fermoy to do last bit of filming? Best wishes, Barry.'

I wait for a reply, and thankfully an email comes two hours later. Richard is back to using capital letters. 'WORKING BOTH DAYS BUT SHOULD BE BACK EARLY FRIDAY BUT DON,T [sic] WHAT TIME THAT WILL BE UNTIL FRIDAY THANKS RICHARD.'

Kevin and I have already arranged to go back to Youghal on the Wednesday morning to interview local journalist Ann Mooney of *The Irish Sun*. Ann was the first reporter to interview Richard, shortly after the garda search of the property in June 2017. As we travel down, I ring Richard to tell him. I want to let him know everything we're doing, and I feel it's important to keep him in the loop about our filming.

He is out working when I ring but says he would actually be able to meet us in Fermoy late that same afternoon. 'That's perfect, thanks, Richard,' I reply. 'Kevin the producer will be with me once again, and Shirley is the camerawoman who you met before. She'll be with us today. See you later.'

'Okay,' replies Richard, sounding busy, doing whatever he was doing. I hang up the phone and we continue driving to Youghal.

Ann Mooney succinctly sums up the mystery during our

interview a short time later, which we film outdoors and overlooking Youghal from a height. 'Tina wasn't working. Her whole life seemed to centre around Richard. They certainly were a couple that were very close – they seemed to live in a bubble. According to Richard they were still very much in love, even after all this time.'

Ann points out it is striking that no one saw Tina on the day she was said to have left her home. 'She would have been quite remarkable, as she was very much into her style and her make-up and her hair and fashion – she would have "cut a fine figure" as they say.'

As myself, Kevin and Shirley travel from Youghal to Fermoy, I text Richard. 'Hi Richard, we'll be there around 3.30. Cheers, Barry.' He replies quickly saying, 'Okay I'm in the town park.' A short time later I get another text: 'Will you be much longer.' I ring him to say we are just arriving in Fermoy and that I'll come to meet him in the park. 'I'm in the car park at the swimming pool,' he says. That's where Tina went swimming almost daily for years, I think.

From my brief interaction on the phone I get a feeling that Richard is more agitated than when I've met him previously. I say to Shirley and Kevin that I should go to meet Richard by myself and then walk back with him to meet them at the bridge. There is a good spot to film there, with a backdrop of Fermoy town and the bridge over the river Blackwater.

Shirley parks her van close to the bridge, and I walk around to meet Richard. I find him standing at the back of his car with Ruby and Heidi. He has just taken them out of the boot and is locking the car. I shake hands with him again. I make sure not to say 'Happy New Year' or anything stupid. 'Good to see you again, Richard, and thanks for your time today,' I say. 'We will definitely have our report on air in a week or two, and this filming today is the last filming we need.'

Richard doesn't answer me directly but rather tells me what is on his mind. 'That's the swimming pool where Tina used to go, and I'd walk the dogs around here waiting for her. Heidi used to do this walk with me for seven years before we got Ruby as well. Even now today, Heidi is looking around to try and find Tina here.'

Richard seems very preoccupied with the dogs as we walk, via a long laneway, to the bridge. He keeps looking down at Ruby and Heidi, and I notice that the dogs seem particularly active. Normally they would walk in a straight line, but today they are walking across each other – they seem excited to be back in Fermoy.

We meet Shirley and Kevin near the bridge, and they say hello to Richard. Shirley gives Richard and me microphones and asks us to clip them on. Richard puts on his mic without any fuss – he's well used to doing interviews by this stage. He is wearing a dark jumper, workman's trousers and heavy-duty runners; I'm wearing a suit.

Darkness is already beginning to fall, the cars travelling over Kent Bridge into and out of Fermoy have their full lights on, and the traffic is noisy. Whereas the first interview with Richard in his house and the second in my car were very controllable in terms of sound, this interview will be at the mercy of passing traffic.

I ask Richard to walk across the bridge with me to get

more footage of us walking together. We go over the long bridge then wait there for a wave from Kevin to signal that we can walk back. Richard is holding the leads of both dogs in his right hand and Ruby's carrycase in his left. I'm standing to Richard's right, so the dogs are centre stage. While we wait, we make small talk. I don't want to ask him anything that I wish to ask during the interview, so I find myself saying things like 'There's a lot of traffic in Fermoy' and 'It's a busy town, isn't it'.

As I stand on the far side of the bridge from Shirley and Kevin, I'm struck that the local garda station is just 100 metres away. This was where Richard reported Tina missing. I wonder to myself why he waited four days to do this. Was he really thinking she'd be with family here in Fermoy? Is that credible?

Momentarily, I think of a long-term missing person case in Fermoy, which was eventually solved. Bill Fennessy was missing for 12 years, last seen in March 1990. His body was found by chance in the river Blackwater in Fermoy in October 2012 by local divers on a training exercise, still inside his car, which had become embedded in silt beneath the water. The chance solving of the case shows how a missing person case can sometimes be solved purely by good fortune rather than planned searches. The river had been searched many times without Bill's car being spotted.

I'm shaken out of my thoughts by a call and a big wave from Kevin. Having spotted the signal, Richard and I walk with Ruby and Heidi back over the bridge. I find myself raising my voice above the passing cars to say I feel it is important that we do this last bit of filming in Fermoy. Richard is not very chatty. He is still friendly, but seems lost in thought. He hasn't said much since telling me in the park about the dogs missing Tina.

The light is falling even more, so we move quickly to do the interview, about 15 feet in off the main road and close to the entrance to the park. We momentarily discuss whether to do a sit-down interview on a bench, but Shirley says the bench is wet. We decide to do the interview standing up, Richard with his back to the river and the bridge.

As Shirley does some last-minute adjustments to her camera, Richard bends down to the dogs. Ruby lifts her two front paws up onto Richard's knee, putting wet pawprints on his work trousers. 'You'll have me destroyed,' he says to the dog, who he then lifts up towards him. He lets Ruby lick him on the face, including on his lips. Richard makes a particular sound to the dogs, by sucking air in as he presses his tongue against his upper teeth. He does this a few times. I'm struck by how odd this all is, but I don't say anything. Instead, I turn back to Kevin and Shirley to get the nod that we are ready to begin the interview.

Only as I start does Richard look straight at me. His eyes are wide open, he is alert, he is staring at me. I notice that he rarely blinks. He holds my gaze as I ask him the first question, and I get the sense he has prepared for this meeting: there is something on his mind.

'We last met before Christmas; here we are in January 2018. How was Christmas for you?' I ask, my voice raised to beat the din of passing traffic.

Richard looks down at the dogs. 'How was Christmas,

lads?' he asks them. 'Miserable,' he says to me, looking back and holding my gaze. 'Miserable,' he repeats, looking down at the dogs again. They are very active and won't sit down – they are looking in different directions.

A group of teenagers walk by in the distance and wave at the camera. This is a common occurrence when filming outdoors in public spaces, and Kevin quietly says to me to wait a few seconds until they have passed us. I look at Richard, who is looking down at the dogs again, and I see he has grown a small beard, or something close to it. He is halfway between being unshaven and having a beard. I sense there is anger within him – it's his body language. He is friendly towards me, but he seems angry about something.

As the teenagers walk on, I persist with questions about Christmas. 'I've seen the lovely photos you sent me of Tina from Christmas a year ago. What were you doing this Christmas?'

'Nothing,' replies Richard forcefully. 'Nothing, I didn't have a Christmas dinner, nothing.' He sucks in more air between his tongue and teeth, looking down at the dogs. 'I took these out for a walk, and that was it for the day.'

'Has the new year brought anything new in terms of the case?'

Richard is shaking his head even before I finish the question. 'No, or nothing that I've been told anyway.'

That's a strange thing to say, I think. An indication of a schism or a divide. Is Richard insinuating gardaí wouldn't tell him if there were new leads?

Richard looks down at the dogs again. They are taking up a lot of his attention. 'Do you want me to take them?' asks Kevin from behind me.

'They won't go with you,' replies Richard.

'Would they not?' says Kevin.

'No,' says Richard, looking at the dogs. It's clear he is not letting anyone else hold the leads.

As if to assert his control, Richard suddenly bends down and commands Ruby to get into her carrycase. The dog duly walks into it, but quickly turns and walks back out again. Shirley has tracked the movement and panned down to capture the interaction. It's all part of the story. A man and two dogs, and a missing woman, and something very amiss.

I move the interview on. I want to keep this interaction short given the falling light, and I want to keep it moving given Richard's somewhat prickly demeanour. It's feels like he's very angry and trying not to show it.

'We're here in Fermoy because it was such a large part of your life and Tina's life. What is important for people to consider?'

'Well, it's her hometown, it's where she was brought up, it's where all her friends are. We spent the best part of 30 years here. It's been a big part of my life as well.' Richard bends down, picks Ruby up into his left arm and rubs her stomach with his right hand.

'Do you still believe that there are people who know more than they are saying?' I ask.

'Well somebody has to know something.' Richard is quite dogmatic in his response, forceful. 'Somebody had to give her a helping hand somewhere. You can't just get up and disappear like this without help from somebody.' His face is showing flickers of anger.

'If someone did help, do you have any idea where that may have come from?'

'No,' says Richard, looking me straight in the eye. 'Family say [sic] didn't help her so I have to take their word for that. As for friends, the town is full of them. So, where do you start?'

I am fascinated by this response, but don't show it. Richard is clearly indicating that he is no longer on good terms with Tina's family. I was convinced, having previously met Tina's niece Sarah Howard, that Tina's family had no know-ledge of where she had gone, so Richard's newly expressed slight on Tina's family is an indication of something else.

I keep probing. 'What are your thoughts now, almost ten months on since Tina disappeared?'

'I just want her back. What's gone on has gone on and can't be took [sic] away. I just want her back.'

Years later this comment will come to be analysed by gardaí in a very specific way. As he stood in Fermoy with me, was Richard angry at himself and wishing he could undo what he had done? Having spent almost ten months with Tina's body so close to him every single day, he must have been tortured in some way, surely?

Richard is taking deep breaths through his nose. His breath is visible in the air. He is looking directly at me, rarely blinking. I feel as if he's trying to read my thoughts.

I mention that if there is no breakthrough in the next few months, it will be approaching one year since Tina disappeared. 'Do you think like that, days have become weeks, have become months?'

'I count every day,' Richard replies. He repeats this comment as a car drives by playing loud music. We pause for a moment to let the music die down. I realise I'm raising my voice even more. It's time to finish this interview, I decide.

I tell Richard I've one last question – what is his appeal this January night?

'My appeal is that somebody has to know something. My appeal is just to ring the guards and say you know she's alright. Anything like that, that's enough for the time being.' I notice immediately that Richard has not spoken directly to Tina, hasn't appealed to Tina. And he's all but told me that he now has a difficult relationship with Tina's family, and he doesn't seem happy with the gardaí either. This interview was well worth doing, I think to myself.

'Just stay where you are for a two-shot,' says Kevin, and I ask Richard to keep his place so Shirley can film both myself and Richard together. All of the interview was filmed with just Richard in vision, from his waist up, so we need to film a wider shot which shows me too. 'Take your hands out of your pockets, Barry,' calls Kevin, and I obey his instruction. I thank Richard again for doing the interview and I repeat that I felt it was important to bring part of the filming to Fermoy.

Richard's face becomes more animated and he has a very slight smile as he remembers something. 'This is where that photo was taken, at them gates over there,' he says, gesturing with his right hand towards the entrance to the park. I know the photo he is talking about. We have previously spoken about an image of Richard and Tina taken without their knowledge as they walked in Fermoy town park. It was taken by local photographer John O'Connell, as he photographed different scenes and people around Fermoy in April 2015. The image emerged publicly after Tina disappeared, and it showed Richard holding Tina's left hand with his right as they walked Ruby. Tina was holding Ruby's lead and Richard held the carrycase. The image was important as it was the only photo of Richard and Tina together in more recent times. I was planning to include it in my upcoming report.

Shirley is now focusing the camera on the two dogs. She has filmed Ruby in Richard's arms as he strokes her back and chest, and now Shirley is focusing on Heidi, who is standing in front of Richard on the footpath and looking around. Just as Shirley puts the camera on Heidi, the dog turns her back. Richard senses what we are trying to do and calls to Heidi 'Heidi, who is it, who is there?' gesturing towards the camera. I find myself joining in. 'This way, over here,' I gently call to Heidi. It's all somewhat surreal, but she eventually turns towards the camera and Shirley films a good image of her.

Richard seems to have gone back in time in his thoughts. He tells me that he and Tina used to walk the dogs three times a day in the park in Fermoy. He says he took photos of Tina lying in snow in the park with the dogs, but the photos are on one of the computer discs that the gardaí took last June. 'They've been telling me since June "Oh, you'll get them back next week", but here we are,' he says.

We do one final bit of filming, where me and Richard and the dogs walk back into the park, then turn and walk back towards the camera. As we do this, Richard says he will email me a copy of the photo of himself and Tina in the park. He says he has copied it from the internet. 'It shows us naturally, no posing, it shows us in us [sic] natural form.' He tells me another man previously asked if he could take their photo in the park. 'You see, we was [sic] always happy.'

I take Richard's microphone and turn it off and turn off my own, and I walk him back to his car. I tell him I'll be in touch very soon with news about what specific day the report will be broadcast. I shake his hand again. He seems less angry now than when we were doing the interview just a short time before. I thank him again for his time, and I walk back to meet Shirley and Kevin to drive back to Dublin. I don't yet know it, but this is not the last interview I will do with Richard Satchwell.

17.

Transmission

After some last-minute tweaks, the *Prime Time* report on Tina's disappearance makes air on Thursday, 25 January, with a duration of 24 minutes 53 seconds. The full length of a *Prime Time* programme is 33 minutes, and Kevin and I know we could have filled an entire programme – indeed, we could have filled an hour-long slot if there was one available. But an editorial decision is made that we need to be careful in how we treat the story. Despite my strong suspicion that someone has killed Tina, we have to consider the possibility that she chose to disappear and that, however unlikely it may be, she might reappear the day after our report is broadcast. Although I don't think Tina is alive, I understand the need to acknowledge that possibility, so I agree that our report should not be a full programme, but rather will fill the bulk of that night's programme, to be followed by a separate story, by reporter Richard Downes, about the dangers for children who are accessing the internet.

The previous Friday I give video editor Liz Walsh my draft script, and she spends a full day in Edit 6 getting to grips with all the material we have filmed. Edit 6 is a small room which can fit three chairs at best. It has multiple screens and a special keyboard which Liz uses to compile the full report. Liz first views every frame of the hours of footage from inside Richard and Tina's house, and then she watches the imagery filmed by both cameras in my car when I drove Richard around Youghal. She also views all the other interviews I have done, including the much shorter interview with Richard in Fermoy. Liz is as fascinated by the story as Kevin and I and is on our wavelength in terms of telling a story which is respectful of Richard as an interviewee, but which also shows a strange man and the peculiar life he and Tina had inhabited.

———

Monday, 22 January – three days before transmission – sees me calling in a number of times to Liz in Edit 6. There's not much I can do, as I've given Liz the script and she is assembling all the elements – my voice, my pieces to camera, the soundbites we have chosen of Richard, Sarah Howard, Ann Mooney and Detective Inspector Brian Goulding. We also have footage from inside Midleton garda station, as well as powerful footage of Richard showing me personal items of Tina's in the house. While Liz is busy putting all this together on a visual timeline, all I can do is offer thanks and cups of tea.

On Tuesday afternoon we have a legal viewing of the report

When they met Tina was 17 and Richard was 22.

Richard and Tina lived in Oldham before moving to Fermoy.

Tina on her wedding morning with
a puppy Richard had bought for her.

Tina and Richard on a visit to Sligo.

Tina and Richard celebrate St Patrick's Day.

A smiling Tina learning to drive in England.

Tina had a love of animals, including parrots.

Tina with her beloved grandmother Florence.

Tina on a visit to her young niece Sarah in Fermoy in 1989.

Best friends – Sarah and her aunt Tina.

Tina had a passion for fashion.

Tina with Pearl the parrot and Ruby the chihuahua on Christmas Day 2016 in the sitting room where Tina's body was buried under the stairs three months later. The stairs are just out of shot, to the right.

Tina with Ruby on Christmas Day 2016 at Old Pier in Youghal.

James O'Sullivan of Cork Business Association, former Deputy Lord Mayor Patricia Gosch, student chef Tina Dingivan and former Fine Gael TD Deirdre Clune at a food festival in the English Market in Cork City.

One of first images provided to the author after Tina was reported missing in 2017.

Richard Satchwell poses with Tina's belongings in their home as he appeals for help finding her. (© RTÉ)

Richard Satchwell showing the author photographs of Tina. Her body lay buried under the stairs on the other side of the door behind the author. (© RTÉ)

The author and Richard Satchwell drive around Youghal. (© RTÉ)

The author with Richard Satchwell and the dogs in Fermoy in January 2018.

The scene outside 3 Grattan Street in Youghal shortly after Tina's body was recovered from her understairs grave. (© Provision)

Arms folded, Richard Satchwell speaks with three gardaí moments before he is arrested on a street in Youghal, in October 2023. (© Provision)

Detectives Dave Noonan and Dave Kelleher walk Richard Satchwell into court to be charged with murder. (© PA Images / Alamy Stock Photo)

Tina's sister Lorraine and niece Sarah, with family members, address the media at the end of the murder trial in June 2025.
(© PA Images / Alamy Stock Photo)

Superintendent Ann Marie Twomey and the investigation team address the media at the end of the trial. (© PA Images / Alamy Stock Photo)

with two RTÉ solicitors, Patricia Harrington and Anne McManus. A legal viewing is crucial with a story like this. Everything I say, everything I broadcast, will be parsed and analysed. It is essential that my report is balanced and fair and that it stands up to legal scrutiny.

We have the legal viewing in Edit 11, which is thankfully much bigger than Edit 6. There is no way we would all have fitted in the smaller edit suite; as well as the two solicitors, the two editors, Donogh and Paulette, have joined Liz, Kevin and me. The legal viewing is the first opportunity for us all to see what Liz has assembled from my paper script.

The solicitors say they are happy with the overall tone of the report, including my voice. It is important that I don't sensationalise any aspect of the story. Innuendo can be created by a raised tone or sarcastic-sounding delivery. I am always careful to ensure my voice is steady and clear, and this is particularly important in a case like this. After a few small points of guidance are raised by the solicitors, they say there is no issue with the overall report: it will be good for broadcast.

During this time I make sure to keep in contact with Richard. I email him on the Wednesday to alert him that a radio advert for the *Prime Time* report will be played next morning. That evening he replies: 'HI BARRY THANKS FOR YOOUR [sic] HELP AND I ALSO HOPE SOMEONE COMES FORWARD WITH SOME NEWS SORRY IT,S [sic] LATE BUT I WAS ON AN OVERNIGHT RUN THANKS RICHARD.'

Late on the afternoon of Thursday, 25 January, I go to the dubbing suite with Kevin, where I do my voice-over for the report. After all the work over many months, it comes down to a short time 'in the dub' before the report is fully complete. I am careful to again be steady in my delivery, not to insinuate any wrongdoing by anybody.

———

At 9.35 p.m. *Prime Time* goes on air, and the report is finally broadcast. 'Hello and welcome to the programme,' presenter David McCullagh says while standing in the studio. Two images of Tina appear on large plasma screens behind David as he continues his introduction. He outlines how Tina Satchwell has been missing for 10 months. 'To all intents and purposes she seemed to vanish into thin air,' he continues. 'Tonight, in an in-depth report, Barry Cummins speaks with her husband Richard Satchwell about Tina, about the investigation and about why she might have disappeared.'

And then the report is played to the nation, the first minute of it being an amalgamation of voices and pictures from different occasions during the investigation, and within two minutes I am shown inside 3 Grattan Street, sitting with Richard as we look at photographs of Tina, while Valentine squawks in the corner. A short time later, the short piece of video of Tina is played and we hear her voice.

I watch the report in a quiet room in RTÉ, wanting to be alone for a number of reasons. I find it emotional seeing the last two months' work finally appear on screen, but it also makes me feel uncomfortable. The various emotions that Richard has exhibited at different times – sadness, hurt, anger – it all swirls around in my mind.

I know from my conversations with Richard earlier in the week that he is also tuning in. As I sit alone in an empty edit suite watching the report, I know that Richard is sitting alone at home in his house in Youghal and he is watching too.

The report ends and David McCullagh appears once again live in the studio. This is the most important element to me now: I have ensured that David will read out the phone number for Midleton garda station. David delivers the line perfectly. 'If you have any information about Tina's disappearance, this is the number to call, and gardaí are at that number tonight.'

My phone lights up with texts of congratulations from family and friends, but I don't respond to anyone just yet. I ring Richard and he answers immediately. I know he has been watching but I ask anyway. 'Hi, Richard, did you get to see the programme?' He says he did, but doesn't say anything else. His tone is friendly, but he also seems a little distant. He might be upset, I think. 'I hope the programme will help with generating leads,' I say.

'I'm going on Red FM tomorrow to talk about the appeal, and TV3 have been in contact and they might do another interview,' he says, sounding more animated now.

I say it was important to put out the number to contact gardaí at the end of the report, and that I know many people will have watched and hopefully someone will now tell what they know. I wish Richard well and say goodnight.

I arrive home late and with a headache; it is tension. Everything has worked out well tonight, but I am still tense. I am hoping that all the effort will lead to a breakthrough in the case.

———

Around 10 a.m. next morning I follow up with gardaí. It's only 12 hours since the programme aired, but what has the reaction been – has the appeal worked? 'We've got 15 phone calls since the programme was broadcast, all 15 with potentially new leads to be followed up,' I'm told. That's great, I think. That's a good response, and it's still early in the day.

I don't yet know it but, within a matter of weeks, one of those calls will lead to the most extensive search to date in the investigation into Tina's disappearance and, ultimately, my fourth and final interview with Richard Satchwell.

18.

Castlemartyr

Late on Sunday, 4 March, I get a tip-off about Tina's case that will see me meet Richard Satchwell once again within 48 hours. The information stops me in my tracks, and for a moment I wonder if a big breakthrough is about to come.

The information I get is short but concise – a major search of a forest for Tina's body will begin at first light the following day. The search will involve the army as well as gardaí and will be focused on an area of woodland at Castlemartyr – about 20 kilometres from Youghal on the road to Cork city. I know the area well, having filmed along the N25 for the report I had broadcast about Tina's disappearance five weeks before. That's the road Richard and Tina would have driven on the way back from the car boot sale on the Sunday Tina was last seen by anyone other than Richard.

It's the final line from my source which makes me feel strangely happy. 'It's apparently a tip from someone who saw a man and woman at the wood. The woman was blonde. They can't be identified. The witness says they saw two people go into the wood, but just the man coming out again. The caller came forward after watching your programme.' Yes, I think, the appeal has worked. A lead deemed credible enough to warrant a large search has come as a result of my report.

My instinct is to contact Richard immediately and see if he will do another interview with me. This new information is the first potential breakthrough to come in the case. It's now almost 12 months since Tina disappeared.

I decide to text Richard rather than ring him. I know that gardaí will have told him about the search by now. I want to give him time to consider my request for an interview; I want him to be in control. He likes being in control of deciding where and when he will talk, if he'll talk at all.

Just before 10 p.m. I text him. 'Hi Richard, I've heard about the search that's beginning tomorrow. I'll be filming all day tomorrow in the area for a follow-up report. Are you free to meet tomorrow to do an interview? Cheers, Barry.' I put in the word 'cheers' as I want Richard to know that my view of him is still the same. Although I have private thoughts where I wonder if he might be capable of attacking Tina, I also constantly counter those thoughts with the possibility that he is an innocent man and someone else may have caused harm to Tina.

Richard doesn't reply to my text that night, but I don't worry. When I'm in County Cork I can ring him or call direct to his door. No matter what, I will make contact with him.

I don't sleep much that Sunday night, and I make sure to get up early next morning. I make contact with Rhona O'Byrne (a wonderful colleague and friend who sadly passed away in 2024), the office manager in *Prime Time*, who assigns the camera crews each day. Rhona is fascinated by Tina's case, and we have had many discussions about it in previous weeks. I tell her I am going to County Cork as soon as possible and will be filming at Castlemartyr, and I will be trying to interview Richard as well. The next *Prime Time* programme is not until the following night, and I don't know what form of report I might be able to compile. It's possible Richard won't want to talk, or that he will talk to everyone, but having spent so much time in his company I feel he will still be selective in whom he speaks with.

Rhona tells me that Eddie Duffy is available to head to Castlemartyr. Eddie is an experienced cameraman and we have worked together on many sensitive stories. I arrange to head directly to County Cork and meet Eddie there. 'We'll figure out what we are at when we get there' is all I can say to him by way of a plan.

My early-morning travel to Castlemartyr is entirely on spec, I don't know if I'll have anything exclusive to report for *Prime Time*, but my instinct has told me to head to County Cork. On route I ring editor Donogh Diamond to alert him that I've headed for Castlemartyr. He knows it's worth getting to the scene of the search to see what's going on, especially as the tip-off has come as a result of the *Prime Time* programme that featured Tina's case. 'Let's see what comes out of today's reporting,' Donogh says. 'And then we can see if there's any report left for us to do tomorrow. If Richard will speak with you, then there's definitely a report, so let's see what happens.'

On my drive from Dublin to Cork, Richard rings and leaves me a voicemail. I pull over to listen, and he is saying he doesn't know if he will be able to do an interview. He says he was only told about the search the evening before and that his head is 'here, there and everywhere'. I don't even think about turning back to Dublin. I am chasing a story, which may or may not work out, but there is only one thing to do, and that's to keep heading to Cork to see how it all plays out.

I decide not to ring Richard but rather text him back. I need to get to the scene and then decide on the best approach. At 8.15 a.m. I text him: 'Got your message Richard. I understand. Talk soon. Barry.' By saying 'talk soon' I am letting him know I'm around and that I haven't given up on speaking with him, but again I'm leaving the ball in his court.

When I get to Castlemartyr I quickly find the search location. It's easy to spot, with uniformed gardaí standing at the entrance, stopping anybody trying to get access to Mitchell's Wood close to the N25. As I walk up and down the road getting a sense of the scale of the search, I ring *Prime Time* producer Kevin Burns in Dublin. 'Kevin, I want to get the band back together,' I say by way of asking him if he is free to work with me once again on Tina's case. I've no idea if I'll have nothing to show for my travels, but if anything is going to come of it I want Kevin with me again. Kevin says he's definitely free but, just like Donogh, he points out that there might only be a report if Richard will do an interview. From the large media presence gathered at the garda cordon it is clear that the search will be covered extensively on the news today, and there may be very little left to report by tomorrow. 'I don't know if Richard will talk,' I tell Kevin. 'But if he will talk, I know it will be with me.'

A large press conference is held at the entrance to the woods. 'Are you looking for a body?' asks Paschal Sheehy of RTÉ News. 'What we are looking for today is evidence in relation to the investigation into the disappearance of Tina Satchwell,' replies Chief Superintendent Colm Noonan. 'The search is going to be conducted extensively,' he adds.

I film a one-on-one interview with Detective Inspector Brian Goulding, who outlines how over 220 separate lines of enquiry have been followed up as part of the ongoing investigation. Forty acres of woodland at Mitchell's Wood is now being assessed as part of this latest search for Tina. A forensic archaeologist is on site advising on the search strategy. A sophisticated grid method is to be deployed to ensure a complete search of the area is conducted, which may take a number of weeks.

Richard Satchwell arrives at the search, and a number of cameras film him peering in through the railings to see what gardaí are doing in the woods. He has answered a call from Paul Byrne of TV3 and agrees to do a short interview. I'm not surprised. I still feel Richard will speak with me, and I know the only other journalist he engages with is Paul. If he's talking to Paul, he will talk to me, I say to Eddie. But I don't want to do it here – I want to do a sit-down interview. His interview with TV3 is short, as it's for a news bulletin – if and when I get to Richard, I want to ensure my interview is long and probing.

I hear from Donnybrook that a reporter from the RTÉ newsroom has called to 3 Grattan Street looking to interview Richard, but he wouldn't answer the door. I'm not deterred by this; indeed, I'm not surprised. I have built up a relationship with Richard over the past five months. I am convinced he will speak with me – I just have to figure out how to get to him without anyone else knowing, so I can get the exclusive long interview.

By the end of Monday evening I make a decision to ring Richard. I deliberately wait until after the TV3 news has been played. I am sure Richard will want to see himself and how he is portrayed. I ring his number and it rings and rings. I decide not to leave a voicemail just yet, thinking I'll give it another half an hour and ring again. But before I get a chance to call, Richard rings me.

'Thanks for ringing me back, Richard, how are you?' I ask, genuinely wanting to know how he feels about what is clearly a search for his wife's body. Richard replies that he's a little better now than earlier, but that it has all been a shock, since gardaí contacted him the day before. 'I saw your interview on TV3, Richard. I want to talk with you as well. Would you come to Fermoy tomorrow – will you sit down with me there? I was thinking the Grand Hotel would be a nice quiet place we could talk properly.'

I have been thinking about where I could interview Richard and decide that Fermoy is the place. I know he has an emotional attachment to Fermoy, and I was transfixed by the two dogs and their reaction to being in Fermoy when I met him there for the interview in January. If he's going to meet me, Fermoy is probably the most comfortable place for him. It's also a good location to avoid other media; I know that the hunt is on for any and all imagery of Richard while the search in Castlemartyr is taking place. The fact that he won't engage with most members of the media has upped the ante in terms of photographers trying to get candid shots of Richard in Youghal and elsewhere. If I can get him to Fermoy, we might have some privacy.

'Okay,' he says, 'I can meet you tomorrow.' I am sitting alone in my car at this time, and I punch the air silently in a mark of achievement. I have been so convinced that Richard will speak to me on camera once again that I haven't really considered how I would tell my bosses if he had said no. All my efforts to keep in touch with Richard are paying off once again. I say I'll book a room in the Grand Hotel and ask if midday would suit him. 'Okay,' he says, and I decide to end the call, again wishing him the very best. I say I'm thinking of him and I'm thinking of Tina.

I ring Rhona back in Dublin to tell her the news, and we make arrangements for a second cameraman, Cormac Downes, to travel down to Fermoy the next day. By coincidence Cormac filmed Richard's overly emotional appeal on *Crimecall* the previous June which raised the suspicions of many people, including myself. I ring the hotel and book a conference room for RTÉ for the next day, not saying that it's an interview with Richard Satchwell. I text Richard back just after 10 p.m. 'Hi Richard, we've a room booked for 12 tomorrow at Grand Hotel Fermoy. The cameraman with me will be Eddie Duffy. Thanks again for doing this at this time. See you tomorrow Richard, Barry.'

As I go to sleep that night I know that the following day's interview will be unlike the three previous ones I have done. No more sitting at ninety-degree angles on a sofa or sitting in a car looking out the window. This interview will be in a controlled setting, quiet, intimate, and with Richard sitting right in front of me. It's time for uninterrupted direct eye contact.

19.

Face Off

I meet Richard on the stairs of the hotel. He is early; I have walked downstairs to meet him as he arrives, but he surprises me by meeting me halfway. 'I've left the dogs in the car outside,' he says by way of a greeting.

'We've a room upstairs here Richard, and we've two cameramen today – Eddie and Cormac, and Kevin is with me again.' I know the room isn't ready, so I say to Richard, 'Sure let's step outside for a minute and have a quick chat,' and we walk out the entrance of the hotel. Richard is showing me that he has parked his car nearby on Ashe Quay, when he spots a woman in another car who is about to drive off. Richard walks to the driver's door of the car to say hello and introduces me, and I say hello. The woman says she is thinking of Tina, wishes Richard well and drives off. 'That's Tina's hairdresser – she used to cut her hair even when she was younger,' Richard says to me.

Richard and I walk back into the hotel and up to the River Room, where the camera crew are doing last-minute adjustments for lighting. I tell Richard to mind himself as he walks over to the chair we want him to sit in, as there are cables going to and fro on the ground, connected to the cameras and the lights. Kevin sits off to the side, ready to take notes of the interview and make sure I ask all the questions we have talked through earlier. As always, I don't have any questions written down: they are all in my head.

We settle into our hard chairs, which have been set up three feet apart. We will be sitting directly facing each other. Eddie's camera will be trained on Richard the whole time and Cormac's on me. I have a sense of urgency about the interview – I am delighted that Richard is doing it, but I also know the time pressure I will be under to get back to Dublin and consult with the editors and legal department before I broadcast it on tonight's *Prime Time*. The time pressure is eased somewhat by Kevin being the producer. He knows the story inside out and knows that this interview needs to be gritty and probing. I am as always respectful of Richard, but gardaí are now looking for a body, and although Tina's disappearance is still officially a missing person case, a lot of media focus is now on who the killer might be.

For once I'm not wearing a suit. I've made a conscious decision to dress casually for this interview. It's a sort of reverse psychology: because this interview will be the first formal-style interview I've done with Richard, I don't want to dress formally. I want to dress more like Richard normally does, so I wear a blue shirt and navy jumper, and Richard is wearing a grey T-shirt and brown hoodie. I've always worn glasses when meeting Richard, but today I wear contact lenses, again changing it up so he can see my eyes.

As we start the interview, I have no idea that this filming

will one day be shown in court as another exhibit in the prosecution case against Richard Satchwell.

I get right down to business, first thanking Richard for his time and then saying that gardaí are focusing their attention now on the wood at Castlemartyr. 'Richard, have you ever been to Mitchell's Wood? Has Tina ever been to that wood?'

He is shaking his head before I get to the end of the question. 'Never' is Richard's answer to whether he's ever been in the area now being searched. He says he doesn't believe Tina has ever been to Mitchell's Wood. It's a cast-iron denial of his ever being in the woods, and it's his first answer. I need to probe more, but will take my time.

Unprompted, Richard says that the only wood he knows Tina ever went to was Corrin Wood near Fermoy, and 'that is the only one she ever trusted to walk with me as well'. That's an odd thing to say, I think. Why would Tina not trust going into woods with Richard? Or am I picking him up right?

Richard continues to speak, so I just listen. 'Tina is just not a trusting person, so I know for a fact, 'cause she wouldn't walk any strange woods with me, so there's no way she'd do it on her own.'

I run this answer over in my mind quickly. The terminology is strange – perhaps Richard is saying Tina is simply fearful of woodland, but the answer makes me wonder if Richard caused Tina to be fearful. Richard is holding my gaze as we speak. I am comfortable sitting with him. I am being quite direct in my questions, but he is not fazed, and he is coming across as well able for difficult questions. This garda search is all because of a report of a man and woman in the woods, so I remind myself to come back to that question later.

Okay, I think, if you're saying you've never been in the woods, how close have you been? 'Do you know Castlemartyr? Would Tina know that village?'

'The only way we know the village is passing through it,' replies Richard. I'm watching his demeanour, and he is very relaxed. He does not seem stressed or under pressure. I'm suddenly struck by a thought – if he has buried Tina somewhere, it's not in Castlemartyr. It's hard to know how someone should act if their wife's body might be about to be found in a wood, but Richard's body language seems to indicate a confidence. He doesn't seem particularly worried.

'Occasionally if we was [sic] late to do the lottery we'd stop off at Centra in Castlemartyr.' I listen to Richard outline normal things he and Tina used to do. He's putting himself physically in Castlemartyr on occasion, but he's already firmly said he was never in the nearby woods.

I continue pressing him on the woodland. 'So any of the woodland around there, Mitchell's Wood or elsewhere, to the best of your knowledge, Tina has never been there?'

'Never been there,' Richard replies. 'She never has, while she's been with me, and she's been with me since she was 17.'

'Given all the resources gardaí are putting in to this search, what are you thinking? Gardaí believe she may well have been there.' Richard is licking his bottom lip on occasion during this interview. I haven't noticed him doing that before. I've seen him bite gently on his bottom lip while thinking, but licking his lip is a new thing. I'm studying every element of Richard's demeanour, trying to get a read on him.

'Well, there is one thing that a relation has been saying for a little while now to me,' Richard replies. 'What if the person who helped her get away has done something to her?' Richard is staring at me as he says this line. He seems to be earnest in his delivery, but I am listening to his words as well. This reply suggests he is in contact with Tina's family, but his interview on the bridge in Fermoy two months previously indicated that was no longer the case.

This is the first time Richard has acknowledged to me that Tina might have suffered a violent attack, but he immediately follows it with a caveat. 'I don't believe that, but a part of it is the fact that mentally I don't want to believe that.'

Richard continues to talk about why a search is underway at Mitchell's Wood. 'I read a newspaper report today about a man walking with a blonde woman. I've no more information officially than what has been given out to the press.'

I am thinking quickly. If Castlemartyr is not the answer, perhaps Tina's body lies in other woodland. Perhaps gardaí are on the right track to presume she has been killed and buried somewhere, but they just have the wrong location. I ask Richard, 'When you heard there was this big search about to take place, what did you feel?' My voice is slightly clipped, as I seek to ask Richard direct questions about his immediate thoughts.

'You've got two feelings,' he begins, and I immediately note that he's reverted to generic rather than specific – 'you've got' rather than 'I had'. He brings his right hand to his forehead and points. 'Your head's telling you she's out there, she's fine, but then you get this awful feeling in your stomach. On the Sunday night I didn't sleep at all because I felt too sick to be able to. Last night I just crashed out on the couch, I didn't go to bed at all. It just leaves you totally off.'

This interview is the first time Richard is acknowledging to me that Tina might be dead. He's not using that word, but he's giving signals in his speech and his demeanour that she may not still be alive. He keeps talking, and I maintain eye contact, listening carefully.

'To be honest, I live by two four-letter words – the love I feel for her and the hope that I just have to keep there, because without hope you've got nothing.' That's strange, I think – not the declarations of love and hope, but it sounds rehearsed, odd. Richard stares straight at me after delivering this line, and I see a flicker of defiance in his face. That could be a sign of determination to keep fighting, to continue to keep hope alive, or it could be something much more sinister.

I change tack. Time to ask an important question I've asked before, but which needs to be asked again now that gardaí are searching for a body. 'You waited four days after Tina disappeared before contacting gardaí. If she did go away it allowed her that time to get away, but also if somebody caused harm to her, it gave them a bit of time.' Richard says the word 'time' just as I say it, a recognition of knowing what I'm asking.

'I am reflecting on that time period, and I reflect on the months leading up to the disappearance, and I'm my own worst critic.' I notice Richard says 'the disappearance' rather than 'Tina's disappearance'. It's a small thing, but I can detect an emotional distance in Richard.

He continues by saying he wonders if he should have contacted the doctor about his concerns about Tina in the months before she went missing. This is a topic he has raised with me previously, the suggestion that Tina was depressed. There is no one to verify this, as the couple largely kept to themselves, but I know that no one at the car boot sales had described seeing Tina in a low mood.

I move the conversation back to the woods. 'If the woman at Mitchell's Wood was Tina, is there any explanation as to why she was there, either alone or in the company of someone else?'

'It makes no sense at all,' Richard replies. 'I know Tina, and I just know, and I can vouch for this now, as much as what [sic] I'm sitting here, Tina would not go near those woods either on her own or in the company of anyone. She wouldn't even go near a strange woods with me.' Richard is emphatic in his delivery. He is clearly saying there is no way she is in Mitchell's Wood. I feel there is something strange about his answer, but I cannot put my finger on it.

I need to persist with the possibility that someone forced Tina to go into the woods – she may not have gone willingly. Richard says Tina is a fighter and would have defended herself. 'I'm telling you now that if any harm has come to Tina in that woods, somebody would have seen somebody else, in my opinion, pretty severely damaged.' Richard's eyes drop from holding my gaze as he finishes that point. Another strange thing to say, I think.

Richard refers to people who have shaken his hand and wished him well. 'People come up and say "Oh, I'm sorry for your troubles" and it's a nice gesture, but it also reminds me of people walking up to you when you're at a funeral.' His voice catches with emotion as he says 'funeral'.

I move to a question I know needs to be asked. 'You have said you would never lay a finger on Tina, and any physicality was love, was emotion. Describe what you mean?'

Richard says that one of the things that originally attracted Tina to him was his demeanour. 'It was my quietness; it was the fact that she felt safe. I'm not the type of person just to fly off the handle. My arms have only ever held Tina in a loving manner,' he says, looking me directly in the eye once again.

As we finish the interview, I say it's now only two weeks away from the year anniversary of Tina's disappearance. Richard looks troubled, as if there's a weight on him. 'These things are never out of my head,' he says. 'Tina used to say, "out of sight out of mind", but that's not the case with me. I've got anniversary presents, birthday presents, Christmas presents, Valentine's presents and everything at home.' Richard is looking at the ground as he says this, but then looks back at me, as if inviting a further question.

'They're there to give her?'

'Yes.'

'You're keeping all those?'

'Every occasion that comes up I'm buying presents and cards.' Richard's voice has reduced to just a whisper as he says 'cards' and I can see he is emotional. The interview has come to a natural end. I have got strong and new material from it.

Richard seems keen to get back to the dogs, who are in his car nearby, and Kevin suggests that Eddie film myself and Richard one last time with them. Richard says he's happy to do this as he wants to give them a walk anyway. We go to his car and he gets Ruby and Heidi, and we walk over Fermoy bridge once again, just like in January. Two passing motorists beep their horns in a gentle way and wave. Richard seems to think he knows them and waves back. We return our microphones to Eddie, and I say I'll walk Richard and the dogs back to his car.

As Richard puts the dogs into the boot, his demeanour suddenly changes. He becomes a little more excited in his tone. 'Did you know I had an ASBO?'

'Oh, did you?' I say, taken aback at this sudden declaration, which has come out of the blue.

'Yes, they said I was shouting at a neighbour's daughter,' he continues, but then doesn't say anything else.

'Oh, right,' I say, and I am suddenly struck that I haven't got this interaction on tape and we are no longer on microphone.

I'm now under time pressure to get back to Dublin, so I steer the conversation to the interview we have just done. 'Thanks again, Richard, and I'm thinking of both yourself and Tina.' I have always been careful to mention her being in my thoughts.

'Thank you,' he replies, and I shake his hand again. Richard seems to be standing a little taller than he might normally, as if he is emboldened having let me in on a secret about the ASBO.

The next time I see Richard in person, I will be filming him at a court appearance as he walks handcuffed into court, charged with his wife's murder. He will have his head down trying to shield his face.

I head back to the hotel to say thanks to Eddie and Cormac. Kevin and I then immediately set off for Dublin to consult with our solicitors and editors and ensure we get the powerful and exclusive sit-down interview with Richard onto that night's *Prime Time*. At the end of that night's report, presenter Miriam O'Callaghan reads out the number once again for Midleton garda station.

I ring Richard the next day to say thank you once again for his time. He tells me that he didn't get to mention yesterday that he has lost his job as a truck driver. I say I'm sorry to hear that, but he says it's okay – all the stress and coverage of the case didn't help, it affected the job, but he's happy to have done all the interviews. I again wish him well and we end the call. I will ensure I keep in contact with Richard, but it will become more sporadic.

The next day a researcher with the *Ray D'Arcy Show*, broadcast on RTÉ One on Saturday nights, contacts me. The programme has managed to make contact with Richard and he has agreed to be a guest live in the studio the following Saturday. The researcher wants to know if I'll take a call from Ray D'Arcy to brief him on Richard in advance of his interview.

On Saturday afternoon Ray rings me and I find myself walking around my kitchen giving him my insights into Richard. I am momentarily struck by the thought that, in my younger years, I used to watch Ray on television with the puppets Zig and Zag, and now I'm helping him prepare for a serious interview about a missing woman who may have been murdered.

I tell Ray that every time I meet Richard I learn something new and that he is a man for whom time has stood still ever since March 2017. I say that I think the one element which will be different with his programme will be the live studio audience, and it will be interesting to see how Richard deals with the studio lights and the gaze of so many people so close to him.

As it transpires, Richard is well able for the studio setting. During his live interview he repeats his love for his missing wife, and he namechecks me a number of times. It's clear that I've established a rapport with Richard that has enabled me to get insights into his character which no one else has.

———

On Friday, 16 March, I hear that the search in Castlemartyr has ended without any trace of Tina being found. I'm conscious this news comes just four days before the anniversary of her disappearance. I text Richard, saying, 'I hope all the recent interviews you have done help in getting a breakthrough. I know gardaí say more people have come forward in recent weeks.' He doesn't reply.

A few months later, Kevin Burns moves to a different role in RTÉ. This means I no longer have my original producer to bounce around ideas with on how to progress the story. But the truth is there is nothing to report – nothing is happening. Tina's case is fast becoming consigned to the long list of missing persons cases which may never see a breakthrough.

I move onto other stories, compiling a full programme in 2019 about the murder of 'Mr Moonlight', Bobby Ryan, whose body was found in an underground tank on a farm in County Tipperary. I work closely with producer Sallyanne Godson on what will be one of the most watched *Prime Time* documentaries in the programme's history. Sallyanne also works with me on a full programme on the conviction in August 2020 of Aaron Brady for the murder of Detective Garda Adrian Donohoe.

Along the way I also compile special extended reports with another producer, John Cunningham. My years of watching numerous court cases about kidnappings pay off when Paul and Marie Richardson bravely do an exclusive interview with me about the ordeal they and their sons faced when they were targeted during the armed robbery of cash from a Securicor van. In 2019, John also works with me on one of the most emotionally challenging reports I have ever compiled, when I report on the case of Ana Kriégel, a 14-year-old girl who was murdered by two 13-year-old boys, only ever named publicly as Boy A and Boy B. Ana's parents give me video footage and photographs of their daughter to be shown on RTÉ once the verdict in the case is announced.

Later in 2019, my expertise and ability to secure exclusive interviews and imagery are recognised by RTÉ when I am appointed security correspondent with *Prime Time* on a fixed five-year contract.

As I subsequently work through the Covid pandemic, I often think of Tina, and I think of Richard. I occasionally send him a text or email, but he doesn't respond. He has gone quiet and has stopped doing any interviews. I still hope that one day I may report on a development in the case, but that will only be if Tina's body is found by chance or if gardaí make a breakthrough.

20.

Dave Knows Nothing

On Sunday, 20th June 2021, Richard Satchwell sits down and gives a lengthy statement to a garda. It's the first time since 2018 that he has spoken at length to anyone about Tina's disappearance. Three years since the search at Castlemartyr ended without any trace of Tina being found, the investigation has run into the ground. There have been more than 60 reported sightings, in Ireland and beyond, of a woman matching Tina's description, but all reports have been followed up and have led to nothing. Gardaí have decided to go back to the primary source of information: Richard.

Since 2017 detectives have known Richard has told different stories to different people. He has told journalists, including me, of a loving relationship between himself and Tina, but he has told gardaí he had been the victim of domestic violence. There are no medical records or eyewitnesses to support his claim.

For three years, from shortly after his second *Prime Time* interview in 2018, Richard has gone quiet. He stays living at 3 Grattan Street and is a familiar sight walking Ruby and

Heidi along the pier. Having stopped doing interviews, his circle of friends has diminished. It is now just Richard, the dogs and the parrot.

―――

The man meeting Richard this Sunday is Detective Sergeant Dave Noonan, a specialist garda interviewer and one of the newer members of the team investigating Tina's disappearance. The investigation is now into its fifth year, and a number of gardaí involved in the original case have retired or moved to other districts. The case needs an injection of life, and today is an important day in this regard.

Dave Noonan has worked in the Cork division for many years and has conducted many complex interviews with witnesses and suspects in various cases. He was one of the garda team that, in 2019, interviewed a woman suspected of murdering two-year-old Santina Cawley, who was found critically injured in an apartment on the southside of Cork city. Karen Harrington was later found guilty of Santina's murder and jailed for life.

By 2021, when he sits down to interview Richard, Detective Noonan is working with the local Garda Protective Services Bureau, conducting various investigations into sexual crimes, child exploitation, domestic abuse, human trafficking and missing persons.

―――

The interview will be recorded with Richard's permission, but the style and format, and even the location, of the meeting will be different to most garda interviews. The meeting is not in a garda station, but rather in a specialist interview suite in a nondescript building that members of the public wouldn't normally associate with the gardaí. A small number of such interview locations have been established throughout the country to enable lengthy and potentially stressful interviews to be conducted in a more relaxed and private setting.

On this Sunday afternoon, Richard is sitting in an armchair in a room in Blackpool, north of Cork city. Detective Noonan, who is as tall as Richard, is sitting in a similar chair facing him. The garda doesn't have a pen and notepad like in a traditional interview. He tells Richard he won't write down what Richard says, but rather it will all be typed up later from the DVD recording being made. The idea is to keep the flow of conversation going and to allow Richard to do most of the talking. Richard says that is fine – he is there to help.

The type of interview the two men are about to embark on is an enhanced cognitive interview (ECI), which is the gold-standard in getting detail from someone who has endured or witnessed a traumatic event. It involves deep concentration – the witness can close their eyes if they wish to recall certain things – and is witness-led, whereby the interviewer will say very little unless more detail is required about something specific. Such interviews are relatively new, but have been accepted by Irish courts as fulfilling the criteria to be admitted as evidence in criminal trials.

By June 2021, evidence from one of the first ECIs conducted

by gardaí has been admitted in a murder trial at the Central Criminal Court, where a college student described witnessing the traumatic killing of a man, Neil Reilly, in Lucan in 2017. The witness in that case gave her interview to gardaí seven months after the event, recalling how, after hearing a commotion, she had looked out the window of her house and seen a man being run over by a BMW. The witness told gardaí that, after the car had driven over the victim, he was then held up by two men and the car reversed over him again, and the vehicle then drove over him a third time as he lay on the ground. Two brothers, Dean and Jason Bradley, were later jailed for life for their part in the murder. The Bradleys subsequently brought an appeal challenging the admission of the ECI into evidence, but the appeal court rejected the argument and upheld the convictions.

Gardaí think an ECI will greatly assist Richard Satchwell to give more precise details about the day Tina disappeared. Detectives know from previous meetings with Richard, and his interviews with me and other journalists, that he often uses phrases like 'we would always' or 'we would usually' to answer questions which required specific answers about specific events, times and locations. Detectives have also learned what I had learned in 2017 and 2018: the more Richard speaks, the more new information he gives.

Dave Noonan tells Richard that a garda colleague, Detective Sergeant Jason Wallace, is outside the room monitoring what is being said, but it is just the two of them in the room, and they won't be disturbed. Another garda, Dave Kelleher, who will later play a crucial role in the case, is also observing from outside the room. Richard is told the interview can go on for as long as is needed. Dave Noonan explains he is looking for as much detail as possible but asks Richard not to fill in gaps unless he is sure of the information. The garda uses the example of a red water bottle sitting on a table nearby. 'It looks like a water bottle,' the officer says, 'but how would you know for certain that it was water in the bottle?' The detective's message is clear – avoid guesswork. You can certainly say it's a red bottle, but you'd be speculating to say that the liquid inside is water.

The detective continues to focus on the bottle to illustrate how he will be looking for precise detail. He shows Richard how the bottle is not only red, but there is also writing and measurements printed on the bottle: there is more to describe about the bottle than just its colour. That is the level of detail the garda is looking for from Richard. 'Today will take a lot of concentration,' the detective says.

The interview begins and the detective asks Richard to describe his relationship with Tina.

'What to say, really, we met in 1989. I was a lot heavier then, and it wasn't until three months later that we began going out ... I broke the law to give her stuff. All I ever wanted was to keep her happy.' It is clear, as Richard begins to speak, that he has listened to Dave Noonan's request and will give a lot of detail. Over the following hours, the interview will go off on various tangents, and sometimes Dave Noonan steers it back on topic, but mostly he just listens. Richard calls the detective by his first name, in the same fashion he previously spoke to me, using my first name and telling me information as if he was confiding in me, as if we were friends.

―――

The first few minutes of Richard's garda interview show a man who hasn't spoken with someone in quite a while. His thoughts are scattered; he has much on his mind. He talks about when their first parrot died and in the next breath moves immediately to another thought. 'When Pearl died it was like losing a child. It got bird flu and we got an autopsy done. Someone gave Tina a box of Quality Street after that happened. We then bought Valentine. Tina used to have the TV licence in her name …'

At this moment the detective introduces what he calls the 'Dave knows nothing' concept, saying that he doesn't want Richard to assume that he – Dave – knows anything about the details of Tina's case, but rather he wants Richard to go back over everything.

Richard is very talkative and recounts that he and Tina used to keep cash in the attic when they lived in Fermoy, and he mentions the house improvement works he had been doing in Youghal and that the plasterboard work had been done 'before she left'. He then refers to the fact that he is now left alone with the animals, saying 'silence can be deafening …

did I once take a box of tablets? Yes.' Much later in the discussion he will return to the issue of the tablets, claiming Tina attacked him in 1995 and he took an overdose.

Richard's thoughts are both plentiful and disordered, but Dave Noonan doesn't interrupt. So much information is coming as Richard relaxes in the armchair and recounts memories of Tina and the life they had. He mixes happy memories with claims of domestic violence. The detail he is giving will provide lots of new leads for gardaí to follow up to check their veracity.

'You would want to be in a coma for the last four years … My feelings are altered a bit … Tina once had a Nokia … And she later had a Samsung Galaxy … In the weeks before she went Tina was constantly writing down her PPS number and her mobile number … Tina could be mean and angry, other times she could just go up to bed … I would sometimes have black eyes and swollen lips … I would have bites and cuts on my head and scrapes on my back … There was a girl who knew Tina who I met again on the day I was filming with *Prime Time* … Soon after she disappeared I got a job … I was working on doing the stairs when she left … I got replacement timber in Flavins … The wood was white.'

Dave Noonan tells Richard he can close his eyes if it helps him remember, and he asks Richard to concentrate on details about Sunday, 19 March 2017, when the couple went to the car boot sale in Carrigtwohill, and also the following day, when he last saw Tina. Richard gives very precise details of the clothes Tina wore to the car boot sale and what they ate that morning for breakfast. His mind wanders at different stages, at one point saying, 'one of two things will happen, she's probably with another fella, or I'll get a registered letter demanding we sell the house'.

Richard continues to be very talkative, exclaiming at one point, 'You've never seen the dogs.' He shows Dave Noonan photos of them. 'The dark one is Heidi, a Jack Russell we got in 2008 – we saw an ad in SuperValu for a rescue dog. And Ruby was bought for €150 when the seller wanted €250.'

As Richard sits with Detective Noonan, he is free to leave at any time, but he seems happy to stay and keep talking. He says various things that will later give gardaí pause for thought, things that don't marry with Richard's previous persona in interviews. His language is coarse at times. At one point Richard refers to the parrot Valentine by saying 'she was a nasty bitch when we got her first', and at another, referring to Tina, says, 'I've bought a shitload of jewellery for her.'

At times Richard speaks in intimate detail about Tina, describing rubbing baby oil into her body the night before she disappeared. He says that when Tina's brother Tom died tragically in 2012 'we never touched sexually after that'. He continues by saying 'she had got the looks, the figure, the tattoos, the body piercings'. Richard has considerable knowledge of his wife's measurements, saying she wore a size 10 top, her bust was 34DD, she wore a size 4 shoe and was always between eight and eight and a half stone.

Richard also gives the detective his memories of going to Dungarvan on the day Tina disappeared. But the timings are completely inaccurate. He tells the detective he arrived at the church in Grange, en route to Dungarvan, 'about 10.30 or

11' and claims 'I got back to Youghal around 12 or 12.15'. Dave Noonan doesn't challenge him about this during the interview – he is happy to let Richard continue to talk.

After several hours the interview is complete. There is a lot for gardaí to digest from what Richard has said. He has voluntarily given this interview in what is still officially a missing person case. Dave Noonan thanks Richard; the next occasion the two men will spend so much time together will be in two years, when Richard will be under arrest, as excavation work begins at 3 Grattan Street.

In late summer 2021 there is growing momentum in the case. The ECI has resulted in many 'jobs' which will need to be followed up. Richard is claiming a doctor will be aware of injuries he previously suffered at the hands of Tina: that needs to be checked. Richard's timeline of his movements on the day Tina disappeared doesn't tally with the CCTV evidence from the post office in Youghal and Aldi in Dungarvan, so more work will need to be done to establish if this is just Richard misremembering or if it is something more sinister.

Detective Dave Kelleher, who has monitored every word Richard has said in his ECI, is now assigned to gather all the case materials for review, including the laptops seized by gardaí four years previously. The next six months will see substantial garda work behind the scenes. Detectives will uncover a lot more evidence, casting even more suspicion on Richard William Satchwell.

21.

Incident Room

In the summer of 2021 Dave Kelleher sets up office in Carrigtwohill garda station with the files from the Tina Satchwell case. He gathers all 170 witness statements from Tina's investigation. The recent ECI with Richard Satchwell, which Detective Kelleher had watched from outside the room, is also written up. Already 370 'jobs' have been issued from 2017 to mid-2021 in relation to the case, including 60 reported sightings of a blonde woman matching Tina's description.

On Monday, 16 August, Detective Inspector Ann Marie Twomey is appointed the senior investigating officer for Tina's case. She and Dave Kelleher review every piece of paperwork already assembled, every lead followed by gardaí over the previous four and a half years. A native of Mallow, Ann Marie Twomey has spent much of her career in County Wexford. She has also served in Kosovo, as part of the garda team assisting local policing in that region. The Tina Satchwell case is one of a number of investigations that she is put in charge of upon her return to her native county.

The new garda team want to be discreet as they begin

reviewing Tina's case file – they don't want media attention. A room in Carrigtwohill garda station is the perfect location. It is quieter than Cobh station, where Dave Kelleher is normally based, and provides space to assemble all the case materials from Youghal station, Midleton and anywhere else work has been done on the case. It is not lost on Dave Kelleher and Ann Marie Twomey that the garda station in which the case is now being assessed is very close to the GAA grounds where Tina Satchwell attended her last car boot sale. Carrigtwohill is part of Tina's story, as are so many other locations throughout the county.

Ann Marie Twomey studies each of the 60 reported sightings of Tina that have been followed up with no positive result. A Yellow Notice has been issued to Interpol, alerting police forces in 196 countries to Tina's description. Gardaí know Tina has a small tattoo of the cartoon character Tweety Bird on the left side of her upper chest. This distinctive detail is important in an international appeal for assistance. But despite a massive trawl, none of the thousands of unidentified female bodies found around the world match Tina's description. Dave Kelleher takes a DNA sample swab from Tina's mother, Mary, and a profile of Tina's own DNA is generated from her personal belongings. These samples ensure that, if ever she is found, Tina can be identified.

Gardaí are aware of false hope, which has previously arisen in the case, where bodies of women are discovered and, for a few hours or days, it has been thought they might be Tina. In January 2019, two women, Audrey Jacob and Angela Kehoe, go for a walk near their homes at Ballyandrew, near Ferns, and find skeletal remains and clothing in a ditch. A full head of dark hair is attached to the skull, and a muddy blanket covers part of the body. Neither woman has a phone; they are understandably in shock at their discovery, but they manage to say a prayer beside the body before rushing to raise the alarm.

Gardaí arrive at the scene within minutes and seal it off. Given the long hair attached to the skull, officers assume the body is female. It is obvious the body has been in the ditch for a significant period of time. Some detectives immediately think of Tina Satchwell; the hair colour is different to Tina's, but there is still a chance it is her.

However, DNA analysis later confirms the body is that of Geraldine Maginnis, an English woman in her mid-50s who had been living in County Wexford and was last seen in mid-October 2018. She had not been reported missing, as she had not been in contact with family members for almost a decade. The subsequent garda investigation establishes there is nothing suspicious about Geraldine's death; it is simply a tragic loss of life of a woman without any friends or family close to her. Her body had lain undiscovered in the ditch for three months. For detectives investigating Tina Satchwell's disappearance, the case serves as a reminder that bodies can lie exposed to the elements for significant periods of time without being discovered.

In early January 2021 gardaí phone Richard to alert him that skeletal remains have been discovered in east County Cork after construction workers clearing a site in Midleton found a human skull. The discovery was made on the greenway on the Youghal side of town. They tell him a full investigation, including an extensive search, is underway.

Over the next nine days gardaí from the Cork North division search along the greenway, and a complete skeleton is recovered along with some clothing. State Pathologist Dr Margot Bolster examines the remains at the scene and subsequently at Cork University Hospital, and despite initial feelings that the body might be Tina, it is soon established that the body, although female, is that of a much older woman. Forensic tests reveal she was in her 70s, large framed, about 5 feet to 5 feet 2 inches tall, wore dentures and had suffered from arthritis. Despite several public appeals, the woman is not identified.

At the incident room in Carrigtwohill, in late 2021, Dave Kelleher is assessing the physical items removed from the Satchwell home during the search in June 2017. Two laptops owned by Richard Satchwell are of particular interest; they had been labelled DB6 and DB8 when seized from the house four years ago. They have been kept in safe storage since 2017, but crucial details within them are not retrieved until 2021, when Detective Kelleher gets his hands on them. No explanation for this four-year delay is given during the subsequent murder trial.

Dave Kelleher knows his way around computers and is up to speed on the latest ways to access the information on them. The detective arranges for the use of Magnet Axiom software to make a copy of all data on both laptops. This will allow for analysis of the internet search histories on both devices, including all emails sent and received.

The digital deep-dive pays off significantly. DB6 shows that on 24 March 2017 a search was made for 'quicklime' and at 9.08 p.m. a YouTube video, relating to quicklime was watched twice. The timing of the internet search is not lost on the team of officers now working on this fresh investigation. On the night Richard Satchwell walked into Fermoy garda station to say his wife had left the family home, someone later searched the internet on a laptop in the Satchwell home for 'quicklime'. Detectives know one of the common uses of quicklime is to speed up decomposition of human bodies.

Dave Kelleher contacts the dedicated law enforcement portals provided by Google and Microsoft. The two companies are well used to police forces across the world seeking to unlock phone and computer data. Detective Kelleher has obtained the necessary warrants from the District Court and asks Google and Microsoft to assist garda enquiries. Among the information retrieved are details of emails which outline how Richard and Tina spent considerable time and money trying to acquire marmoset monkeys from abroad.

One of the email addresses found within the DB8 laptop is richard.richardsatchwell.satch@gmail.com and Dave Kelleher asks Google for details relating to this address. The detective's methodical approach to following leads within the devices is about to unleash a treasure trove. Google tell gardaí there are 25,000 GPS co-ordinates for a phone attached to that Gmail address – Richard Satchwell's 085 phone, a number he has kept all this time, the same number he was using in 2017 when Tina disappeared. This is how detectives are now able to track Richard's location on the day Tina disappeared. The data shows Richard travelled to Dungarvan much later than he has always claimed, and he didn't go directly home to 3 Grattan Street on his return but rather drove to another part of Youghal. In all his dealings with gardaí, including his ECI, he has never told them that fact.

The cold-case detectives also analyse detail of the advert Richard put on DoneDeal offering to give away a chest freezer, placed shortly after Tina disappeared. It's just one of many suspicious elements to Richard's actions and demeanour, but officers know they are going to need much more than suspicion to break open the case.

As Ann Marie Twomey continues to study the case file, she is monitoring other cases of missing women. There may be no link between any other case and Tina's disappearance, but the detective is keeping up to speed with the investigative methods being used by gardaí investigating cold cases in other parts of the country.

In October 2021 a two-week search is undertaken in woodland at Brewel East in County Kildare, close to the Wicklow border. Gardaí are searching for the body of Deirdre Jacob, following an analysis of new information which has come into the incident room in Kildare town. It is now three years since Deirdre's case was upgraded to a murder investigation, and it is 23 years since the 18-year-old was last seen at the gate of her home near Newbridge.

The methodical search at Brewel East is overseen by forensic archaeologist Dr Niamh McCullagh. The Cork woman has worked for well over a decade throughout Ireland and abroad searching for human remains. She has worked with the Independent Commission for the Location of Victims' Remains, successfully finding the bodies of men shot dead by the IRA in the 1970s and secretly buried in bogland and other terrain in counties Monaghan, Antrim, Louth and Meath. Dr McCullagh was also part of the team to recover Séamus Ruddy's body in France in 2017, after a fresh search found the exact spot where his body had been buried, after being killed by the INLA in 1986.

Since 2014 Niamh McCullagh has been advising gardaí on how best to search for the bodies of homicide victims. She has also been the lead scientific advisor on the planned excavation of the site of the Tuam mother and baby home, where the remains of many infants are believed to be buried.

During the search at Brewel East, traces of centuries-old human activity are discovered, but no trace of Deirdre Jacob is found. The search has been slow, painstaking and exhaustive. Inch by inch, layers of soil have been removed from a large area as part of a deep excavation. The information leading to the search may have been given with the best of intentions, but it's a dead end in the investigation into Deirdre's suspected murder.

Ann Marie Twomey picks up the phone and rings Niamh McCullagh. She wants to get the archaeologist's opinion on the Tina Satchwell case. There have been three major searches for Tina: the search of her house in June 2017; the search of Youghal Bay near her home in August 2017; and the search at Castlemartyr forest in March 2018. Niamh McCullagh knows all about the search at Castlemartyr – she oversaw it, giving her expert advice on how to use a grid method to ensure the area was completely and properly assessed. She tells the detective she is happy to look over Tina's case and give her opinion on the search strategy.

On Sunday, 23 January 2022, Richard meets gardaí again. When he had agreed to the ECI seven months previously, he knew the entire interview was being recorded and would be typed up so he could read it back. In the January follow-up meeting Richard is invited to read over the notes and sign the statement as being correct. He clarifies it was three or four weeks after Tina disappeared that he began working for a tyre delivery company. He also has another comment he wants added. During the ECI Richard had said Tina's mood changed after her brother's death in 2012 and that she had often said she would leave him. Now Richard wants to add more detail. 'What I believe is that when Tina was planning to leave in 2013, that when we got Pearl, Tina was happy again and decided to stay. Depression can do stupid things to you. I personally think she is still out there somewhere.'

While Richard Satchwell is still claiming his wife is alive, Ann Marie Twomey is coming to a different view. At the end of January and into early February 2022, the detective inspector has read the entire case file and ensured all proof-of-life enquiries have been carried out, both in Ireland and abroad. As the senior investigating officer, she comes to a decision: she now believes missing woman Tina Satchwell is not a living person. While it's not known where she is, Tina is dead. This decision will refocus the investigation on a simple but crucial question: if Tina is not alive, where is her body?

In late March 2022, on the fifth anniversary of Tina's disappearance, gardaí issue a fresh appeal on *Crimecall*. Members of the investigation team phone Richard and seek his approval to show a photograph of himself and Tina on the programme. It's the image taken in Fermoy in 2015 without the couple's knowledge, which captures them walking in the park with Ruby. Richard gives his blessing for the photo to be used. Gardaí are happy – it is good to keep in contact with Richard and good that he is continuing to engage with them.

Ann Marie Twomey gives Dr Niamh McCullagh a USB stick with a copy of the entire case file. She wants Niamh's expert advice on where Tina's body might lie. The forensic archaeologist becomes an essential part of the team investigating Tina's case. She is aware that only one in five missing persons, who are actually homicide victims, is found during a planned search, and she wants to improve on that figure.

Among the case materials given to Niamh are the two *Prime Time* reports I filmed with Richard, including the exclusive imagery of myself and Richard in the front room of the house from November 2017.

———

One year after becoming the senior investigating officer in the Tina Satchwell case, Ann Marie Twomey comes to an important decision. In August 2022 the detective decides the investigation has reached a stage where Richard Satchwell could be arrested as part of garda enquiries. There are enough elements of Richard's narrative which either don't make sense or are completely and demonstrably inaccurate. There are many questions which could be put to Richard if he was formally arrested. But the desire to find Tina is paramount; gardaí know that a suspect could seek to destroy evidence if arrested and then released without charge. Arresting Richard now might not lead to any development in finding Tina and might actually damage the chance of finding her body. Richard is still living in Youghal at the same house from which Tina vanished; he is not going anywhere. There are other lines of enquiry which need to be followed up. While there might be enough evidence within the casefile to arrest Richard now, gardaí will actually wait a further 12 months, as they continuously ask themselves – where is Tina?

22.

Door Knock

My last personal contact with Richard is in March 2023. Monday 20th is six years to the day since Tina disappeared. I am back in work full-time after a health scare the previous summer and have been thinking a lot about Tina and Richard. I decide to email Richard rather than ring him. I haven't been in touch in a while, and I think an email is better; he can decide to reply to me whenever he wants, if he wants.

'Hi Richard,' I type. 'Very best wishes at this time. I haven't been chatting with you in a good while. Thinking of Tina today and I hope an answer will come soon. I saw the garda appeal issued today. I've retweeted it. Best wishes, Barry Cummins.' I put 'Best wishes at this time' in the subject line and I send it shortly after 5 p.m. I have thought about the best time to send the email. I decided I shouldn't send it during the morning or afternoon, but rather wait until evening – until well after the time of day Tina had disappeared. Knowing Richard, I have a feeling he is living each minute of this particular day, thinking about what he was doing in those very moments six years ago.

Before I send the email, my thoughts are a mix of all the strange things Richard said to me during our meetings and the different personalities he has displayed. He had seemed to act like a softie at some points, as if he was a gentle giant. Other times I felt as if he was staring me down, challenging me with eyes that rarely blinked. He definitely seemed a 'Walter Mitty' type – prone to exaggeration or overly romantic descriptions of his relationship with his missing wife, and I constantly wondered if there was anything more sinister to him.

There is no reply to my email that night, nor the next day, nor the next or next. I am struck by that. What is Richard doing? Is he lost in his own thoughts in the house in Youghal? Is he thinking back over his actions six years ago? Despite the lack of response, I am sure Richard will get back to me at some point. It is five years since we last met in person, but I have kept in touch sporadically by text and email. Although I can't figure out what makes Richard tick, I know he likes our interactions, he trusts me. I have come to believe his private comment to me in 2018 – that he had been given an ASBO – was a test. I believe he deliberately waited until our microphones were switched off and we were alone before telling me this detail. I had later checked it out and confirmed he had indeed been given an ASBO while living in Fermoy, but I never made that detail public. I figure I am one of a small number of people who knew about the ASBO, and if word gets out, Richard may break off contact with me.

On Friday 24 March, four days after contacting Richard, an email reply via rickiesat@live.ie finally lands in my inbox just after 7.30 p.m. That's interesting, I immediately think. If Richard is living with thoughts of what he was doing at this very moment six years ago, he had just left Fermoy garda station, having told Garda Conor Gately that Tina had left home. I am struck by how this week is an exact replica of the calendar in 2017. Monday was the 20th, the day and date Tina was last seen by Richard in their home; Friday 24th is six years to the day that Richard went to Fermoy.

I study Richard's email and reread it a few times, trying to read into every word and decipher what it all might mean. This email is short but it seems more sophisticated than previous interactions. There are a few spelling errors, but gone are the capital letters for every word, and he is now using emojis.

'Thanks Barry,' he begins. 'It means a lot to me that you wasn't [sic] looking for storey [sic] because you meet my Heidi the older of the to [sic] dogs passed away in November last year at the age of 18 she was brown one it broke 💔'

I look at the red broken-heart and I am taken aback. Richard never struck me as the type of man to use emojis, but he has obviously changed. My other immediate thought is that he has not used Tina's name. I am struck by a feeling that this has been intentional – he is putting some distance between himself and Tina. I am sad to hear that Heidi has died. I think of the walks I took with Richard and the two dogs, both in Youghal and Fermoy.

I note that Richard believes I wasn't looking to do an

interview with him. To be honest I wasn't, but I would never turn one down. My email to him was simply to keep in contact and a genuine expression of good wishes. I have been constantly torn between thinking either he killed his wife and hid her body, or someone else killed her and is laughing at Richard being the prime suspect. I really don't know what to think, but I don't regret sending him good wishes. I was fishing for information, but I also know from his reply that he won't be doing any more interviews. He has cut me off at the pass by saying it means a lot that I 'wasn't looking for storey [sic]'. I know he's telling me he won't be talking to media anytime soon.

I decide not to reply for now – I feel I should just leave Richard alone for the time being. I know that gardaí are investigating Tina's case, and I can read between the lines. A nationwide appeal for information has been made on the sixth anniversary of Tina's disappearance, but no garda spokesperson was available for interview. From my decades reporting on crime stories, I know that means a specific line of enquiry is being pursued, something gardaí don't want to be questioned on publicly. I decide to sit and wait. Something is going on, but it is not for public consumption, not just yet.

———

As 2023 continues, Niamh McCullagh is studying the full file on Tina Satchwell's disappearance. It's not the only work the forensic archaeologist is doing. She is separately assessing how best she and colleagues can excavate a 1,000 square metre section within the grounds of Mountjoy Jail. The Department of Justice has approved an excavation to search for the body of a man executed by the Irish State for a crime he didn't commit. In 1941 Harry Gleeson was hanged and his body buried within the grounds of the prison. He had been convicted of the murder of a single mother of seven, Moll McCarthy, who was shot dead in County Tipperary.

A lengthy campaign in recent decades by Harry's family, and local people in Tipperary, assisted by a number of experts, had uncovered new evidence, which in 2015 led to Harry Gleeson being granted a presidential pardon. The one part of the sentence, imposed in 1941, which could be undone was that Harry's body be recovered and reburied with his family in his native County Tipperary, but that was easier said than done. Niamh McCullagh and her colleagues knew Harry was buried somewhere under an area which had been tarmacadamed in recent decades, and over a dozen other bodies of executed prisoners were lying in unmarked graves under the tarmacadam in the same general area. A lengthy search was due to commence in the eastern part of the prison grounds, near the Royal Canal, in early 2024.

Niamh McCullagh has come to a firm view, which she shares with Detective Inspector Ann Marie Twomey on 6 September 2023. Having spent months looking at all the media interviews Richard Satchwell had given, reading all the witness statements and knowing Tina was not sighted on the many hours of

CCTV harvested after 20 March 2017, Niamh has zoned in on 3 Grattan Street. She has read the report of the search of the property in June 2017 and knows no excavation work was undertaken. Niamh has also studied numerous cases of homicide victims being hidden and knows that, statistically, female victims are often likely to be within a kilometre of their home.

Niamh tells gardaí of various possibilities. Tina may have been killed in the house and her body later removed, while intact, for clandestine burial elsewhere. It is also possible she was killed in the house, her body dismembered and her remains disposed of in one or more locations. Or there is another option, one which jumps out as a credible theory – Tina never left her house. A strong possibility exists that Tina died inside her home and has been buried within the confines of the property. Her body may be buried under the extension work undertaken in recent years in the kitchen at the back of the house. But Niamh McCullagh is clear in her view: the entirety of 3 Grattan Street needs to be searched. Dr McCullagh's report recommends an 'extensive and invasive search to include an exploration of the potential for further forensic evidence that may be concealed by the recent refurbishments made in 2017, specifically the plasterboard, stairs and ground floor of the sitting room, the recent extension and rear yard'. She also recommends that a cadaver dog be brought into the house to determine the possibility of buried remains.

As gardaí consider the recommendations, they feel it is less likely that Tina's body was removed from the house, if indeed she was killed inside the property. The only way in and out is via the front door and, despite the poor CCTV coverage in the area, it is felt someone might have spotted Richard carrying a body to his car. There is still a chance he might have taken Tina's body away from the house, but it would have been risky for him to do so. The possibility that Tina's body was dismembered in the house and then removed is not as likely. The special forensic search in June 2017 by Dr Edward Connolly had found no traces of blood in the property whatsoever, and dismemberment would have caused significant blood staining.

Spurred on by Niamh McCullagh's report, gardaí begin to focus on the house. The cost of such an extensive search is analysed. Adding together all the costs of garda manpower and equipment, hiring of building contractors and the demolition work which might ensue, it is likely such work will cost in excess of several hundred thousand euro. If Tina's body is recovered no one will raise an eyebrow about the cost. If Tina's body is not found after such an invasive search gardaí need to show it was essential and that every other line of enquiry has been completely exhausted. While a lot of focus now turns to Tina's home, detectives also run down all new recently reported sightings of Tina. Once all proof-of-life enquiries are ruled out, the momentum to get into 3 Grattan Street for a more detailed search than the one in 2017 is unstoppable.

In mid-September four builders who work for Henry Connolly Ltd in County Limerick are summoned to a meeting with their boss. Pat O'Connor, Philip Burke, Gary Twomey and James McNamara are asked if they'd be interested in a State job in Youghal. They are not told what the job is but that it will be in mid-October. All four men say they are happy to travel and stay overnight for the job, which will take a number of days, whatever it is.

Detective Superintendent Seán Healy chairs a conference of detectives and experts who will all have a crucial role to play in the upcoming search. The arrest of Richard Satchwell is also part of the plan. He will be taken to Cobh garda station for questioning, and efforts will be made to divert anyone else who happens to be arrested that day, for other offences, to alternative garda stations in the region. A cadaver dog named Fern is to travel down from County Antrim along with her PSNI handler, Sergeant Alan Ward. Fern will enter the house once the members of the Garda Technical Bureau have taken video and photographs of the house as it exists when taken control of by gardaí.

Seán Healy is one of the older members of the investigating team. With almost 40 years' service as a garda, he has investigated many types of serious crime, including major multi-million euro drug seizures made off the south-west coast of Ireland. He has come face to face with many criminals who thought they could pull the wool over the eyes of gardaí.

The garda operation is kept tight and quiet. The goal is to ensure Richard Satchwell's arrest and secure 3 Grattan Street before the media get wind of what's happening. The builders arrive from Limerick and are brought into the fold, being told exactly what is happening. As James McNamara would tell me years later, the message was simple: 'we were told we are going looking for a body'.

Ann Marie Twomey knocks loudly on the door. She knows Richard Satchwell is at home. It is 5 p.m. on Tuesday, 10 October 2023, and this is the moment the cold-case garda team have been waiting for. Ann Marie has search warrants in her hand, warrants to search 3 Grattan Street and to search Richard Satchwell's personal car. The detail of the warrants specifies they are to facilitate the investigation of a crime – the murder of Tina Satchwell.

Richard opens the door. The television is playing loudly inside. Detective Dave Kelleher is standing beside Ann Marie. She identifies herself to Richard, telling him she is the detective inspector in the Cork North division. She tells him she has a warrant for an intrusive search.

Dave Kelleher steps forward. It is 5.06 p.m. After two years working discreetly on this case, the detective has a very specific task: he arrests Richard Satchwell on suspicion of the murder of his wife. Richard makes no reply. The only sound is the television playing loudly in the sitting room. As gardaí move to seal off the house and allow the forensic officers to begin an assessment of the property, Dave Kelleher puts Richard into a garda car, where he is brought at speed to Cobh station, arriving at 5.53 p.m. There, Richard is fingerprinted and has his height recorded by Sergeant Shane Prendergast, who will be responsible for Richard's welfare while in custody.

Meanwhile, back in Youghal, as the builders await instructions and the cadaver dog waits nearby, as do Niamh McCullagh and her fellow forensic archaeologist Aidan Harte, members of the Garda Technical Bureau pull on their white forensic suits and approach the front door of the home of Richard and Tina Satchwell.

23.

Discovery

Cadaver dog Fern is the first to indicate there is something hidden within the house. She is a three-year-old springer spaniel from Enniskillen, who normally works with the PSNI north of the border. But because gardaí don't have their own cadaver dog within the Dog Unit, they had to call in outside assistance. The force's lack of its own dog, skilled in detecting human remains, has long been criticised, given that more than 900 people are long-term missing in Ireland. Similar to machinery like ground-penetrating radar and metal detectors, cadaver dogs are an important tool which can help find bodies. Dr Niamh McCullagh's recommendations have been followed to the letter, and when she advised a cadaver dog was necessary for the search of 3 Grattan Street, the garda team made sure to request this expertise from the PSNI.

Fern has proven in other searches that she can detect the scent of decomposed human remains. The signal she gives, when she finds the scent of bone or blood, is to go down on all fours and freeze completely.

Before Fern enters the house, Tina's beloved chihuahua, Ruby, is taken out of the property. The parrot, Valentine, is also removed by gardaí, still in her cage. The house is a mess, full of clutter, and there is a distinct smell of dog faeces. In the six years since I filmed there, Richard's living conditions have disimproved significantly; he is living in squalor.

Fern doesn't enter the house until two hours after Richard has been arrested and taken from the property. In the meantime, Detective Garda Mairéad Crowley is the first member of the Garda Technical Bureau to enter; she walks through the entire property filming video footage which will later be played at Richard's murder trial. The video shows that a whitewashed brick wall has been added either side of the front part of the hallway. Just another step into the property, and a white shelving unit is to the left, extending from floor to ceiling, while a large mirror hangs on the back of a door to the right. This door has long been blocked off by a couch on the far side of the door in the sitting room – the same couch where Richard and I sat for hours all those years ago.

As Detective Crowley walks further down the hallway she turns slightly right into the dining room and the extent of the clutter and dirt is more visible. A cement mixer is in this room, close to the stairs, and various other building materials lie scattered on the floor. Beneath the mess on the ground you can see square black and white tiles laid from the front door right through to the kitchen at the back of the property.

At the side of the stairs is a red-brick wall and a cubbyhole door for access to the understairs storage. The kitchen is composed of old, brown-coloured cupboards and a large fridge, which sits to the side of the interior door beside the dining room. There is a skylight window in the kitchen.

DISCOVERY

The video also shows the sitting room, the location where Shirley, Kevin and I spent two hours with Richard in November 2017. The room has not seen any upkeep in those six years. The wallpaper is peeling. The loud sound of a television dominates the audio, and the TV is visible in the sitting room: a large screen in front of the mantelpiece that marks the shrine where Richard has kept Tina's nail varnish and the bottle of cava marking their 25th wedding anniversary, a bottle which she never opened.

A British gameshow is playing on the television, and a studio audience claps as a contestant wins a prize. Mairéad Crowley takes video of the rest of the house and also a laneway to the side of the property, which has been blocked off and cannot be accessed by passersby. But it could have been accessed by Richard to hide Tina's body, or any evidence of what happened to her. Having captured this imagery, Mairéad is joined inside the house by her colleagues in the Garda Technical Bureau, detectives Shane Curran, Brian Barry and Karen McCarthy. They will be in charge of directing the scale and scope of the search. Over the next few days the sound of the noisy television will be replaced by the sound of gardaí and workmen clearing the house to prepare for a thorough examination of the property.

Just after 7 p.m. Fern is brought into the house. She is wearing special forensic boots, so as not to contaminate the scene, and her harness has also been specially cleaned. Fern is a very active dog and is keen to get inside. Her only reward for doing her work – seeking the scent of decomposed remains – is a ball. At the end of her search work, whether Fern has detected the scent of a human body or not, she will play catch with a ball that Sergeant Ward always has. Later, some distance from the house, he will throw the ball for Fern and give her plenty of water. First, Fern has work to do inside 3 Grattan Street.

Dr Niamh McCullagh also enters the house when Fern does. After studying maps of the property and watching footage broadcast on *Prime Time*, this is her first opportunity to assess directly what parts of the house should be the first for examination. The scientist has marked out 10 search zones covering the entire property, and decisions will be made on which zones to search first, once the house has been cleared and made ready for closer examination.

Alan Ward and Fern start at the top of the house and work their way down. Fern sniffs at everything and moves on, but at the bottom of the stairs, in the hallway, she is particularly active. She keeps sniffing and moving around, wagging her tail and returning to the bottom steps of the stairs. She's not giving a firm indication that she's found something specific, but she's showing great interest and that she's trying to figure out what she can smell and where it's coming from.

Approaching 8 p.m., after an hour in the house, Fern is taken outside for a rest and a play with a ball. Ten minutes later another dog is found inside the property. Gardaí are surprised at this. They knew Ruby was in the house, and they knew Heidi was dead, but they didn't know Richard had taken another dog in. The fact this small dog is only found three hours after officers have taken control of the property is a clear indication of the amount of clutter inside.

The newly discovered dog is removed, and at a quarter to nine Fern is brought back in. Sergeant Ward brings her to the stairs once again, and it's clear that she is now showing huge interest in the red-brick wall to the side of the stairs. It's impossible to access this wall right now, as it's blocked by a couch and other materials. They will all have to be moved by the builders and gardaí, but it will be tomorrow before this area will be cleared. It is now completely dark outside, and a decision is made to begin afresh the next day. At 9.06 p.m. Fern leaves the house – she needs to rest after her intense sniffing and searching. Gardaí remain at the property, which will continue to be sealed off, being treated as a potential crime scene.

———

I am on annual leave the day Richard is arrested and the house sealed off. Before Richard has even arrived at Cobh station in the back of a garda car, I get word from a contact that an arrest has been made and a major search is about to take place. I am stunned by this news; I have been expecting something dramatic to happen, given the reluctance of gardaí to speak publicly about the case in recent months, but I still take a sharp intake of breath when I get news of this development.

Early on this Tuesday, 10 October, the first of three days'

leave I have taken, I think about leaving RTÉ. I am upset at the financial scandals that have hit the organisation in recent months, there has been an erosion of public trust in RTÉ. I am also disillusioned following a recent decision by RTÉ to refuse me permission to volunteer my time as host of the annual National Missing Persons Day event. I have worked for the previous ten years at the event, and RTÉ has previously approved my involvement. The reason given for the refusal to allow me to participate this year is that the event is organised by the Department of Justice, and RTÉ is concerned by any potential conflict of interest. As I begin my annual leave I am very disappointed at RTÉ's decision given my close involvement with the memorial event over the previous decade, but I understand that I have to abide by the rules. Before the day is done, I put my work woes to the back of my mind.

Once I get word around 5.50 p.m. of the arrest of a suspect in the Tina Satchwell case, I know instinctively who it is. I also know immediately that, despite my work frustrations, there is one last big report I would certainly want to do before ever actually leaving RTÉ, if indeed this is the breakthrough everyone has hoped for in the search for Tina. I think about all the time I have spent with Richard. I know gardaí have previously searched his home, but it's now becoming clear that parts of the property were never searched. If Richard is the answer to what happened to Tina, I know I am the journalist who spent the most intimate time with him, in his house and my car and on our walks with the dogs. Not for the first time, I begin working on my days off, tipping off *Prime Time* that something big is potentially happening.

DISCOVERY

The first garda interview with prisoner Richard Satchwell begins at 8.05 p.m. that Tuesday night. As Fern is sniffing around 3 Grattan Street, showing interest in the bottom steps of the stairs, Richard is sitting in a chair fixed to the floor in the middle of an interview room at Cobh garda station. His solicitor, Eddie Burke, is now with him, sitting a few feet behind Richard and to his right. In front of Richard sit two detectives, Noelle McSweeney, who is taking notes, and Dave Noonan. The last time Richard and Dave met for a long discussion, they had sat in armchairs during the ECI; Richard is now sitting on a chair which doesn't move, and the encounter is far less comfortable.

Richard's arms are folded, and he is wearing a dark coloured T-shirt and dark trousers. The detectives read Richard his rights, telling him anything he says will be taken down in writing and can be used as evidence. He is being held for questioning on suspicion of the murder of his wife. Richard says he understands his rights, adding it was 'what myself and Dave did before'.

Dave Noonan stands up at various stages during the interview, which will last for almost three hours, while Richard stays sitting. During all this time, Richard keeps to his narrative that Tina had left the family home on 20 March 2017. As he sits with his arms folded his muscles are visible – he has not lost his strength. His legs are spread as he sits in the immovable chair.

Richard and Dave know each other well, having spent a long day together conducting the previous interview. Dave's interviewing style is both probing and disarming. When Richard refers to the two pizzas he bought the night before Tina disappeared and says you wouldn't eat a 22-inch pizza on your own, Dave Noonan quickly replies, 'I might chance it.'

―――

Richard recounts his memories of the day Tina disappeared. He gives precise details of what he says he bought in Aldi in Dungarvan: a six pack of pork chops, two steaks and five pieces of fish. The CCTV footage from the store doesn't show him carrying those items, but Dave lets Richard continue. Richard moves on to talking about Tina's love of swimming, saying she would also use the steam room or sauna. 'She might wear a swimsuit and then put on a bikini to get the full benefit of the steam room.'

When Richard says there were 'a thousand tell-tale signs' that Tina was going to leave him, he refers to her changing the TV licence into his name and says, 'little things like that', saying 'lickle' rather than 'little'.

Dave introduces the concept of 'the wall of truth'. He points to one side of the room and says that is where they can put anything that is completely correct. He is trying to figure out what is true and what is not. He tells Richard that gardaí have been able to access GPS co-ordinates which show where his phone was at various times in March 2017.

At one point while being interviewed Richard suddenly clicks his fingers – it's a loud click, like a jolt. 'Tina was calm,' he says, as he clicks his fingers again, 'and then changed to violence.' His narrative of being an abused husband continues throughout his questioning at Cobh. 'She could chuck a plate or a knife at me – she threw a lamp at me around Christmas time,' he says at one point.

Richard is held overnight, and his questioning continues at 8.25 a.m. the next morning. During his time in custody he recounts multiple memories of discovering that Tina had left the house. He also strays off in conversation, at one point saying he had three clear rules which he lived by and which everyone should live by – 'don't hit partner, don't cheat on partner, don't abuse kids'. He later makes a comment that 'a slap from a woman can be sexy'. He states on a number of occasions that Tina had threatened to leave him.

On Wednesday morning, 11 October, at 8.22 a.m. Fern goes back into the house. The settee which had been in front of the side of the stairs is moved. General clutter from under the stairs is removed via the cubbyhole door. Fern is again very active, indicating great interest inside and outside the red-brick wall area and around the second step of the stairs. She is sniffing in various places and moving around quickly, as if trying to figure something out. She keeps going to the stairs area. Only if she freezes completely at any spot will searchers know Fern has detected human remains, and she hasn't done that yet. But by her furtive movements, she is clearly indicating that the stairs area is somewhere she wants to explore more. A metal detector and ground-penetrating radar are brought in and used to assess the area around the stairs, but neither indicate anything suspicious beneath the ground.

The stairs area is definitely still a place of interest and will need to be properly examined, but a lot of attention is also being placed by searchers on the kitchen area, which is at the back of the stairs. They also feel the small garden, directly outside the back door of the kitchen, might need to be dug up. But significant clutter needs to be removed from the house first so search equipment can be further deployed.

Just after 4.30 p.m. on Wednesday afternoon Richard is released without charge. Under the law governing his arrest he cannot be held more than 24 hours in custody without being either charged or released, and he's been held for almost the full period allowed. He hasn't made any admissions, and nothing of significance has yet been found in the search of his home. The house is still sealed off – significant excavation work is planned to begin the following day. Because he can't be allowed back into an active crime scene, gardaí arrange accommodation for Richard in a hotel in Cork city. He is also given a new mobile phone, as his own was seized when he was arrested and is still being forensically examined. Plain-clothes detectives maintain a discreet watch on Richard as he settles in for the night in the hotel. He is under constant surveillance, which will become extremely important, given that events are about to move very quickly back at 3 Grattan Street.

While Richard Satchwell is being released from Cobh garda station, Detective Brian Barry from the Garda Technical Bureau and builder Pat O'Connor are standing in the dining room of Richard and Tina's home. It is around 5 p.m. and the men are discussing what preparatory work they might need to do for excavation next day. The builder advises that the kitchen extension is unsafe for demolition, and they discuss if an electrician might be required before any ceilings, walls or floors are removed. Pat's colleague James McNamara is also in the dining room and stops to chat about next steps for the following day. The three men find themselves looking at the red-brick wall to the side of the stairs. Fern has indicated great interest in this area, but the ground-penetrating radar and the metal detector have not shown any anomaly beneath the flooring on either side of the wall – either within the dining room or behind the cubbyhole directly under the stairs. But now, with the settee and cement mixer and various other items of clutter removed from the area, the three men can look more closely.

An old piece of green and yellow 1970s-style linoleum covers the floor under the stairs. The builders have small powerful lights which they shine into the space, and they pull back the lino. Brian Barry immediately spots that the concrete is a light colour, meaning it's a relatively fresh pour. The concrete on a section of floor beside it is darker and older.

Under the direction of Detective Brian Barry, James McNamara gets a Kango hammer and lifts it under the stairs. There is very little room to manoeuvre, and Pat O'Connor and Brian Barry crane their necks to watch what James is doing. James breaks the concrete easily – it crumbles as the hammer digs down. 'It was an area about six foot by three foot,' James later tells me. 'I started digging down, but when I took up the floor it was only a small bit of mortar. It should have been four inches of concrete, but it basically fell apart. The filling underneath was pure loose soil. I couldn't use a shovel, it was such a confined space. I was down on my knees, using a trowel to dig down and down. I went down the length of my arm, about two and a half feet. That's when I came across the polythene plastic.'

The moment James finds there is plastic buried deep in the soil, Brian Barry immediately tells him to stop digging. The detective thanks James and Pat for their work and tells them they need to leave the scene. It is 5.21 p.m.; after all this time, the discovery beneath the ground has been made just minutes after ground was broken. The detective immediately phones Midleton garda station, where a case conference is being held. He alerts investigators to what James McNamara has just found.

Niamh McCullagh's colleague Aidan Harte enters the house at 6.45 p.m. He examines the area under the stairs and confirms that it looks like a clandestine grave. Niamh arrives from Midleton a short time later. The two forensic archaeologists are wearing special clothing so as not to contaminate the scene. They get down on their hands and knees in the small area beneath the stairs and begin slowly, delicately, clearing away a little more soil from the hole which James had dug.

The scientists continue to dig methodically, scraping gently at the soil. At 8.35 p.m. Niamh McCullagh suddenly spots something in the soil. Based on her experience, she believes there are human remains in the ground.

A wooden plank is placed over the hole, and weights are put on top to seal the entire space where it's now believed a body may lie two and a half feet beneath the ground. It is too late to continue any further work. The scientists will need the red-brick wall removed so they can properly excavate the entire area where a full body may lie. Niamh McCullagh and Aidan Harte leave the scene, knowing the following day they will expose and recover whatever human remains lie beneath the stairs of 3 Grattan Street.

News of the discovery of what appears to be a clandestine grave is relayed to the garda team discreetly watching Richard Satchwell. The information is kept tight between a small number of people, from the builders to the forensic scientists to the detectives who have pursued this cold-case investigation. While the media is now aware that a search is taking place, they are not told on Wednesday night that something very significant has been found, and Richard Satchwell is certainly not told. Gardaí need to know what exactly lies buried beneath the stairs before they make their next move. Thursday, 12 October 2023, is going to be the most dramatic day in the investigation into the disappearance of Tina Satchwell.

24.

Recovery

Early on Thursday morning, 3 Grattan Street is a hive of activity. The hole, which Niamh McCullagh examined the previous evening, has remained stuffed with forensic plastic and covered by plywood overnight, preserving the scene. What is believed to be a human hand has been sighted buried deep in the soil, and now Niamh and her colleague Aidan Harte begin the slow, methodical process to check if other body parts are also deep down under the stairs. One question yet to be answered is whether a complete and intact body is buried in the house. Everyone is assuming that the body is almost certainly that of Tina Satchwell, but the first thing to establish is if the body, whoever it is, has been buried in recent years, rather than decades. The investigation team is aware that Richard Satchwell was released without charge the previous evening, having reached the maximum 24 hours he could be held for. If he is to be re-arrested in the next few hours, detectives know they will need fresh evidence.

Richard leaves the hotel in Cork city that he has spent the night in; detectives are watching him from a distance. He is entitled to go almost anywhere he wants – Richard is a free man. The only place he can't go is into his own home, which is sealed off as a potential crime scene. When arrested two days ago, gardaí told him they would be searching intrusively in his home, lifting floors and pulling apart walls if need be. Richard knows this is a different approach to the first search of his home, in 2017. Deep within his thoughts he must realise Tina might now be found.

As Richard walks out of the hotel, gardaí know that if he decides to leave the county they will have to follow him. They hold off on seeking to arrest Richard just yet: they watch and see where he might travel. He walks to the bus station on the southside of the river Lee, and he boards a vehicle. Richard is on his way back to Youghal.

―――

Just after 8 a.m. Niamh McCullagh and Aidan Harte begin their work, down on their hands and knees. They have small trowels and spoons which they use to begin removing soil from under the stairs. Every bit of soil that is removed is placed in small buckets, before being brought out through the kitchen and placed on planks of wood to be sifted through in the back garden.

The two forensic archaeologists have worked together many times. Both have worked with the Independent Commission for the Location of Victims' Remains and have recovered the bodies of a number of people who have lain dead in bogs and forests, having been shot dead and buried by the IRA. Niamh has been working with Detective Inspector Ann Marie Twomey since the previous year, discussing the various possibilities as to where Tina Satchwell's body may be. Just a few days in advance of 3 Grattan Street being sealed off, Niamh had phoned Aidan and asked if he was free to work on a specific search. Now both experts are wearing full-body protective suits and slowly removing soil above what is believed to be the body of Tina Satchwell.

The soil is easy to remove; it is soft, loose material. Niamh and Aidan instinctively know this soil has been placed into the hole in recent times – it is what they call a 'modern insertion'. The natural soil in Youghal is yellow clay, and it is normally hard compacted material, almost rock-like. But it is obvious that someone has spent considerable time, and energy, digging down into this clay to make a large hole and then put the loosened clay back again. As they slowly excavate the hole, Niamh comes across a small best-before-date tag buried in the soil, the type that might be on a packet of bread. The date reads 3/3/17.

Down and down the archaeologists dig, scooping an inch and a half of soil at a time. They work as a team, ensuring that they dig down in a level fashion, scooping soil from all of the three-foot by six-foot section which is becoming ever more visible as an anomaly. The red-brick wall has been removed by the builders, so there is more space to work and excavate, but the conditions are still cramped.

Down they dig further, and eventually Niamh and Aidan are lying on their stomachs on the tiled floor near the side of the stairs with just their heads and shoulders resting above the grave, which is now empty of several feet of soil. They continue to slowly scoop out the ground, scanning every scoop for material which might be of forensic value. It is difficult work, and the two archaeologists are now reaching down deep into the large hole they have dug. It is almost like hanging upside down while trying to work, and they both need to occasionally stand up, stretch and rest.

Forensic anthropologist Laureen Buckley arrives at the scene, along with Assistant State Pathologist Dr Margaret Bolster. Laureen gives assistance at the hole, removing soil from around the black plastic sheeting which is being revealed. It is becoming clear that what is being uncovered is a body wrapped loosely in plastic. But due to decomposition and various shifts in the soil, what is also becoming visible is clothing, pieces of bone and remnants of soft tissue.

The scientists follow the contours of the body shape as they slowly scoop out more soil. It is becoming apparent that the grave is much bigger than the body in it. About a foot at either end of the body is now clear of soil. The body is face down, and there is substantial decomposition on the back of the remains.

Fern is brought back into the scene. Over the previous two days the cadaver dog had been very interested in the stairs area, but couldn't pinpoint the exact location causing her to continue to sniff around the stairs in the hall. It was as if she had been trying to figure something out, but couldn't. Her constant sniffing had been a hint that something might be amiss in the house.

Now Fern can detect the reason for her interest. With the body now exposed in the ground, when Fern approaches the area she goes into a full freeze, lying down and refusing to move until her handler gives a special call. By lying completely still at the site of the excavation, Fern is confirming what the forensic team already know: a human body lies buried here.

The work under the stairs is done respectfully and professionally. There is occasional talk amongst those present to record various measurements and make other observations. The top of the black plastic is at a depth of 69cm, or more than two feet. The base of the grave is 84 cm, more three feet deep.

The body is photographed in the grave by Detective Garda Mairéad Crowley. Just two days ago she had been the first forensic officer into the house, filming video of the cluttered property. Now she is recording the precise manner in which a body has been found under the stairs.

Richard Satchwell is standing at a bus stop on O'Brien Place at the other end of Youghal. Gardaí are now very visible in the area, and some are speaking directly with Richard. He could have travelled anywhere out of Cork city that morning, but he chose to return to Youghal. He has come near the location where Tina used to sit on a bench and listen to music on her headphones. O'Brien Place extends onto Lighthouse Road; this is where he got me to drive when we filmed in my car six years before. The third bench from the end, close to the lighthouse, was the one Tina would sit on. In those memories that Richard recounted to me, he would walk up with Ruby and meet Tina at this location, and then the three of them would walk back to their house. But that was years ago – that life is gone now. While Richard now stands near Lighthouse Road, with the sea in the background, Tina is dead and buried in their home. Richard doesn't yet know that the understairs grave has been discovered, but he is about to find out.

Detective Superintendent Seán Healy chats with Richard at the bus stop. He is accompanied by two other detectives, Ger O'Shaughnessy and Aidan Dardis. Seán Healy and Ger O'Shaughnessy are in plain clothes, standing either side of Richard, while Aidan Dardis is wearing a jacket with 'Garda' emblazoned on it and standing in front of him. Richard has his arms folded; he is chatting with the officers, but his demeanour is defensive. He is dressed in a black T-shirt, while the three gardaí are wearing heavier clothing on what is a dry but crisp autumn morning. These are the moments just before Richard is arrested for the second time – and the last moments he will ever be a free man. A leaf-strewn footpath 900 metres from his home is the last place Richard will ever be at liberty.

From nearby, Detective Garda Dave Kelleher approaches Richard for the second time in less than 48 hours. He has just got word from the District Court that, based on the dramatic discovery at the Satchwell house, Superintendent Adrian Gamble has obtained a warrant for Richard's re-arrest. At 12.02 p.m. Detective Kelleher arrests Richard for the murder of Tina

Satchwell on or after 19 March 2017. Similar to his first arrest, Richard is brought at speed to Cobh garda station, and Sergeant Shane Prendergast is again the officer in charge who will make sure Richard's rights are protected during his detention. Detective Dave Noonan is ready to interview Richard once again, but this time the tone of questioning will be different, and Richard's narrative will change significantly.

Meanwhile, at 3 Grattan Street, the scientists are still working to recover Tina's body from the grave. The identity has not yet been confirmed, but there are strong indicators that the body is that of a woman who would fit Tina's age and height. The body lies with her feet towards the bottom steps of the stairs and her head towards the kitchen. The skull has become separated from the rest of the skeleton due to natural decomposition. But there is nothing natural about the way the body has been hidden beneath the house. A large stone slab is found in the soil directly over where the head rested. The legs are folded back over the thighs and have become skeletal.

A body bag is laid out beside the grave, and once all possible soil has been removed from around the body, Tina's remains are finally taken out of the ground. Detective Brian Barry and forensic archaeologist Aidan Harte lift the body – still within the black plastic sheeting – into the body bag, which is then sealed.

Word begins to quickly emerge that a body has been found inside the house. I get a call from a contact. It's a short conversation – 'skeletal remains found' is all I'm told. 'Thanks for telling me' is all I can say, and I realise I am somewhat lost for words. I am stunned, and I think of the time I spent inside 3 Grattan Street. I think of Tina; I think of looking at photographs of her while sitting inside her home. I think of Tina's voice on the video talking to Pearl. I think of Richard, and I think of shaking his hand so many times. I can hear his voice in my mind. I think of our knees touching as we sat on the couch inside the house in Youghal. I feel emotional and am compelled to share this news I've just been given.

I immediately text my colleagues Shirley Bradshaw and Kevin Burns. It is close to midday. We have been keeping in touch in recent days about the case, and I know they will want to know what I have learned. We have the shared experience of spending hours in the Satchwell house. 'Skeletal remains found in house' is the message I send to both of them. They both text me back immediately, expressing shock and horror. I quickly text cameramen Nick Dolan and Eddie Duffy, both now retired, who spent considerable time along with me in Richard's company. They are also stunned at the news. I share their feeling, but I don't have time just yet to properly dwell upon it; I am now following my journalistic instincts. I know I am one of the first reporters to learn that remains have been found, and I also soon learn that an arrest has been made. I know the RTÉ news on Radio 1 will follow up on the story in less than an hour. I'm already thinking about that night's *Prime Time*, and I know we need to go big on the case.

News of an arrest is first broken nationally by TV3 reporter Paul Byrne on the station's 12.30 p.m. news bulletin, while Richard is still en route to Cobh station. Meanwhile, I have contacted my editors, Richard Downes and Paul Murphy, to alert them to the news. We are all on the same wavelength – I am still on annual leave, but I will come into the studio tonight and do a live update on *Prime Time* with the latest news on the investigation. I will cue some of the footage to be played, during my update, of my previous visit to the house. I quickly contact RTÉ solicitor Daniel Coady to discuss what I should and shouldn't say on air. The situation is complicated by the fact that Richard will still be in custody when I am live on television, and I won't be able to discuss my previous interactions with him. Already we are thinking that all media coverage of the case will be subject to scrutiny if Richard is charged with any crime.

Myself, the *Prime Time* editors and the legal team are all still happy that I will have more than enough to say without straying into territory which would be legally contentious.

I tweet three photographs of Tina with a message that human remains have been recovered at her home. The three images are a sequence of Tina with Ruby, taken along the seafront in Youghal. Richard had emailed me the images at the end of 2017, and I have kept them on my phone ever since. They are particularly vivid images, and they seem to fit the tone of what so many people are feeling but unable to articulate on this sad and dramatic day. A short time after tweeting the images I am contacted by the RTÉ newsroom asking if they can use them in their online reporting of developments in the case and also if they could be used in the studio wall for the *Six One News*. I immediately say, of course, my news instincts have automatically kicked in and I am happily helping to shape RTÉ's coverage of a story I know more intimately than any other reporter.

A black Ford van, with blacked-out windows, is driven behind the barriers at Grattan Street and parks directly outside the front door of number 3. Away from the TV cameras, which are on the other side of the barrier, the undertakers open the back of their vehicle, and the body bag containing Tina's remains is carried out through the hallway of her home and placed into the van. Local priest Fr Bill Bermingham is invited behind the garda cordon and stands near the house, close to members of the Garda Technical Bureau and the forensic scientists who unearthed Tina's body, who all stand respectfully outside the front door. Fr Bermingham quietly blesses the remains as the search team bow their heads. For a few moments there is silence, then the loudest sounds are the vehicle slowly reversing from the property and photographers' cameras clicking as the van drives along Grattan Street, heading towards the morgue at Cork University Hospital. As it travels out of Youghal the van drives past O'Brien Place where Tina's husband had been arrested three hours earlier.

The post-mortem examination begins that Thursday evening at the hospital. It is led by pathologist Margaret Bolster with assistance from Laureen Buckley, along with mortician assistant Kevin Lynch and the four members of the Garda Technical Bureau – Shane Curran, Brian Barry, Karen McCarthy and Mairéad Crowley – who have co-ordinated the fresh forensic search of the house. A forensic dentist, Dr Paul Brady, is also present, and he takes a dental impression of the teeth, which will soon confirm the body is that of Tina Satchwell.

As the body is removed from the outer sheeting in which it had been covered, debris, soil and leg bones are visible. The body is wearing a dressing gown, and the front of the body is better preserved than the back. Twelve ribs are exposed, three of which are not attached to any other part of the body.

An examination of the spinal column reveals the body is that of a woman who was aged around 45 years at time of death. Dr Bolster examines the upper body, noting that the hyoid bone is present and intact. Such bones can often be damaged during cases of manual strangulation, but no such damage is evident with this body. Laureen Buckley washes the skull, lower jaw, hyoid bone and neck bones. None of the bones show any sign of fracture.

A toe bone from the right foot is removed to be sent to Forensic Science Ireland (FSI) for extraction of DNA. Scientists at FSI have advised that toe bones are one of the best preservers of DNA and give reliable results.

Dr Bolster examines the belt tied around the upper body of the dead woman. It is a belt from the St Bernard dressing gown the woman is wearing but is not attached to the gown at all – instead it's tied tightly around the upper body, extending over the left side of the neck, under the right shoulder and knotted at the front. It strikes Margaret Bolster that such an unusual positioning of the belt means it could be used for carrying a body.

The post-mortem examination provides some definite details. The dental comparison confirms a match with Tina Satchwell's dental chart. The toe bone gives a DNA match with Tina and her mother. The left pocket of the dressing gown holds a wallet with a number of personal cards, including a public services card in the name Tina Satchwell. The wallet is gold and has a Playboy logo. It also contains a Boots Advantage card and cards for Holland & Barrett and Tesco, all in Tina's name.

But the one thing which cannot be established – and never will be – is the precise cause of death. Tina may have been strangled or suffocated, but there is nothing to prove it absolutely. None of her bones show fractures, so she hasn't been beaten to death. Fifteen glass fragments are recovered from her scalp but there is no visible damage to her cranium.

Thirteen of the glass pieces are large enough to be confirmed as toughened glass, the type normally found in a glass tabletop, shower door or window pane. Detectives wonder if Tina was pushed up against a glass object which shattered during the course of her murder. But no matching glass is ever located. The other possibility for the presence of the fragments is entirely innocent and also plausible – they may have already been within the plastic sheeting used to wrap Tina's body and then became attached to her.

Thirty kilometres away from the morgue, Richard Satchwell is now telling a new story, one completely different to the narrative he has held to for six years. Gardaí listen to his fresh story, but tell him it just doesn't add up. However, Richard will stick to this account: that Tina was on top of him trying to attack him with a chisel and that he held her off with the belt of her dressing gown until she stopped breathing. He will claim Tina's death was not intentional. Richard will later decline the opportunity to repeat this story directly during his murder trial; but his garda interview, where he tells this tale, will be played in court. Ultimately, a jury will not believe Richard's account.

25.

Confession of Sorts

When Richard begins talking it is almost like a whisper. He is sitting in the same chair, in the same interview room, as he had been the previous two days. But his reality is now very different; Richard can't hide anymore behind the stories he has spun. A decomposed female body has just been found under the stairs of his home, and the height and shape match that of his missing wife.

The interview begins at 3.35 p.m. while Tina's body is en route to Cork University Hospital. Richard is again sitting in front of detectives Dave Noonan and Noelle McSweeney. His solicitor, Eddie Burke, is back in the same seat behind Richard taking notes.

Richard has his arms folded and legs spread; Dave Noonan sits close, directly in front of him. Dave doesn't ask a direct question to start; instead he has a red water bottle with him, just like in the ECI over two years ago. Richard knows what the bottle means, but Dave says it anyway – give as much detail as possible about what you are going to say if you wish to say anything.

Richard takes off his glasses and wipes his eyes. There is

a shift in the dynamic, a change in his demeanour. He is half crying, half whispering; a flow of words comes, a flow of emotion.

He is talking about 19 March 2017 and saying Tina had hit him in the face during their drive home from the car boot sale in Carrigtwohill. This is new information; despite his claims of being attacked on various occasions by Tina, he has never said she struck him the day before she vanished.

Richard says Tina knocked his glasses clean off his face as he drove, and he completed the journey to Youghal without the glasses, which lay on the car floor. He says he made a cup of tea for them both when they arrived home, and later he got pizzas and ran a bath for Tina. He repeats his story about rubbing baby oil all over Tina's body, a nightly ritual he says they had. 'It was one of them [sic] days it could be nice or nasty,' Richard says.

In the first few moments of his interview Richard is setting the tone for his defence – accounts of domestic violence, which he says he long endured, and his love for Tina.

He moves on to Monday 20th and says he was up early and made breakfast for Tina. 'I always tried to make the breakfast special,' he tells Dave, as Noelle takes notes beside her colleague. 'I had got grapes and mandarins and yoghurt.'

Richard is speaking very fast, a stream of information; what he says during this arrest is the first and only time he will give an account of how his wife died and how he buried her body. He tells Dave he was out the back and heard a noise inside, went in, saw Tina in the hallway and 'she flew at me'. He says he fell backwards and Tina was on top of him trying to hit him with a chisel in her hand. He says he held 'the belt of her bathrobe' she wore to hold her off him. He uses his hands to show the gardaí how he held the belt up away from his chest, and he uses his right hand to demonstrate the downward motion he says Tina was making with the chisel.

Dave Noonan just listens. He will have time for follow-up questions, but Richard is in full flow, outlining his version of the moments of his wife's death. 'I honestly didn't know what to do ... I held her for 20 minutes, half an hour ... the dogs came over ... there was no taking back ... shame, panic, I don't know ... I went into the church to light a candle for her ... when she's calm she's lovely ... I buried her under the stairs ... muck and stones ... I wanted to get roses ... I got tulips ... I've got no excuses for not coming forward ... once it was done I couldn't take it back ... you can ask what you want now, Dave.'

Dave takes a breath and says, 'I do need to ask you questions to get a better understanding of what you just said.' The detective is now half off his seat, leaning in towards Richard, who uses his left hand and arm to wipe his nose. Dave first asks more about this new claim that Tina struck Richard on the car journey from Carrigtwohill. He then asks for more detail about their interactions in the house that night, before probing Richard's details of the next morning. Richard provides a lot of information, from the type of pizzas they ate and where they ate them to the talcum powder he says he rubbed into Tina's feet after her hot bath. He describes how, as he ran the bath, Tina was playing downstairs with the parrot Valentine who had recently learned to say, 'Tina's going for a wash'.

Some of Richard's account of the Sunday night is perhaps steeped in fantasy. Richard tells the detective that 'Tina loved being covered by suds'. Richard says she spent two hours in the bath and 'she then lay on the bed naked with steam coming off her body, and I rubbed baby oil into her body all over. And I rubbed in between the catch between the toes.' He says that as Tina lay on the bed 'letting the baby oil dry into her body' he got into the same bath water 'and had my own bath'. He says he then went back to the bedroom and gave Tina's feet a rub and put talcum powder on them. 'No sex,' says Richard to Dave. 'Didn't have sex for a lot of years.'

He tells Dave Noonan that a bottle of purple nail polish was taken out to put on a fresh coat on Tina's toes. Richard is continuing to speak in a low voice, and his speech pattern is fast. He says the two dogs slept up in the bedroom that Sunday night, and that around midnight Tina went to sleep. At one point during this intense garda interview in Cobh station, Richard says 'not everything I said to cover it up was a lie', claiming he would have preferred to stay living in Fermoy, but Tina wanted to move to Youghal. 'She'd go asleep crying on my shoulder ... even if an hour before she'd black and blue me, she'd cuddle into me ... in reality I think she was missing Fermoy ... never tears until Youghal ... I'm not a psychiatrist but I think she was missing Fermoy.'

Tina's friends and family would later tell me they believed Tina never wanted to leave Fermoy, but it was Richard who had decided the couple would move to Youghal, which had allowed him to further isolate his wife.

Dave Noonan moves the interview on to get more detail about the morning of 20 March 2017 and the moments Richard says Tina died in their hallway. At this point the post-mortem examination is only beginning; it is not yet known that no precise cause of death will be determined for Tina. Every detail Richard gives is important in assessing the veracity of his account of her death.

Richard describes getting up that morning, saying, 'I left Heidi up onto the bed, left Ruby up ... I went downstairs to the bathroom ... I put on old clothes, dirty old jeans, T-shirt, cheapest possible jeans ... I'm not into clothes, Dave.' The way Richard speaks with Dave Noonan reminds me of the way he often spoke with me – as if, despite the incredibly harrowing situation, they are mates having a chat.

'I washed the apple and sliced it, the mandarins were seedless, and then the grapes and natural yoghurt on them ... I was working on the sink next to the washing machine in the shed ... the two dogs came out into the shed, tails were wagging ... I could hear a scrape ... sounds ... Tina was scraping away at the plasterboard with a red-and-black wood chisel ... I might have startled her ... and she just flew at me ... I don't know why her belt was loose ... my arms were tired ... her reaction was that of a startled person ... one thing I can tell you, she was angry ... It happened so fast, Dave ... her hair wasn't brushed, her face was red.'

Richard uses his right hand to demonstrate how he says Tina wielded a chisel. 'Feeling of knowing you're on the full flat of your back ... that chisel coming like this ... Tina was standing right at the bottom of the stairs ... she lurched at me.'

Dave Noonan stands up, moves towards Richard and asks him to stand too. Dave offers Richard a yellow marker and asks him to demonstrate what he says Tina did, as if the marker was the chisel. Richard makes a forward swiping motion with the yellow marker and sits down again, still holding the marker. 'She just pounced at me, flew at me,' he tells the detective.

Dave asks Richard to stand again and help him understand the distances involved. Richard says he was 8 feet away from Tina when the confrontation occurred. 'Within seconds it was over,' Richard continues. 'I remember thinking "What are you doing?" and then the feeling of falling ... when on the floor, Tina on top of me ... hands on the bathrobe holding her up off me ... she was really trying to get me with the chisel ... across her throat ... her head above my head ... purplish colour ... she didn't get me ... next thing I remember is her body going limp ... she fell on top of me ... I was fearful ... I was afraid ... Don't know how many times she went for me.'

It is now one hour since the interview began; Richard has more to say. 'Chisel is somewhere in the house or shed ... I lay there and Tina was lying on top of me ... belt is with her ... I grabbed out when falling back.'

Dave Noonan is now holding a belt from a pair of trousers, and he offers it to Richard, asking, 'Hold the belt the way you were holding it.'

CONFESSION OF SORTS

'Please don't,' replies Richard, and he refuses to take the prop, but he doesn't stop talking.

'I was numb, not numb in body, Dave, numb in brain ... I walked up to the post office with the dogs ... she was on the floor beside the double doors going into the sitting room ... I'm going to say this, genuine, worst day of my life ... after the post office I sat there, pulled her to my arms ... got out of dirty clothes to look normal before going to the post office ... there's a sense of unravelling ... you know it's happened but part of you is telling you it's not reality ... I held her all night long where she was ... even last night Tina came to me in my dreams.'

Richard's narrative is moving around, from different days and times of day. Dave is so close to Richard that their knees are almost touching as he asks, 'Why didn't you call anyone?'

'Panic, shame,' Richard replies. 'When I was holding her she was the 17-year-old girl I met ... I felt it should be me ... I can't say her neck was broke or strangulated ... I know you're thinking "fucking eejit" ... I laid Tina on the couch next morning ... I know I buried her ... on the Sunday afternoon ... I laid her in the freezer, away from the dogs ... I was robotic ... times I thought of committing suicide ... and other times, thoughts of walking in and saying what happened ... I sat in places we had sat ... walked in places we had walked ... in some sick retarded way I wanted to be arrested in Youghal.'

Richard is crying again as he speaks about burying Tina's body under the stairs. 'It's been killing me since I did it ... wrapped in black plastic and I threw flowers in ... the number of times I sat and talked to that piece of ground ... I used a spade to mix a bit of concrete ... laid her down in the kitchen ... I had all of these illusions, a funeral, a burial.' Richard is sobbing as he utters the next line – 'The hand that killed her is the hand that loved her.'

Richard is handed a roll of toilet tissue for his tears, and he unravels some of it so he can blow his nose. 'Tina in the plastic ... I carried her down in the hole in my arms ... I didn't drop her into the hole ... I wasn't disrespectful ... I didn't get her dirty ... I put wedding rings in the pocket of her robe.'

Sergeant Prendergast knocks into the room to make sure Richard is okay, asking if he would like some water. 'Can I get a coffee?' asks the prisoner. Everyone in the room needs a break – it has been an emotional and exhausting few hours. This is just the first of many interviews Richard will face during his time in custody over the next two days. He will be challenged repeatedly on his narrative of how he says Tina died.

As he waits for his coffee, Richard tells the detectives that he would sit and speak to Tina's body buried beneath the stairs and would recount stories from his new job delivering tyres around the country. He refers to the cement which he poured over the soil covering Tina's body, saying he already had it for house renovations. 'Didn't buy the cement especially ... I started filling the hole and the next thing I knew I was sitting there with it done.' He is asked to draw a sketch of the downstairs of the house to indicate where Tina and he were standing when the confrontation occurred, and he takes up a marker and sheet of paper. 'Now, it's not to scale,' he says, drawing a map of the hallway and stairs.

On the *Prime Time* programme that same night, I am interviewed by presenter Fran McNulty about the fast-moving developments in the case. I say that DNA results are awaited which are expected to confirm that the skeletal remains recovered from within Tina's house are those of the missing 45-year-old. I speak about a man currently in custody, being held on suspicion of murder, but I don't identify him as Richard. Although I already privately know there is ample evidence to charge Richard with some form of crime, even if only concealing a body, there is an established protocol whereby a prisoner is not publicly identified while they are still being questioned by gardaí.

I quickly guide the studio conversation towards the victim and cue inserts from the documentary myself and Kevin made in 2018. I show the footage of Tina's newly purchased clothes which were hanging on the back of the door of the sitting room, and I show her nail varnish and other personal belongings, which had a layer of dust on them when I visited the house. I also show various images of Tina which I had exclusively obtained from Richard down the years. As my studio segment ends, it is clear to everyone that I will be following this case to its conclusion. I have exclusive imagery and I know I have a responsibility to tell Tina's story and also my story of being inside 3 Grattan Street. While only recently I have been thinking of leaving RTÉ, I now know I have a duty to stay and compile a full programme on the Tina Satchwell case, to be broadcast whenever Richard faces justice. I have kept all the tapes of my interactions with Richard, hours of footage, some of which has never been shown publicly but will now, one day, be aired in a special documentary.

Shortly before going on *Prime Time* I contact Tina's niece Sarah Howard by text to express my best wishes to all of Tina's family. I know gardaí are liaising closely with them and have kept them up to date on all developments within the last 48 hours. I can't imagine the shock and upset they are now facing, and I think of how Sarah had met me in Fermoy six years ago, appealing for help in finding her aunt. It was obvious Sarah and Tina had been very close.

The news is being relayed from Cork University Hospital to gardaí in Cobh that Tina's hyoid bone is intact, and there are no fractures to her body. There are some small fragments of glass in her scalp, but they may already have been in the black plastic which her body was wrapped in. The post-mortem examination concludes there is enough evidence to prove the body is that of Tina Satchwell, but there is no evidence to determine how exactly she died.

Noelle McSweeney and Dave Noonan conduct another interview with Richard. While Dave led the first interview, both officers now address questions to Richard, and both make clear they don't think his narrative of how Tina died

CONFESSION OF SORTS

makes any sense. Dave asks Richard what he thinks was the cause of Tina's death. Richard replies that the weight of her, and him fighting her off, was too much for her throat and it 'blocked her breathways [sic] or something'.

Noelle notes Richard is six-foot-two inches tall and has done a lot of house renovations by himself involving heavy lifting. Richard is a strong man. Noelle asks why he hadn't tried to take the chisel from Tina. Richard replies he was holding her up and couldn't. He adds that a small person can be stronger than a big man, and he hadn't been expecting Tina to lurch at him.

The detective says Richard's doctor has no record of seeing him at a time he claims he tried to take his own life due to violence carried out by Tina. Richard replies that people had seen bruises on him, but he doesn't name anyone specifically who can vouch for this. He adds that he should have gone straight to the gardaí after Tina died but he hadn't and couldn't take it back now. 'It started with a lie, and the lie escalated,' he says.

Detective McSweeney says it seems to her that Richard is being selective with what he remembers. She suggests that, based on the timings gardaí had established, there was an hour and 37 minutes where Richard had managed to kill Tina, come up with an alibi and begin to create a cover-up. She says this doesn't suggest the actions of a panicking man. Richard denies there was any premeditation involved in Tina's death.

Dave Noonan says Richard's account doesn't make sense, and he repeatedly asks for details of how exactly Tina died. Dave observes that Richard can give so much specific detail about the day before Tina's death, but is excluding detail about her actual death. The detective says there is no logical reason to do this, other than there is something to hide. Richard replies that he was defending himself and that he wasn't looking at Tina's face or her clothes but at the chisel. He says he was full of fear.

Richard says he has a vision of having positioned Tina's body, in the hole, in a sleeping position. When he is told Tina's body is pretty well preserved, he says that means he did 'kind of make her comfortable'.

Richard says the last six years have seen him working, but at home he has had no quality of life, no motivation. He has been sitting on a couch with 'mouldy dog shit' on it. He hasn't changed the sheets on the bed in years. He describes himself as 'living the life of a homeless person with a roof over my head'.

Richard says he came to gardaí and put his hands up and told them 'I'm the reason she's no longer with us'. Dave Noonan reminds Richard that he had actually been arrested and had consistently lied to gardaí until after his wife's body was found. Richard says he had intended ringing gardaí earlier today, and there was no need to arrest him.

Richard spends Thursday night in a cell in Cobh station, just like he had done on Tuesday night. There is no other prisoner in the station. Richard has the full attention of all the officers working through the night. Richard sleeps on a blue thick sponge mattress which fits the width of the cell. Gardaí occasionally keep watch through a viewing hatch to ensure the prisoner is okay.

CONFESSION OF SORTS

On Friday, 13 October, the post-mortem is complete. Gardaí consult during the day with the Director of Public Prosecutions. Richard has clearly confessed to the crime of concealing a body, but the big question is what other crime he might be charged with. He claims Tina's death was non-intentional. Gardaí have amassed evidence of Richard's strange and deceitful actions in the minutes, hours, days, weeks and months after Tina's death, all of which created a false narrative about her disappearance. Officers also have copies of all the television interviews Richard gave, including my four separate interviews with him, which clearly show how conniving he was. At 7.28 p.m. Detective Inspector Ann Marie Twomey receives advice from a legal officer as to what should now be done in the case, and she informs her team of what has been decided.

At 8.07 p.m. Detective Garda Dave Kelleher approaches Richard in Cobh garda station. Although he has been involved in many serious criminal investigations, Dave has never charged someone with murder before, but that is about to change right now. The detective tells Richard he is being charged that 'on the 20th March 2017 at 3 Grattan Street, Youghal, Co. Cork in said District Court Area of Youghal did murder one Tina Satchwell contrary to common law'.

In the seconds after being formally charged with the murder of his wife, Richard utters five words: 'Guilty or not guilty, guilty.' It seems at this point he is taking responsibility for the violent death of his wife. While being questioned earlier in the day, Richard said he would be going to prison and there would be no jury as he was going to plead guilty. He said even if he was advised to go to trial and try for 'a lesser charge', he would not do that. However, despite these pledges, Richard would eventually change his mind and opt for a trial so a jury could determine the level of his guilt.

The morning of Saturday, 14 October 2023 is bright and crisp in Cashel, County Tipperary. Photographers and camera crews stand with journalists, and a number of uniformed gardaí stand along Commandant P.J. Hogan Square to ensure an imminent arrival gets in and out of the local courthouse without hassle. The word has gone out: a man is due at a special early-morning sitting of Cashel District Court charged with the murder of Tina Satchwell.

The two unmarked Hyundai garda jeeps turn off Main Street and drive slowly towards the courthouse. The occupants have travelled the 100-kilometre journey from Cobh garda station; it would normally take a motorist over an hour to travel the distance, but these two vehicles have the benefit of flashing lights and sirens, and the journey has been more speedy.

Richard Satchwell is in the second jeep in the convoy. The lead car, a silver Hyundai, parks in one of two spaces which have been specially kept free, and the darker Hyundai parks behind it. Richard is in the back passenger seat of the second vehicle, handcuffed, with his hands in front of him.

As the cars pull to a stop, the camera crews and photographers move closer; the goal is to get as much imagery of Richard Satchwell as possible without hindering his walk to

CONFESSION OF SORTS

the courthouse. Within seconds of the cars stopping, it is clear Richard is not hiding his face. Sometimes prisoners cover up with hoodies, jackets or Covid face masks, but not Richard, not today.

Dave Noonan holds Richard gently by the right elbow, and Dave Kelleher takes Richard's left arm, and they guide him towards the court. It's a walk of 30 feet to the door, and Richard keeps his head down, staring at the ground. Other detectives who have travelled in the convoy – Dave Barry, Stephen Fuller, Diarmuid O'Neill, John O'Donovan and Ger O'Shaughnessy – walk behind the two Daves and Richard.

There is silence but for the constant clicking of cameras, multiple photographers recording these moments. Richard keeps his eyes to the ground, not meeting anyone's gaze. It will be for a jury to decide whether Richard is guilty of murder, but it is clear he has lied to the media, Tina's family and gardaí, right up to the moment her body was found.

Irish Daily Star and *Irish Mirror* photographer Mick O'Neill is right at the court door getting close-up images of Richard before he goes inside. (A wonderfully talented photographer, and a friend, Mick was tragically killed in a road accident in 2025.) I later joke with Mick that it looked like he was actually going to go into the courtroom and lay the charge against Richard himself, such was his enthusiasm to follow the prisoner right up to the court door.

Over recent days I have been running on adrenaline, excited by the developments in this story, but not really stopping to think of the enormity of what it all means. It is only much later that I will begin to properly process the fact that I sat so close to where Tina's body lay buried, and that I walked on the stairs above where she lay, and that I shook hands multiple times with the man who took her life. In the meantime, I am doing what I always do – simply chasing the story.

The court formalities take just four minutes. Judge Miriam Walsh remands Richard Satchwell in custody. His solicitor, Eddie Burke, successfully applies for free legal aid, saying his client is unemployed. At a later stage Richard will apply for bail but he won't get it. His days of freedom are over.

Richard is quickly brought back out the front door of the court and placed in the back of a prison van. Again the clicking sound of cameras dominates – the only voice is a uniformed garda calling out to the media to 'give him room, lads'.

And then Richard is gone. The black Hyundai leads the way with sirens blaring, and the garda van follows quickly behind. Richard is on his way to Limerick Prison to await trial.

26.

At Peace

Tina's body is cremated two weeks after her remains are found under the stairs. Once all forensic testing is complete, Tina is formally identified, and undertaker James Ronayne collects Tina's remains from Cork University Hospital. Her mother, Mary, previously gave Dave Kelleher a DNA sample, and a DNA profile has also been extracted from personal belongings of Tina. These match the sample from the toe bone sent to FSI. An analysis of Tina's dental chart had already given a visual match with the body recovered from 3 Grattan Street, and the DNA results confirm this.

Tina's remains leave Ronayne's Funeral Home on Patrick Street in Fermoy after midday on Wednesday, 25 October. There are no flowers in the vehicle. Tina's family are in the cortege directly behind the hearse. Tina was a much-loved daughter, sister, aunt and cousin; this is obvious from the gathering which marks her final journey. This is a very different kind of funeral service. The indignity which Tina faced in death is being undone by a simple, dignified and heartfelt tribute from her family, friends and the people of Fermoy. Tina's family have made this journey 11 years before; her brother Tom reposed at the same funeral home, following a sudden, tragic death.

The week before Tina is laid to rest, her niece Sarah had gone to the dog shelter where Ruby was taken by gardaí after being removed from 3 Grattan Street. For years Tina had doted on Ruby, they were always together. Sarah took the chihuahua from the shelter and brought her to live in Fermoy, where her mother Florence took Ruby into her home.

Tina's coffin travels slowly over Kent Bridge in the centre of town. Traffic stops, people stand in tribute, no one speaks. Tina Dingivan was born here, in St Patrick's Hospital, on the last day of November 1971. She spent the first 17 years of her life in this town, before she ventured to England, met Richard and her fate was sealed. She later spent two more decades in Fermoy, living with her husband at an end-of-row semi-detached house at Liam McGearailt Place. Tina knew so many people in Fermoy, and they knew her.

The funeral cortege continues over the bridge, passing the entrance to the town park, on the left. This is where I interviewed Richard in January 2018, when I'd noticed a more confident and confrontational demeanour. He'd stared at me while telling me he believed that someone in Fermoy might have helped Tina to disappear. Fermoy was where he had first told gardaí his wife had left him, where he had thrown suspicion and innuendo, claiming someone had 'given her a helping hand' to leave him.

The town park is also where Fermoy fought back, honouring Tina in an emotional vigil held two days after Richard was charged with his wife's murder. On Monday evening, 16 October, 300 people had gathered in front of the bandstand. Tina's mother was there, and other members of the family, including Sarah Howard, whom I had interviewed in 2017. A large vibrant photograph of Tina was placed to one side of the gathering, Tina beaming at the camera, wearing a soft-blue patterned scarf and dark jacket, a black handbag over her right shoulder. This is how Fermoy will remember Tina, a woman who always had a smile, always had time for a quick word with people. Some also had memories of Tina's husband not allowing his wife to stop and talk for too long with people – Richard was always with Tina, always ensuring people didn't get too close to her.

The vigil in the town park saw hundreds of candles lit and a minute's silence held. Some of the candles were arranged to spell out Tina's name. A family friend spoke of Tina's love of fashion, her friendly nature, her impact on those who had the privilege of meeting her. Richard Satchwell had isolated his wife in Youghal in the last months of her life, but she had left a lasting impression on all who had met her in previous years in Fermoy, and they would remember her with dignity and respect.

The town park was also where Richard walked his wife to the swimming pool when they lived in the town. Her time swimming was the longest period in any given day that Tina was away from Richard; but he was never far, waiting outside with their dogs to collect Tina and walk her home again. It was in this park that the chance photo of the couple had been taken by local photographer John O'Connell, the image showing Richard half a stride ahead of Tina, holding her left hand with his right, Tina holding Ruby's lead in her other hand.

Now Tina is free of Richard, and she will soon be at rest in the same cemetery where her brother and grandmother are buried.

Onwards the cortege travels from the bridge, turning off the N72 to the right of Christ Church, rising high above the town. Tina's body is driven up Oliver Plunkett Hill, a road she walked up and down countless times in her early life. At the top of the road the cortege turns left into St Bernard's Place. Tina's old neighbours, and newer arrivals, are standing outside their homes, waiting to honour a local woman whose name is now synonymous with a horrific story.

There are 62 houses in St Bernard Place, a proud, old council estate in a jumbled gathering of small roads. Tina's coffin is slowly driven past her old home at number 39. People bless themselves as the coffin passes. These streets are where Tina played as a child; one neighbour who stayed living locally remembers how he played hopscotch and marbles with Tina Dingivan in the late 1970s and early 1980s.

The hearse leaves St Bernard Place and heads slowly back to the crossroads where the Dublin Road meets Oliver Plunkett Hill. Tina's family follow the coffin in a small convoy of vehicles. Tina's funeral service is private, one last dignity which can be afforded to this native of Fermoy and her family who are reclaiming her. Local people have known from the death notice that Tina's journey from St Bernard's Place will be the last opportunity to pay respects. 'Tina's funeral will take place privately and quietly, as she lived', is the message attached to the funeral details.

The funeral cortege travels from Fermoy to south of Cork city, through Ringaskiddy and on to the Island Crematorium, close to Haulbowline. At the crematorium Tina's family pay their final farewell to her. Tina is a beloved daughter of Mary and dear sister of Lorraine, Shane and the late Tom. She is a dearly loved granddaughter of the late Florrie and Patrick Dingivan, a niece of Stephen, Margaret, Teresa, Florence, Frank and Patrick. Tina is mourned by other family members, including her good friend Sarah, and also Linda, Noel, Cindy, Gemma, Mathew, Amy, Amanda, Isabrina, Scarlet, Elvis and Stephanie.

The family later receive Tina's ashes, and they bring them to Kilcrumper New Cemetery at Ballyvoskillakeen, two kilometres outside Fermoy. For over six years Tina's body was entombed by her killer within her own home. Now, Tina is free, she is at peace. Half of Tina's ashes are buried with her brother Tom; the other half are laid to rest with her grandmother Florrie.

27.

Court Thoughts

Gardaí are busy on New Year's Day 2024. It is 11 and a half weeks since Richard was charged with Tina's murder. Events in October 2023 had moved very quickly and, although a massive amount of work had gone into finding Tina, a similar effort is now required to present a criminal case against Richard. He had not helped detectives find Tina, nor did he give any indication she was buried in their home until after Tina was found. The only witness to what happened to Tina was Richard, but his story, as outlined in Cobh garda station after his second arrest, simply did not stack up for detectives. Richard's account of Tina falling on top of him, and him holding her dressing-gown belt against her with outstretched arms to ward off an attack with a chisel, seemed very hard to fathom.

But finding a cause of death was now impossible. The post-mortem examination had failed to establish how Tina died. Her hyoid bone was not fractured, she might have been strangled to death, but because her body was so decomposed it was impossible to ascertain.

COURT THOUGHTS

Older detectives remember the case of Michael Bambrick, who suffocated two women to death, in 1991 and 1992, and cut up their bodies with a hacksaw before dumping them in west Dublin, then had the charges reduced to manslaughter when the case finally reached the Central Criminal Court. This reduction is still shocking to many people but is exactly what happened.

In 1996 at the Central Criminal Court Bambrick offered to plead guilty to the manslaughter of his wife, Patricia McGauley, in September 1991 and the manslaughter of Mary Cummins, whom he killed in July the following year. He had been due to go on trial charged with two murders, but the Director of Public Prosecutions ended up accepting guilty pleas of manslaughter.

After his initial arrest in 1995 Bambrick had at first denied knowing anything about the two missing women, but he eventually confessed to hiding their bodies, and he brought officers to two locations at Balgaddy near Lucan where the women's remains were recovered. Bambrick told gardaí he had tied both women up and stuffed tights in their mouths during sexual intercourse at his home at St Ronan's Park in Clondalkin. He said he panicked when both women choked to death, and he then dismembered them before hiding their bodies in a field and in a ditch less than a mile from his house.

The fact that Bambrick killed Mary Cummins in the same fashion as his wife, eight months after his first killing, led gardaí to believe they had a very strong case against him for murder. However, because he had dismembered their bodies, no cause of death could be established for the deaths of Patricia and Mary. In the absence of a medical cause of death, and in circumstances where the only living witness was the man who had caused their deaths, the Director of Public Prosecutions agreed to drop the murder charges against Bambrick in exchange for his guilty pleas to manslaughter.

The Bambrick case served as a stark reminder that, despite whatever wealth of evidence there might be in a murder case, nothing was certain until the case reached court. Bambrick was sentenced to a total of 18 years in jail for two crimes of manslaughter – nine years for each killing – but was released on good behaviour in 2008 having served only 13 years in Arbour Hill Prison. More recently, he was living a quiet life in Dublin city and was not subject to any ongoing monitoring. If he had been convicted of murder, Bambrick would have received a life sentence and been subject to post-release supervision if and when released from jail.

Officers who know of the Bambrick case wonder if Richard Satchwell will seek a manslaughter conviction rather than murder. If no medical cause of death can be established for Tina, it will be up to the prosecution to prove in other ways that the crime amounts to murder. Gardaí already know Richard is blaming his wife for what happened, claiming he was a long-time victim of domestic violence. Despite his original statement while in garda custody that a trial would not be required, it is looking more and more likely that Richard Satchwell is going to contest the murder charge. He might not even offer a plea to manslaughter, but rather might seek an acquittal on grounds that he had been provoked or was attempting to defend himself.

Gardaí work through Christmas to ensure the file on Tina's case is assembled and submitted to the Cork State Solicitor on 1 January 2024. That the file was despatched on a bank holiday shows the dedication of detectives, keen to ensure the case not falter due to any perceived delay on their part. Any alleged murderer has a right to a speedy trial, especially if they are in custody, and Richard Satchwell is no different. He has legal rights which need to be protected.

I drive to Clonmel District Court on 2 January 2024. It is another remand hearing for Richard, and a chance to glean what I can about the case. I want to know when and where a trial is likely to take place or if Richard will give any indication he might plead guilty.

Once in position inside the District Court in Clonmel I quickly realise that Richard won't be in court in person today. The court registrar is checking the video link to see if contact can be made with Limerick Prison. Suddenly Richard appears on screen. I study him closely: he now has a thick beard and wears a light-coloured sweatshirt. He looks much better than I've ever seen him – prison food, proper routine and rest are having a good effect on him.

'Are you Richard Satchwell?' asks the court registrar.

'I am, yes,' replies Richard, his voice clear and distinct. I haven't heard him speak in a long time, but I'd recognise his voice anywhere.

'Can you hear us okay?' the clerk asks.

'I can,' replies Richard. I'm suddenly struck by the thought Richard can also see us. I'm sitting at the back of the room, a few rows behind where Richard's own solicitor, Eddie Burke, is sitting, and I figure Richard can see me too. I don't change my demeanour; I am craning to listen to everything and quickly scribbling notes of what is being said in court.

Eddie Burke rises to his feet to address the court, saying his client has been in custody since 14 October and is seeking an update on the status of the prosecution file. A garda responds that the file is with the State Solicitor since the previous day and will be with the Director of Public Prosecutions by the end of that week.

Now I start to really get a feel for how this case is going to pan out. Eddie Burke tells the court his client is not consenting to a four-week remand, but rather wants an update on the case in two weeks' time. I know from my experience as a court reporter what this most likely means. It's an opening salvo in a legal tussle, as close an indication that can be gleaned at this early stage that Richard Satchwell is going to contest the murder charge.

COURT THOUGHTS

It seems Richard has been doing a lot of thinking. By not complying with any request to allow the State extra time to prepare the case against him, I am now wondering if he will even offer a plea to manslaughter. I've nothing to base these feelings on, other than my knowledge of Richard through my many meetings with him years before and my 'read of the room' in terms of what is being said in court.

Looking at Richard on the video screen as he stares back at the courtroom, he is polite and seems confident. I just know that whenever this case is finally heard we are going to have a trial. No way is this man pleading guilty, I think to myself.

Driving home that afternoon I think about the fact that Richard is not charged with any specific crime relating to concealing Tina's body. He could have been charged with perverting the course of justice or with committing an act to prevent the lawful burial of a body. But in Richard's case the State has decided to simply charge him with one count – murder. All the evidence of hiding the crime, and hiding the body, will form part of the case seeking to convict him of murder.

I think of another homicide in County Cork where the body of a victim was hidden. Wayne O'Donoghue killed 11-year-old Robert Holohan in Midleton in January 2005. O'Donoghue compounded the horror of his actions by taking part in searches for Robert, whose body was found at Inch Strand eight days after he vanished. After a trial at the Central Criminal Court in Cork city, a jury had found O'Donoghue not guilty of murder but guilty of manslaughter. He was given a four-year sentence and served three years in jail before leaving Ireland for a new life in the UK.

Despite hiding Robert's body and then taking part in searches for him, Wayne O'Donoghue was never charged with perverting the course of justice or any other crime to mark specific actions after Robert's death. Instead, the Director of Public Prosecutions decided to keep matters legally simple and bring just one charge for a jury to decide upon. The same is now being done in the Richard Satchwell case. The State is going all in on the murder charge. It is all or nothing. The prosecution will allege this was murder most foul. If a jury agrees, Richard will be going to prison for life, but, if a jury finds him not guilty of the homicide he will walk free, despite burying his wife under the stairs.

I have no doubt the prosecution file will be properly presented to Richard Satchwell within the time allowable. I know authorities will be working night and day to have a prosecution case ready for whenever the trial will take place. I know deep down it will indeed be a trial; it will need a jury to decide the guilt or innocence of the man now a comfortable prisoner on remand in Limerick Prison.

28.

Seven Women, Five Men

'Not guilty ... Not guilty.' Richard Satchwell professes his innocence twice as a jury is sworn in to decide whether to believe him or not. These are the first words he has spoken in court number 9 at the Central Criminal Court. It is 2.27p.m. on Monday, 28 April 2025 – 565 days since the body of his wife was found buried in their home, and 3,042 days after Tina disappeared, Richard Satchwell is facing trial charged with her murder.

I am sitting 10 feet from Richard, the closest I have been since we took our last walk together with the dogs in March 2018. At the time of that last meeting Richard had been living almost 12 months with Tina buried under the stairs. Now sitting in court, I find myself stealing glances at the man who sat in my car and whose hand I shook so many times. I am searching for answers in his demeanour, in his expression, something to tell me what kind of person he actually is. Richard lied to my face so many times, and I have had a long time to think about it all. I had always thought he might be capable of harming his wife, but I'm still coming to terms with the fact that he spun such a web of lies.

Richard doesn't return my glances – indeed, he never turns his face to his right, where all the wooden benches in the centre and back of the room are full. I'm among a large group of journalists squashed into the rows just behind the legal teams. The garda team involved in the cold-case investigation are gathered in a corner on the opposite side to where Richard sits. Right towards the back of the room are members of the public, all craning their necks to look at the man who has just recently emerged from a holding cell to the side of the court.

We are all in this room for the swearing in of the jury. Once 12 members of the public have been empanelled, we will all move to another court on the same floor of this large modern building, where the trial will be heard. Both the prosecution and defence teams believe the case will last a maximum of five weeks, meaning it will all be over before the June bank holiday weekend. Through the five large windows behind Mr Justice Kerida Naidoo you can see the tops of lush green trees in the Phoenix Park a few hundred feet away. This judge's function is to get 12 people onto a jury for this case, a dozen people who will be available for the next five weeks and will give their complete attention and focus to deciding if the defendant is a murderer or not.

No jury members are in this room yet; for now, they are among the throng assembled downstairs in a large room, like an airport waiting area. There are enough seats for everyone in this large jury holding area and space to walk around, but not too much space.

'Put forward Richard Satchwell,' calls the registrar, standing just below the judge, whose seat is higher than anyone else to observe everything and everyone in his courtroom.

Richard stands and holds his arms behind his back. He is freshly shaven and wearing small-rimmed glasses. He looks well-fed and has taken off a pale-green sports jacket, which he places to his left on the bench he has been directed to sit at – the dock, where defendants sit. He is wearing a blue shirt and dark trousers. I find myself studying every part of Richard, noting the blue trainers he is also wearing. They have a white sole, and the sports jacket he's taken off has a purple inner lining. Richard is better dressed than I've ever seen him, a form of smart casual that he will try and keep up over the course of his trial.

Behind Richard, and to his left, is court artist Mike O'Donnell, who is a familiar fixture in courtrooms, capturing moments where cameras are not allowed. Mike's position is the perfect spot to sketch a side profile of Richard, who is turning his head slightly in that direction anyway, keen to avoid looking to the pack of journalists to his right.

Look at me, Richard, I think. Though I don't know what I will do if he actually does look in my direction and catch my eye. I know I won't look away, but will I acknowledge him, give a tiny nod of my head? Down the years I've met criminals and suspected criminals at social gatherings, in supermarkets, in pubs – people I have seen face trial in court. Some were convicted and are now back out after serving prison sentences; others were found not guilty and never spent a day in jail. Often they have looked me in the eye, as we passed each other by, and simply nodded a form of greeting. I have nodded back or said hello. I've never demonised anyone convicted of a crime – I've always stuck to the facts in my reporting, and I think most people who have been in the dock respect that in some way.

The two bearded prison officers who brought Richard into court now sit towards the back of the room. Key to the effective running of a trial is that a jury should not know if a person is being held in custody or not. In recent years a number of people facing trial for murder have been granted bail while they await trial. One killer who was on bail, until a jury found him guilty, was Noel Long, who was convicted in 2023 of the murder 42 years previously of Nora Sheehan who was strangled to death in a random attack in County Cork. Another high-profile case where the killer was only taken into custody when a jury returned a guilty verdict was Patrick Quirke, who murdered Bobby Ryan in County Tipperary and hid his body in an underground tank on farmland.

Richard Satchwell had sought bail before his trial was heard, but a judge had denied the request, citing the fact the defendant was originally from England, and that gardaí had concerns he would not turn up for trial. And so, while Richard will be brought into court for the duration of the trial from a custody holding area, the jury will never know that. The idea is that the jury won't know anything about the defendant which might colour their view before they hear the evidence. A defendant is entitled to the presumption of innocence, so prison officers always sit away from any prisoner they have brought into the courtroom. The officers accompanying Richard today make jangling sounds as they take their seats, the keys of handcuffs, doors and the prison van hanging on their belts.

The prosecution team is all female: Gerardine Small is the lead barrister, and she is joined by Imelda Kelly and Maria Brosnan. Catherine McAleer is the solicitor for the Director of Public Prosecutions. Her seat is facing the barristers, one of the few seats which faces away from the judge, high behind her. To Catherine's right, about 10 feet away, is Eddie Burke, Richard's solicitor. In 2023 Eddie sat in the interview room at Cobh garda station during both of Richard's arrests. Now Richard sits six or seven feet diagonally to Eddie's right.

Directly in front of Eddie is Richard's defence counsel, Brendan Grehan, joined by Paula McCarthy and Mahon Corkery. In recent years I have reported on a number of cases that Brendan has been a central figure in. I have followed the successful prosecutions he has led against Boy A and Boy B, both convicted of the murder of 14-year-old Ana Kriégel, and I have also compiled a *Prime Time* programme on his prosecution of Aaron Brady for the murder of Detective Garda Adrian Donohoe. Brendan Grehan works as both a prosecution and defence barrister, so I have also watched him successfully defend Gerry Hutch against the charge of murdering David Byrne at the Regency Hotel. Will he also now ensure Richard is acquitted of murder, I wonder, as the jury minder walks from the jury box and around to the body of the court. The jury minder has an earpiece in his right ear and wears a black blazer with a harp crest. He approaches some of the detectives sitting on a particular bench. These gardaí are more used to being in court in Cork and don't realise that this area will be commandeered by would-be jurors once their numbers are shortly called out. The detectives will be able to reclaim these seats once a jury is sworn in, but until then, they must stand towards the back of the room to give the jury panel space.

'Good afternoon,' Mr Justice Naidoo says to the screen which is relaying proceedings live to the jury holding centre downstairs.

The registrar faces Richard, who is standing 15 feet away. 'Are you Richard Satchwell?'

'I am,' responds Richard.

'Richard Satchwell, you are charged that between the 19th and 20th March 2017 within the State you did murder Tina Satchwell.'

The registrar hasn't finished speaking but Richard says, 'Not guilty' just as the registrar says, 'How do you plead?' They have spoken over each other, so Richard repeats his answer, his denial – 'Not guilty'. I immediately register the fact that Richard has not offered to plead guilty to manslaughter – he is simply denying he is guilty of any crime whatsoever.

Richard sits back down as Mr Justice Naidoo tells the jury panel that the trial may last up to six weeks. The prosecution and defence have indicated it may last five weeks, but the judge is experienced enough to know that estimations can be inaccurate. Jurors need to be able to give up six weeks of their lives to sit in judgement in this case.

The judge then reads out a list of names of proposed witnesses, including many gardaí and people Richard and Tina would have known from car boot sales in Cork. Because the trial is being heard in Dublin it is unlikely that anyone on the jury panel will know any of the witnesses, but the judge wants to ensure this doesn't happen.

Fifteen minutes after Richard has pleaded not guilty, the registrar begins calling out names of potential jury members. Eighteen names are read out, and those 18 people are then escorted from the holding area into Court 9. It takes three minutes for these people to arrive, and during that time there is silence. I am still glancing occasionally at Richard, not turning my head towards him, but turning my eyes to my left to catch glimpses of him.

The first 18 prospective jurors come through a door at the back of the jury box and stand in the body of the room. It's a daunting experience for these people, coming into a packed courtroom where everyone is looking at them. The first of the 18 approaches the judge and has a private whispered conversation; the judge then announces this man is excused from serving on a jury in the case. The same thing happens with the woman whose name is called out next. The third person called is challenged by the defence team, meaning they don't want that person on the jury. Both the defence and prosecution can challenge prospective jurors if they want. The fourth name called is not objected to by anyone, and that woman is sworn in as a juror in the case.

A total of 72 names are called out before a jury is empanelled. The whole process takes 48 minutes. During most of this time Richard sits with his arms folded, looking forward at a fixed point midway between the jury box and the bench in front of him. Occasionally he looks up at the jury members whose number are increasing slowly. Just after 3.30 p.m. the final member is sworn in and she takes the final seat in the jury box. There are seven women and five men on the jury. Their names are called out once again by the registrar, and at 3.38 p.m., with the process now complete, they are told they can go home and to return the following day for the start of the trial.

Once the jury has gone, the judge also departs, his work on this case complete. The trial will now take place before Mr Justice Paul McDermott in Court 6.

Even with court now finished, Richard never looks over to his right to the rows of journalists watching his every move. Richard speaks with his legal team for a short time, he shakes hands with his solicitor and then the two prison officers take him out a side door to a prison van at the back of the court building. For the duration of the trial Richard will be an inmate of Cloverhill Prison in West Dublin.

29.

Prime Time

'The next interview is with RTÉ, and was on 25 January 2018, and was with Barry Cummins of *Prime Time*.' Gerardine Small is standing at a lectern at the prosecution bench. It is day four of the trial, and the jury is about to see video footage taken from inside 3 Grattan Street in Youghal. They are about to see Richard's demeanour within the very house where his wife's body lay buried under cement, footage recorded as I sat less than ten feet from the concealed grave. My report is entered into evidence as Exhibit 18 in the case.

I've known this moment is coming for two days, since the opening statement was made by the prosecution. I know the entirety of certain media interviews are to be played to the jury. While certain evidential material is not available to the prosecution, most notably a precise cause of death for Tina, one very strong plank of evidence is Richard's demeanour during television interviews in the months after Tina disappeared. Richard's *Crimecall* interview has already been played to the jury, where he tearfully pleads for Tina to 'come home'. Short interviews he gave to RTÉ News and TV3 News have also been shown, but now the most detailed and lengthy of all the television reports is to be played to the jury and everyone else in this packed courtroom.

It is only following the recovery of Tina's body from under the stairs that certain things Richard said can be properly considered in the round, his multiple lies laid bare.

I am sitting two rows behind Gerardine Small, in the middle of a row of journalists. It's a tight squeeze in court, given the big media interest in the evidence. I am sitting between Liz Dunphy of the *Irish Examiner* and Paul Healy of the *Irish Daily Star* and *Irish Mirror*. Both Liz and Paul are part of a new batch of journalists who have come up behind my generation, and there is healthy competition and camaraderie between all the 'hacks' who are in court. Everyone is seeking a fresh angle on the case and looking to see what type of evidence might emerge to sustain the murder charge against Richard. If the prosecution doesn't have a cause of death, what exactly does it have?

Detective Garda John O'Donovan is the technical expert within the cold-case investigation team assigned to play all video clips during the case. He takes a seat beside the registrar, close to the jury, and cues up Exhibit 18. There are a number of screens in both rows of the jury box, the judge has his own, and there are a number of other large screens on walls within the courtroom and smaller screens in front of the barristers. I am suddenly very self-conscious, realising my voice is about to boom around the courtroom and my footage will be on show for all to see.

I glance to my left at Richard, who is wearing an unbuttoned short-sleeved check shirt. It is intensely sunny all this week, and despite air conditioning the room is hot. Beneath his shirt Richard wears a white T-shirt, untucked from his dark trousers. I notice he is the only person not looking at a screen to see the report he and I will feature in. He keeps his head down, looking both at the bench in front of him and down towards his deck shoes. He hasn't looked up at any of the other TV reports which have already been played.

The studio introduction to my report stands the test of time. David McCullagh consulted with me all throughout Thursday, 25 January 2018. He had just a few lines to say to introduce my report, but every word was important, and he had to deliver them deadpan. The entire *Prime Time* team knew in 2018 it was possible Richard was responsible for his wife's disappearance, but we also knew he might be innocent.

'Ten months ago Cork woman Tina Satchwell disappeared from her home,' said David in the *Prime Time* studio, with a large photo of Tina on a screen behind him. 'To all intents and purposes she seemed to vanish into thin air. Since then there's been a massive garda investigation to try to find her and frequent appeals from her husband Richard Satchwell for her to come home. Tonight, in an in-depth report, *Prime Time*'s Barry Cummins examines the case and speaks to

Richard Satchwell about the investigation, about Tina and about why she might have disappeared.'

The first voice we hear in the actual report is Richard's. Over general imagery of Youghal and some photographs of Tina, we hear the voice of the man now sitting with his head down in the dock of Court 6. Everyone else is transfixed, eyes glued to screens; my report is about to expose lie after lie that came from Richard's mouth. 'She obviously felt she needed a break' are the first words he says. That's the first lie, I think, as I watch a screen on the defence bench, just in front of lead barrister Brendan Grehan. She left 'to get her thoughts together, to get her head straight'. That's the second lie, I note. His third sentence spoken in the report is also a lie – 'I know she took over the 26,000 mark.' 'This is cash?' I ask Richard up on screen. 'Yes,' lies Richard, looking me straight in the eye.

Now my voice is heard, and Richard and I are shown together inside 3 Grattan Street, sitting on the couch in the sitting room. I have rewatched this footage countless times since Tina's body was found; her body is so close to where I was sitting that November night in 2017. Sitting in Court 6 I remember the smells of dog faeces, parrot droppings and general mustiness and neglect.

I keep my eyes fixed on the screen beyond the defence barrister's right shoulder. After a collage of media imagery of garda searches, I am suddenly in vision in the report, standing by the pier in Youghal. I have always been able to do pieces to camera quite easily, but I suddenly feel very self-conscious looking at myself staring back on all the screens. 'Despite a national profile, numerous public appeals, searches both in the water and on land, there has been no trace of Tina,' I say on screen, completely unaware that one of those garda searches had been physically so close to Tina but failed to find her.

The next voice in my report is that of Ann Mooney, the *Irish Sun* journalist who was the first to interview Richard. Ann has a good turn of phrase and nails the big question in one sentence: 'Why does a woman who is 25 years married and who is with the love of her life suddenly vanish off the face of the earth?'

'Quite right,' I think to myself in the courtroom. 'You were right, Ann – it never made sense.'

The report then shows the interior of the garda station in Midleton where I had filmed officers attending a conference on the case. There were over 200 open lines of enquiry by the end of 2017 when we filmed in the incident room.

The man now accused of murder appears on screen walking Ruby and Heidi, as my voice-over states 'Tina Satchwell's husband of 26 years is Richard'. The imagery cuts to an archive quote from the *Crimecall* appeal and the words that Richard tearfully spoke which really piqued my initial interest and made me pursue an interview with him: 'Tina, come home, there's nobody mad at you. My arms are open.'

My voice resonates around Court 6 once again with a pacy voice-over, and I glance up at the judge, noting his eyes are fixed on the screen in front of him. 'As he appeals for information on his missing wife, Richard Satchwell has been thrust into the media glare,' my voice-over booms, as Richard and I are shown walking around Youghal and across the bridge in Fermoy. 'I've spent time with him over the past number of months in the ongoing search for Tina.'

The next line in the report is from Richard, and is one I have long thought about. 'It's like I'm walking outside looking in at the old life. You feel like it's happening to somebody else, that it's not directly happened to you. It's just totally heartbreaking.' What I had never said to anyone, in 2017 or since, was that this description by Richard of feeling he was looking at someone else's life had reminded me of Joe O'Reilly, who had murdered his wife Rachel in 2004.

A mother of two small children, Rachel was found bludgeoned to death in the family home in Naul in north County Dublin. Her husband had gone to work in Phibsboro but then secretly drove back home and killed his wife, before returning to work. He later played the role of grieving husband, going on RTÉ's *Late Late Show*, alongside Rachel's heartbroken mother, Rose, to appeal for help in finding the killer.

I had reported extensively on Rachel's murder and the subsequent trial of her husband, so when Richard Satchwell had said to me in his home in 2017 'it's like I'm walking outside looking in at the old life', it had immediately reminded me of the words Joe O'Reilly spoke as he sat in a studio in RTÉ describing arriving back to where his wife's body had been found by her mother. 'I just literally felt I was at the outside looking in at myself, walking into, running into the house,' O'Reilly had said to the nation. Richard's phrasing was uncannily similar to the convicted murderer O'Reilly's, but when I had composed my original script for that first report I had reminded myself that it might simply be coincidence. Who was I to judge how someone described how they felt when a loved one disappeared? Just because one murderer described a feeling of being 'on the outside looking in' at themselves didn't make the next person to say something similar a murderer. Now, sitting in Court 6, I recognise my original instinct was right: Richard's description of his life in the weeks and months after Tina disappeared was now demonstrably suspicious.

———

While I know that everyone except Richard is watching one of the many screens in the courtroom, I also get the feeling that people are looking at me, stealing glances, nudging each other. I'm now partly the focus of attention in the courtroom, and I make sure to keep my expression neutral, avoiding anything the jury might think looks like displeasure with the defendant. I can see this report stands the test of time; it has captured evidence of lies, evasion and subterfuge – all at the hands of Richard Satchwell. An understandable human reaction, having been lied to so often, might be for me to shake my head in disbelief, but I can't do that here and now. I know as I sit in the middle of the courtroom that I must not betray any emotion. As I look up at myself and Richard viewing Tina's nail varnish on the mantelpiece of the sitting room, I squeeze my toes in court, just like I did when I sat in Richard and Tina's home. I keep calm and composed; people are watching.

The footage of Richard in my car appears on the screens, and I think about the Volkswagen Passat. That car had taken us on family holidays since 2008, including on the ferry to France. Amid the blurred lines where work infiltrated personal life, I had often used my own car to film for *Prime Time* reports, but having Richard in the front passenger seat always stood out in my mind.

After repeat engine trouble, the car was sold for scrap in 2021. But now, here it was once again, up on screen in Court 6, Richard holding the boom microphone in his hand in the front passenger seat, and the windscreen wipers whacking over and back, as the rain beat down in Youghal.

It suddenly strikes me that this is one of the first times that the voice of a murder victim will be played in the trial of their alleged killer. The video of Tina saying, 'Heidi has distracted her' and 'What you got, Pearl?' as she speaks to the parrot is played within my first report. Tina's strong, melodic Cork accent reverberates around the courtroom, just for a few seconds, but it is poignant, the voice of a dead woman. I feel proud of the work myself and Kevin Burns put into the programme, and I immediately think of the other report which will inevitably be played, where I sat down and did a face-to-face interview with Richard, when the search for Tina's body was taking place in Castlemartyr in March

2018. I know the reports are being played chronologically, so that one won't be shown until this afternoon. In the meantime, interviews that Richard did with TV3, a community radio station in Youghal and Red FM will be played. These interviews are all important, showing a man who kept up a charade over years. But my first report, which has been played in full, is different to all the other media reports being put before the jury. Tina's voice is heard, and the interior of the house where her body was buried is shown. And my many meetings with Richard are shown, so that his lengthy and ongoing lies are uniquely summed up within Exhibit 18, the *Prime Time* report.

Approaching midday the last few frames of my report are shown; the music fades, and the closing image of Tina is shown on screen. Music is always an important element in a report – too much melancholy can be overbearing, but soft music, with a rhythm, can create a good editorial pace to keep viewers engaged with long-form reports. In this report it was three simple piano notes. They were not dramatic, but they set a reflective tone, forcing the viewer to think about what they were seeing and hearing.

Michael Doyle of *The Irish Sun* is sitting directly in front of me. Just as my report ends and the next exhibit is being made ready by Detective Garda O'Donovan, Michael gestures to me with a sideward glance, which I know means he found the report to be powerful. Liz Dunphy also gives me a similar nod, and when the court breaks for lunch, and Richard is taken back out to the holding area for prisoners, Paul Healy beside me asks if it felt odd watching my report in court.

'Very odd, very odd,' I reply, struggling to find adequate words to sum up how I feel at this moment.

Rather than go for lunch with the other reporters I find myself walking around Heuston station at lunchtime. I am unsettled, knowing that another of my reports will be shown to the jury after lunch. I know this one is equally powerful in terms of the questions I put to Richard and the overall tone. I'm feeling a little exposed, my work being parsed and analysed by legal teams – one vying for a conviction, the other for an acquittal.

After lunch, my report of 6 March 2018 is played to the jury. Once again, I am introduced by the prosecution as Barry Cummins of *Prime Time*.

This second report is one where I was ill at ease when it was filmed, not only because I felt Richard was hiding something, but also because I wasn't very experienced at conducting fast-paced interviews, which needed to be filmed as if they were live. Immediately after the interview, at the Grand Hotel in Fermoy, Kevin Burns and I had to travel back to the RTÉ campus in Donnybrook in Dublin and edit the interview very quickly. We also had to consult with the legal department, as well as our editors. The most effective way of speeding things up in a situation like this is to ask pithy but direct questions, so there is very little left to actually edit. I was more used to asking questions in a slow fashion, teasing out information from an interviewee, rather like a fireside chat. Kevin had reminded me in advance of the interview to get to the point quickly with my questions, and his advice paid off. I kept to a short, direct question-and-answer format, and it worked well, with Richard again showing various sides to his personality.

Richard's lies were multiple, repeating a claim that Tina was depressed and that 'she went away to kind of sort her own feelings out'. He looked me in the eye during the interview and without a hint of irony said, 'I believe there is somebody out there that actually does know where she is.' While saying that Tina would fight back if someone tried attacking her, he also raises the possibility that someone had caused her harm, saying, 'What if the person who helped her to get away has done something to her? I don't want to believe that.' During the interview Richard dismisses on more than one occasion the possibility that Tina was buried in Castlemartyr Woods, where a major search was ongoing at the time. Only now, seven years after the interview, could everyone see why he was so confident at the time: he knew exactly where she was.

Other comments in this second interview with me reverberate around the courtroom and give everyone pause for thought. He refers to people wishing him well as if they were mourners at a funeral. The evidence now unfolding during the trial is that Richard had performed what he believed to be a 'self-funeral', where he had dug a grave and buried Tina's body under the stairs, where he was the only 'mourner' and had put flowers in with the body.

The report on screen comes to a moment I had always found strange, a comment from Richard which always sounded rehearsed, remote. 'To be honest, I live by two four-letter words,' said Richard, looking me directly in the eye, holding my gaze, not blinking, 'the love I feel for her, and the hope that I just have to keep there, because without hope you've got nothing.'

Another comment from the report hits me hard when it's played. 'Last night I just crashed out on the couch, I didn't go to bed at all.' If this comment is true, it means that Richard was sleeping downstairs on the couch where I had once sat with him, and he was sleeping just a few feet away from Tina's body. That's if the claim is true at all, because with so much of what Richard had said, it was hard to now know what was truth and what was fiction.

At the end of the day's evidence I look at the jury, a mixture of people from various walks of life brought together by a lottery system to pass judgement on another human being. Some are dressed smart casual, others are more informal. One man has arms full of tattoos, most wear short-sleeved tops, some carry bottles of water, some have notepads to record some of the evidence. But the one thing uniting all is their focus, their attention; they have had the same look throughout this first week of the case. They are watching and listening intently to every single bit of evidence.

30.
Cushions and Phones

The prosecution case is relatively simple: what is lacking in forensic evidence is compensated for by Richard Satchwell's own actions after his wife's death. The case against Richard is that his narrative of how Tina died is 'absolutely farcical', as described by Gerardine Small. Richard's account of Tina dying while on top of him, as he lay on the ground holding her away from him with the belt of her dressing gown, is analysed and dissected in Court 6. The prosecution barrister is clear in her view. The defendant's narrative of how Tina died 'has more holes in it than a block of Swiss cheese'.

Gerardine Small points out that, even if it were true that Tina held an implement in her right hand, her left hand would have been free and she could have got off Richard. The barrister is incredulous at Richard's account of the supposed incident in the hallway of 3 Grattan Street. 'Curiously, this eight-stone lady versus a six-foot-two man never manages to get a mark on him. Tina is well capable of getting up, she has her left hand free and can stop her own death, it's absolutely farcical but that is what he is telling gardaí.'

The prosecution is scathing in its view of Richard's failure to give precise details of Tina's death. Gerardine Small notes that when Richard was asked by gardaí to demonstrate what had happened, he said he couldn't. When Richard was asked how he held the belt around Tina's throat, he said he didn't know. When he was asked how close his hands were to Tina's neck, he said he didn't know. 'Think about that,' Gerardine Small told the jury. 'It totally beggars belief.'

The multiple lies Richard told me and other journalists is part of a wider deceit, where he lied to Tina's family, gardaí, car boot sale attendees and anyone else who would entertain his thoughts. The prosecution says Richard was 'shamelessly brazen right up to the very end', pointing out that even after his first arrest in October 2023, and knowing that his house was about to be intrusively searched, he stuck to the story that Tina had left the house while he was out shopping in Dungarvan.

Richard's actions in the minutes and hours after Tina was killed are put before the jury. CCTV footage is shown of him going into the post office and collecting both his social welfare payment and Tina's. By his own admission during his second arrest in October 2023, Tina was dead by the time he went to collect the dole money. Yet the footage shows him walking into the post office with the two dogs, just like everything is normal. As we watch the footage it strikes me that people can often be in shock and appear normal, and it will be for the jury to decide what is at the heart of all the evidence. Did

Richard plan to murder his wife? Did he form the intent to murder even just a few seconds before he attacked her, if he attacked her at all? Was Tina's death simply a horrible accident, and Richard's actions after her death a spiral of bad decisions which left him isolated and living a lie?

Why bury Tina's body? That was a big question which hung over the trial. In the moments after Tina's body went limp, why didn't Richard ring for an ambulance or call the gardaí? How did he come to a decision to dig a grave within the house, and why did he wait four days before alerting gardaí that Tina had 'upped and left'? Why did he go to a truck-driving course on the following Saturday, as if all was normal? And crucially, on the morning Tina died, how did Richard come to write emails outlining his fear that his wife would leave him over a failure to obtain marmoset monkeys?

There is so much evidence for the jury to decipher and distil. It is clear that Richard kept control over his wife after death, deciding where she should be buried, that it shouldn't be in a coffin, that only he should know where she was. How much control he actually held over her during her life was a big question I had, but not one which was crucial to the running of the prosecution case. In recent weeks, *Prime Time* producer Sallyanne Godson and I have met people who witnessed interactions between Richard and Tina which left them feeling uncomfortable, concerned that Richard might be coercively controlling his wife. Such opinions are based on observations of body language or interactions between Richard and Tina. But there was no single 'smoking gun' proving such suspicions. It was as if many people had single pieces of a puzzle, but it couldn't all be joined together until after Tina's body was found. The prosecution case had to be based on provable facts and so, no matter how likely it was that coercive control was part of the marriage, the prosecution did not call any such opinion evidence.

While the trial is ongoing, I am now working with Sallyanne on a full programme about the case to be broadcast once the trial is over. I have a long-running rule in work to 'always keep the tapes'. Every interview I've done I've kept the original recording. I used to have a large cupboard full of discs beside my desk in Donnybrook, but when a decision was made to 'modernise' the offices, all the proper storage was removed. I was left with no choice but to take all my discs home, hundreds of interviews I have recorded down the years. My hoarding of old material paid off when Richard was charged with Tina's murder. I have the original discs with lots of footage which has never been broadcast. The plan now is to compile a full *Prime Time* documentary which will feature elements of the two original reports, but also new, fresh material and some never-before-seen older footage too.

I have always remained loyal to producers when following through on a story. Kevin Burns, my original producer, is now working in management at RTÉ and so is unavailable. I have worked with Sallyanne for a decade on numerous special programmes about gangland crime, and we work extremely well together. It is Sallyanne who makes contact with Tina's former schoolteacher Olive Corcoran, who has stories about witnessing first-hand what she believes was coercive control exhibited by Richard.

We drive to meet Olive in Fermoy, and she describes how, many years after she taught Tina, they would often meet by chance around the town. Richard would always be with Tina and would not speak to Olive, who tells me she has long felt his behaviour was coercive.

Olive is not a witness in the case at the Central Criminal Court, so we record an interview to be broadcast after the trial. We also meet Sara Dobson, who sold Ruby to Richard and Tina. Sara knew the couple from attending car boot sales, and she describes witnessing arguments between Richard and Tina which left her uncomfortable, but when she asked Tina about the confrontations, Tina said it was nothing and that she loved Richard. Tina always said the same thing: she loved Richard and couldn't be without him. Sara describes how Richard would just have to give Tina a certain look and she would stop talking or say she wasn't free to walk around the car boot stalls with Sara.

Sara is a witness in the trial but is not asked about the disturbing interactions she witnessed. Her evidence is purely about Richard's lies, which he spread at car boot sales, saying Tina had gone to England due to ill-health. Once Sara completes her evidence in court, Sallyanne and I make contact with her and we record an interview to be broadcast in the special report after the verdict.

I am doing a lot of travelling during the early part of May, watching the trial in Dublin but also going to Youghal, Fermoy and elsewhere, gathering information and filming segments for the fresh report.

On day six of evidence I am late to court but end up getting the best vantage point to observe Richard. After driving around Infirmary Road and Arbour Hill and failing to find a parking space, I drive to the Dublin Zoo car park, find a spot and run back to the Central Criminal Court, arriving just before the session is about to begin. The room is full, and my usual seat has now been taken by someone else. The journalist who has routinely sat closest to the defendant is Ralph Riegel of the *Irish Independent*, and I normally sit in the row behind Ralph, close to his colleague Catherine Fegan, but not today.

A number of secondary school children have also arrived into court, part of a programme to show teenagers the realities of the legal world. The room is even more packed than normal, but I spot one seat up to the left, near the door from which Richard emerges each day.

This seat actually faces back down the courtroom, so I am sitting with my back to the judge and turning at an uncomfortable angle to my left so I can observe proceedings. That's when I realise it's actually a very good seat from which to observe Richard. Through a pane of Plexiglas, I can see where Richard will sit – I am only six feet away from the dock. Just as I realise this, the door of the holding cell opens, and Richard is brought into court by two prison officers. Richard takes his seat to my left, behind the glass, and the prison officers walk to the back of court.

That's when I notice the cushion. I am craning my neck 180 degrees, but I can see what no one else in court can see: Richard is sitting on a thick, particularly comfortable-looking cushion. For a few moments I am fascinated by it. It is navy patterned and was already there before he came out, so it's been a regular fixture. He must have had it since the trial began. Cushions are not standard for accused persons. Richard may have asked for it specifically, or it might have been left in place from a previous trial – and Court 6 is a busy courtroom, with other accused persons sitting in the dock early some mornings for short appearances as part of the management of their cases before Mr Justice McDermott.

I realise I am the only person who can properly see Richard's lower body. Because of the wooden dock he sits within, the jury, other journalists and other onlookers can only see him from the elbows up. I find myself writing down 'thick cushion' in my notepad. I think of Tina and the indignity of how her body was placed, dragged or thrown face down in the clandestine grave. I think of how Richard backfilled the grave with soil and then poured cement on top, confining Tina to the house in which horror had befallen her. I look at Richard's cushion and I think of Tina, and I feel angry, but I make sure not to show it.

I glance towards the back of the court where Tina's mother, Mary, is sitting with her daughter Lorraine. I know that both women are being escorted by the Victim Support at Court service, and they have cushions provided in their designated seating. It is quite right that both women be afforded every comfort to make their attendance at court as bearable as can be. I look back at Richard's cushion, and I know it is thicker than the ones Tina's family have. I am getting more annoyed, but I distract myself by jotting notes of what Richard is wearing.

He is wearing a light blue shirt, and his hair is very short – it looks like he's had it cut in recent days. His shirt is untucked, and he holds his right hand to his face and rests his elbow on the bench in front of him. This angle normally ensures no one except his legal team can see his expressions. But today I can also see more of Richard's face than anyone else, as I am seated a little bit behind him, while I crane my neck and act as if it's not uncomfortable.

But there is nothing to really see – he seems in another world. He is undoubtedly conscious that so many people are watching him, but he seems like he has zoned out. I look at his left hand, which no one else can see, set on a small bench in front of him. It is resting calmly, it's not shaking, he is not fidgeting, he is still. I find the lack of movement to be quite telling. While Richard cannot control where he is, he can control his reaction to his surroundings. He is not phased, he is not upset, he can zone out. He is using his right hand to shield his face from the gaze of the courtroom, but he seems comfortable enough on his cushion.

'All rise,' the judge's tipstaff calls as Mr Justice Paul McDermott emerges from his chambers. The judge takes his seat at the top of the courtroom and gives a nod to the jury minder, who goes into the jury room to bring in the seven women and five men to hear another day of evidence.

After lunch on this same day, Thursday 8 May, I can't face twisting my neck anymore on the seat close to Richard, so I get into court early for the afternoon session and find a more comfortable seat back amongst the journalists in the centre of the room. A woman in her twenties sits on my right. I don't know her, and at first I assume she is a journalist, maybe up from Cork to cover the trial. The afternoon session begins, and a witness from one of the car boot sales gives evidence of the lies Richard told her about Tina being unwell. I notice Detective Inspector John O'Connell gesture to the woman beside me to come out of court. I assume she mightn't be a journalist at all and might actually be a witness in the case. I don't see her come back into court, but I quickly forget about her as I scribble in my notepad.

The evidence continues with the playing of the first video of Richard's questioning after his arrest in October 2023. His ECI of June 2021 has already been played to the court on a previous day. Now his changing narrative between his first and second arrests will soon be laid bare in court. So much of the evidence against Richard is the lies he told to journalists and gardaí, and over the course of the trial, the jury is being shown a comprehensive video compilation of untruths and shifting stories from Richard.

Later, once court is over, I realise something is afoot.

Gerardine Small waits until the jury has left the courtroom before rising to her feet and telling the judge that an incident has occurred in court which she wishes to bring to everyone's attention.

Mr Justice McDermott looks down towards her with curiosity. I glance over at Richard Satchwell, who looks to his right observably for the first time during the entire trial, taking in a two-second glance at the body of the court. He doesn't catch anyone's eye.

Gerardine Small calls John O'Connell to the witness box, and the detective says that a woman has been taking photographs inside the courtroom. The detective says he spotted her holding her phone and took her outside and asked to see her phone's photo album. That was the woman who was sitting beside me, I think to myself. The detective says he quickly discovered the woman had taken seven photographs and had sent some to a family WhatsApp group. Wow, I think, seven photographs – I didn't even spot her take one. She had been very surreptitious, but the detective had rumbled her.

The rules inside a courtroom are clear and simple: it is forbidden to take photographs or video.

Detective O'Connell outlines that the woman had used her phone in court just after 2 p.m. and had taken a series of photos of Richard Satchwell as he sat in the dock.

None of us in court knows where this is going. Was the trial in danger in any way? The jury was gone home now. The photos were of Richard Satchwell, not of the jury. John O'Connell says he'd examined the woman's phone – she had co-operated fully. She had contacted the members of her family she had sent the photos to, and they had assured gardaí they had deleted the photos on their end. The images would not be spread any further.

It is quickly becoming apparent that this breaking of the rules is foolhardy, but not malicious. The woman is not out to cause a mistrial; she is merely a member of the public who has gone too far in her enthusiasm to share her experience of being in court. Such is the danger, in the digital age, of people feeling they can take photographs of anything and everything. The woman has done something silly, but it is a contempt of court and has to be dealt with.

Mr Justice McDermott is not a man to be trifled with, but he takes a very practical approach to this breach of the decorum of the courtroom. The wrong has been undone by the deletion of the photographs. Given that the incursion will not affect the running of the trial, the judge says he is not inclined to take it further. He reminds everyone that you cannot take photographs of anyone in court. It seems such an obvious thing, but the judge feels he needs to say it again. And so he does.

As I leave Court 6, I spot the young woman sitting to the left outside on a marble seat with two gardaí. She is now free to go. The officers are being nice to her but had needed to keep her close to the courtroom in case the judge wanted to speak with her. The woman knows she's made a mistake, but she's undone it. Thankfully this trial is set to continue as normal next day.

31.

Three Options

Richard Satchwell's defence is that he was a victim of domestic abuse over several decades, and he didn't intend to kill his wife. Among the many prosecution witnesses are two of Richard's former GPs in Fermoy. Patrick Burke tells the jury he was Richard and Tina's doctor from 1999 onwards. The couple almost always came to his practice together and he recalls only one or two occasions when 'one came without the other'. They would attend between eight and twelve times per year. Dr Burke says Richard never made any claim about Tina assaulting him until after she had disappeared. Asked if Tina had any underlying psychological issues, the doctor says she had a background of anxiety, which did not warrant intervention. The doctor describes Tina as always very friendly, very open and a great communicator.

Dr Deirdre O'Grady was the couple's GP before Patrick Burke. She tells the jury she has no recollection of ever being told in the 1990s that Richard had taken an overdose of pills. Defence barrister Brendan Grehan asks if she remembers his client attending her surgery with scratches on his face; the doctor replies she has no medical notes recording this.

THREE OPTIONS

There is no medical evidence to support Richard's story of decades of violence at the hands of Tina. Furthermore there are no corroborating witnesses, nobody to say they saw any of the violence he claims was meted out to him by his wife.

Two weeks after giving birth to her daughter, Sarah Howard sits in the witness box at the Central Criminal Court. Sarah is an important witness for the prosecution – she describes being offered a chest freezer by Richard in the weeks after Tina disappeared. Sarah is emotional in Court 6, saying she found the message about a freezer 'very unusual and very strange'. Richard wasn't the 'kind to just give stuff'.

Sarah is Tina's niece, and they were extremely close. As a child, Sarah would be delighted when Tina would visit in Fermoy; later, as a young woman, she spent many happy times with Tina socialising around the town. Prosecuting barrister Gerardine Small asks Sarah to describe Tina. Her aunt was a 'genuinely lovely person', someone who was 'kind-hearted, loving, a family person, social, bubbly and someone who loved animals'. Sarah cries in the witness box as she is shown her interview with me on the *Prime Time* report broadcast in January 2018.

Before the clip is played on all the screens, I think of what Sarah said to me, which always stayed with me, when I asked her to describe her aunt's disappearance: 'It's puzzling.' They were just two words among many she said that day, but it was the way Sarah said it that always made me think. She had put great thought into what might have happened to Tina, contacting so many people to see if they had heard from her. By simply saying 'It's puzzling', Sarah was getting across a sincere view that it just didn't make sense.

By the time she met me to do that interview in Fermoy in late 2017, Sarah had experienced some of Richard's recent strange behaviour, from offering her a chest freezer for free to offering her tickets for a musical in Cork city. His actions were at odds with the fact his wife of 26 years was missing. Now, in court, Sarah's words are being played back to her and to everyone in the packed room, including the man on trial for the murder of her aunt. 'It's tearing us apart every day not knowing where she is,' continues Sarah in our interview on the screens dotted around the courtroom. 'And every day if you've a missed call on your phone, or you're checking the paper, you're checking everywhere really just to see if there's any information or news. And every day there's nothing.'

My mouth is dry, and I feel emotional watching Sarah in court as we all listen back to what she said over seven years ago. I find myself studying the red carpet in the courtroom, thinking of the upset Sarah must feel. I have met so many families of missing people, and I recognise her description of constantly checking phones or always scanning a crowd for the face of a missing loved one. Now Sarah is sitting in the same courtroom as the man whose lies have compounded her pain.

'What do you think might have happened to her?' I ask in the report being played in court. I am standing along the river Blackwater in Fermoy with Sarah, and Tina is missing eight months by this stage. 'There's loads of different thoughts in my head,' replies Sarah on the video screens. 'But I can't … I don't know what's happened … Or I don't have the answers … Of course everything has gone around in our heads, the possibility that it mightn't be a good result or good news that comes.' Sarah finishes by telling me that 'someone has to know something' and someone 'can't just disappear'.

As the video of my interview with Sarah finishes, I feel proud of the work, glad that I did the interview, but I also feel very uncomfortable, unsettled. Richard Satchwell wasted all of our time, seeking to trick us, trying to fool us. I glance at Richard, but he's not looking at any of the screens. He's keeping his head down, eyes fixed on his feet.

———

Gerardine Small is almost finished the prosecution case. After 14 days of evidence, spread over four weeks, and following dozens of people entering the witness box, Sarah is the last prosecuting witness. Sarah is asked if she ever witnessed Tina being violent or aggressive. 'Never,' she replies.

I think of how Sarah has recently given birth and is now the focus of so many eyes in Court 6. She is a crucial witness, the person that Richard sought to confide in most in the first months after his wife disappeared. Sarah tells the court how Richard told her Tina had left him following an argument and that he claimed Tina had thrown a cup at him.

The witness says Richard told her Tina said she had wasted 28 years of her life with him. Sarah confirms she received texts from Richard asking her to check with other family members to see if Tina had contacted them, and how in August 2017 he had texted to say he'd spotted suitcases at a recycling spot in a shop car park which looked similar to the ones Tina had supposedly taken. Richard had also texted Sarah to say Tina's birth and marriage certs were gone from the house too.

The court hears Richard told Sarah he was going to set up a website dedicated to finding Tina. In one text, sent two months after Tina vanished, Richard told Sarah, 'I know Tina is your family and I'm not, so please try to understand that I love her with all my being. She's my wife, she is my life and my best friend, my everything. I'm finding it difficult to get through the days. You know that I cry all the time even now writing this. I feel I let her down in some way.' The jury is also told that five months after Tina went missing, Richard hand delivered a birthday card to Sarah, which he'd signed from 'Tina and Richard'.

Gerardine Small thanks Sarah for her time in the witness box and says she is finished with her queries. Brendan Grehan rises with some questions on behalf of Richard. He asks Sarah if it's fair to say Richard appeared 'devoted to Tina'. Sarah says this is correct.

The defence barrister asks about Sarah's statement to gardaí that Richard was 'besotted if not obsessed' with Tina; she says he was always with Tina when she was visiting. The barrister asks about a comment Sarah made to gardaí before Tina's body was found that Richard was so besotted with Tina that he couldn't have caused her harm. 'That was before,' replies Sarah.

After Sarah leaves the witness box, the prosecution barrister

THREE OPTIONS

rises again and confirms that this is the end of the prosecution case. The jury is sent home for the rest of the day, being told to return the following morning.

Once the jury has left the room Brendan Grehan says he wishes to make an application that the charge of murder be withdrawn from the case, claiming the prosecution has failed to establish Richard Satchwell intended to kill or cause serious injury to his wife.

In one way, this is what the last four weeks has been leading up to. The defence has not challenged much of the prosecution case – there is not much dispute about evidence leading up to or after Tina's death. But the schism, says the defence, is what happened inside 3 Grattan Street on 20 March 2017. There is only one living witness to those events, and he claims his wife's death was an accident. The defence case is simple: there is not enough evidence to prove murder.

In Irish murder trials a judge has the power to dismiss a charge of murder before a jury has the chance to begin deliberations. Any judge presiding over a murder trial can do this if they feel the prosecution hasn't proven the necessary elements of murder exist in a given case.

In Court 6 Brendan Grehan points out to Mr Justice Paul McDermott that no cause of death could be determined for

Tina. One thing medical experts had been able to say was that Tina did not have any broken bones, and her hyoid bone was not fractured. The barrister maintains there is no medical evidence to say his client's account of holding Tina off him with a restraint against her neck before she suddenly collapsed was not possible.

As I listen to the defence submission, I am aware that, despite being very disturbing, some killings which might be labelled as murder in the initial stages of an investigation can end up being reduced to manslaughter, or indeed in a complete acquittal for a defendant.

Gerardine Small responds that there is 'a wealth of evidence' from the surrounding circumstances in the case from which intent to kill can be inferred, pointing to the deception and plethora of lies which began very shortly after Tina died, on that same day.

Ms Small reminds the judge that the limited results from the post-mortem examination are because Richard hid his wife's body for over six years, and she says there is a motive for murder which the jury should be allowed to consider: that Richard told gardaí Tina had threatened to leave him. 'She has "wasted 28 years" of her life – that is all part of the evidence for the jury to accept or not,' says Gerardine Small.

The judge dismisses the application to withdraw the murder charge. Mr Justice McDermott notes that Richard's immediate response to his wife's death was to create a false impression that Tina was alive, and he had taken every conceivable step to protect himself. The judge says Richard had told lie after lie 'to any journalist who would indulge him', and he says it is a matter for the jury to decide if the defendant had formed the requisite intent and if he was guilty of the crime of murder.

Only one defence witness is called when the trial resumes next day. Tina's sister Lorraine Howard is called to the witness box. The defence wishes to ask Lorraine about specific elements of a statement she made to Detective Dave Kelleher while Tina was still missing. It is a deeply uncomfortable situation for Lorraine, as she is asked personal questions about her family, but she bravely takes the witness stand and answers all questions asked of her. At one point she takes a break but manages to get through the ordeal of giving evidence.

The defence team asks Lorraine about the statement she gave to Detective Kelleher in 2020 where she described Tina as being 'high maintenance'. Lorraine tells the court she had told gardaí that 'Tina wore the trousers' in her relationship with Richard. Lorraine agrees she told detectives Richard would spend 'every penny' on his wife 'to dress her up'.

Lorraine tells the jury that she first met Richard when she was 15 years old. She was three years younger than Tina, and she had spent her early years believing Tina was her aunt. It had only been when Tina went looking for a birth certificate, in preparation for making her confirmation, that she had discovered she and Lorraine had the same mother – Mary – who Tina had previously believed was her older sister. Tina had always believed that her grandmother Florence was her mother, and while Tina remained very close to Florence up until her grandmother's death, discovering the truth had led to tensions between Tina and Lorraine. There were significant periods of time when the sisters would fall out, and then they would make up again.

Lorraine tells the court that Richard used to call Tina his 'trophy wife and girlfriend'. 'I didn't like that as a comment,' says Lorraine in the witness box. 'I didn't think it was right to refer to someone as a trophy.'

Lorraine is sitting ten feet from Richard; the witness box is on an elevated section of the court halfway between the defendant and the judge. Mr Justice McDermott is at another height above Lorraine, to her left, with Richard down below her to her right. Lorraine describes how, for a long time before Tina was found, she believed her sister was alive and had felt anger about what she was putting the family through. Lorraine speaks into the microphone in the witness box, saying, 'I should have aimed this anger at Richard Satchwell', who had been calling to her house 'telling me all these lies'.

Lorraine has been called as a defence witness, but much of her evidence is now painting the accused in an unflattering light. She says Richard was 'possessive' of his wife, 'wanting to know where Tina was all the time, who she was speaking to all the time, where she was going all the time'. She says the accused would find fault with every friend Tina would meet and her 'friendship circle was getting smaller and smaller'.

Lorraine begins to weep in the witness box when the defence barrister mentions her brother Tom, who took his own life in 2012. She says Tom's death affected Tina as much as her. She is asked about a comment she made to gardaí that Tina had a 'Jekyll and Hyde personality', and Lorraine explains that sometimes they could be friends and then they wouldn't be. Lorraine says she told gardaí that Tina had a temper but so did she. She says she never once saw Tina being violent.

Lorraine finishes her evidence, and all eyes and ears are trained on Brendan Grehan. Is he going to call Richard to give evidence in his own defence? Myself and other journalists have been chatting about this moment ever since the trial began. Because of all the lies Richard has told, I feel he may want to give a new narrative in the witness box. I think the jury might also want to hear his side of things. The only version of Tina's death that Richard has ever given is while under arrest for the second time in Cobh garda station in October 2023, and that was shortly after Tina's body had been discovered in the understairs grave. The videos of Richard's interviews from that arrest have already been played before the jury, and during that evidence the defendant sat quietly in the dock, with his hands covering his face. Other than saying the words 'Not guilty … Not guilty', Richard has not spoken at all out loud during the four weeks this trial has been underway. For a man who once spoke for hours to me and to gardaí, Richard has been a quiet presence in court.

The expectation that Richard might give evidence is dashed when the defence barrister announces they have no more evidence to offer. I feel immediate disappointment that we will not hear Richard being cross-examined about his multiple lies.

The charging of the jury is a final and important element of this trial. It is Monday, 26 May 2025, four weeks to the day since the jury was sworn in, when Mr Justice Paul McDermott begins this process of giving the jury instructions on how to go about their deliberations. Over the past month the seven women and five men who have sat in the jury box of Court 6 have watched videos of Richard's various interviews with gardaí and with me on *Prime Time* and in other media. They have heard witnesses in court describe finding Tina's body and have heard her niece and sister outline their memories of their loved one.

The judge looks at the jury as he tells them what they must do and what they must not do. He tells them they must return a verdict in accordance with the evidence and not with emotion, sympathy or empathy. The starting point in the case is that Richard Satchwell is presumed innocent of the offence of murder, and it is up to the prosecution to establish if he is guilty of that offence beyond a reasonable doubt. The judge says the defendant was under no obligation to give evidence, and in terms of determining the case, it 'has no relevance, he has no obligation to prove anything'.

In a packed courtroom the judge outlines how there are lies and a whole web of untruths in this case, and there is a complete difference of opinion between the prosecution and defence relating to Richard's lies to gardaí, media and Tina's family. The prosecution says the lies indicate he was trying to avoid being caught having murdered his wife, while the defence says Richard's 'concocted account' of Tina going missing was because of panic and shame.

THREE OPTIONS

The prosecution argues the motivation for the alleged murder is that Tina was going to leave her husband, and Richard's reaction ensured this did not happen. The judge says the jury is entitled to consider what Richard said and did in the time immediately after Tina's death and in subsequent years to determine his state of mind.

As I sit in court, I know it all boils down to whether the jury believes Richard intended to kill or cause serious injury to Tina. Do they believe his account of Tina falling onto him as he lay on the ground while he held her belt against her neck, trying to ward her off?

The judge tells the jury there are three options. If they believe Richard intended his wife's death, or intended serious injury, they can convict him of murder. If they have a doubt that he intended the result of his actions, they can acquit him of murder but convict him of manslaughter. The jury is told they can consider the issue of self-defence. If the jury decides the force used by Richard was reasonable in the circumstances as he honestly believed them to be, they must acquit him of both murder and manslaughter and return a verdict of not guilty.

I look at the jury as they listen intently to the judge. I wonder what it's like to be in their shoes. I have never been on a jury. Down the years, I've got the summons three times in the post but have always been excused because of my job. I know too much about who is in custody and who is not, who has previous criminal convictions and who doesn't. The jury in this case doesn't know that Richard is in custody or that he has 14 previous convictions dating back 20 years.

From what it does actually know, this jury has much to

consider. There are four weeks of evidence which these 12 people will have to weigh up. The prosecution claims Richard's description of how his wife died is 'absolutely farcical' and that his 'fabricated narrative' was because his objective from the very outset was 'to put everyone off the scent' because he had 'murdered his wife'.

The defence says there is no doubt Richard is guilty of something, but the jury must decide what he is guilty of. Although Richard had lied 'to the people of Ireland', those lies do not make him a murderer, nor do they relieve the prosecution of proving the ingredients of murder.

The judge takes two days to sum up the evidence in the case. The jury retires to begin deliberations at 3.05 p.m. on Tuesday, 27 May, being brought by a uniformed jury keeper into their private room. It's been a long day already, so they spend only 46 minutes considering their verdict before being sent home for the day, to resume deliberations the following morning. Richard is taken back to Cloverhill Prison. Everyone is on edge. Richard's fate now lies in the hands of 12 ordinary members of the public brought together by lottery.

32.

Verdict

The jury takes four days to deliver its verdict, during which time I have a nervous energy I've never experienced before. I am on edge, walking alone a lot around the interior and exterior of the court building. I stop for many chats with fellow journalists, but I also have a lot of time with my own thoughts.

On all four days I am also driving between the court building and the RTÉ studios in Donnybrook. The full programme myself and Sallyanne have put together is almost ready for broadcast – it just needs the verdict to complete it. I have structured my script so that, whether the verdict be guilty of either murder or manslaughter, or not guilty of any crime, I will still have a full programme prepared and can adapt my script according to the finding of the jury.

I walk along the river Liffey several times during these four days, walking the short distance from the Criminal Courts of Justice over to Heuston station, turning left down by the side of the Guinness factory and back over the northside and up to the courts again. There is an intense heat from the sun, which has been shining all through May. I think of Tina and her body lying wrapped in plastic under the stairs of her home. I think of Richard and all the times I spent in his company.

As I walk alone close to the court, I have arranged with fellow journalists to alert me if there is any sign of a verdict. I also repay the favour, sitting for times inside the courtroom or just outside, giving other reporters the opportunity to get a breath of fresh air during the long wait for a knock from the jury-room door.

Among the many memories which come to the fore during this time, I think of the case of Harry Gleeson, whose body was finally recovered in 2024 from within the grounds of Mountjoy Jail. The same pair of forensic archaeologists who recovered Tina's body – Niamh McCullagh and Aidan Harte – were part of the team which found Harry's remains. Eighty-three years after his wrongful conviction and execution, his body was taken from within the prison, in a fresh coffin, home to County Tipperary. I was privileged to attend his funeral, filming a report for broadcast on that night's *Six One News*. My job in RTÉ had given me opportunities to be an eyewitness to historical events, none more poignant than watching a man being finally laid to rest in his family plot more than eight decades after his wrongful death.

By the end of Wednesday, 28 May, the jury has deliberated for four hours and 42 minutes. They are sent home to return at 10.30 a.m. the next day. I study the jurors' faces before they leave court. They seem tired but comfortable; they don't seem rattled; there is no underlying tension, and they seem to be getting on with each other. It's possible they are having disagreements about evidence, but they also seem to be making progress. This is purely guesswork on my behalf, all gleaned from their body language. I have studied juries for a quarter of a century, and I think I have a good read on when a jury is deadlocked or moving towards a verdict. I know, watching the jurors head back into the jury room to get their coats and bags, that they will reach a verdict. I feel a sense of calm among them. A verdict is coming, I can feel it; I just don't know when it will come.

I am immediately struck that the verdict may come the next day, a day *Prime Time* is on air. We have an edit room up and running, and I have no doubt that I can slot the verdict into a report if it comes tomorrow, but I need to alert the editors to the possibility. They decide to have a two-fold idea for the next day's programme – one if there's a verdict, and a second if there's not and they need to fill the programme with other material. This creates a bit of a headache for everyone working on the Thursday programme, but it is unavoidable.

All through Thursday I watch Court 6, waiting to see if there will be a verdict. The room itself remains largely empty all day – only the registrar, the stenographer and the jury keeper are inside for a long period. But the room is packed at 3.46 p.m. when the jury re-enters. As they take their seats, all we know, through hushed tones and reading the body language of the legal teams, is that the jury have something they want to communicate. It's not a verdict, but they have a message. The foreman of the jury hands a note up to the judge. Everyone studies the judge for a reaction – what is going on? Mr Justice McDermott looks at the note and then at the jury and says there is 'no difficulty about that'. It turns out the jury is asking if they can go home now and return tomorrow, but they want to start later than usual, asking if they can resume deliberations at 11.30 a.m. I know deep down that this is it – they are close to a verdict. They just need to rest and sleep and come back together and resume. I quickly alert the editors in *Prime Time* that there will not be a verdict today and Plan B for that night's programme should now proceed immediately.

I have so many thoughts on the Friday morning. I keep close to the courtroom, confining my nervous solitary walks to inside the impressive 11-storey structure. The jury resume deliberations at 11.30 a.m., and just over 45 minutes later the jury minder enters the courtroom and gives a discreet signal to the court registrar. I see the body language, and I know what is happening. Other journalists see it too.

'Verdict.' The message ripples across the first floor of the court building from within Court 6. A flurry of text messages are sent to those who are walking around outside. 'Verdict, now.'

Tina's mother, Mary, sister Lorraine and niece Sarah take their seats, along with other family members. Members of the Victim Support at Court service are with them, ensuring they are as comfortable at the back of the courtroom as they can be. Gardaí gather in a corner to the right-hand side, their faces not betraying anything. They know it all comes down to this moment, right now, what a jury has decided about the man who hid his wife's body.

The legal teams take their seats, and Richard Satchwell is brought into the courtroom, taking his seat in the dock, sitting on his cushion, his head down, occasionally looking towards his legal team but avoiding the intense stares of everyone to his right – the onlookers, the journalists, Tina's family.

The jury comes in and take their seats, five in the back row and seven at the front. Their faces look drained, but a form of relief seems evident. They have done their job, made a determination: they have a verdict.

There is huge tension in the room, and the judge is acutely aware of this. The verdict must be delivered promptly.

In the seconds before the verdict is read out, the jury foreman confirms their decision is unanimous. The jury has spent 9 hours and 28 minutes coming to its decision. I look at the clock: half past 12. The jury had needed just one hour when they resumed deliberations earlier today to ensure they were all on the same page about the evidence and what it meant. They must have been so close to a verdict yesterday, I think, but they needed some time so that it all sits right with them.

Right here, right now, this is justice; this is a jury of Richard William Satchwell's peers deciding if the 58-year-old is to walk free or go to jail. I feel my chest pumping. I think of Richard in my car giving me directions around Youghal, him holding an RTÉ microphone in his hand, pleading for assistance in finding his missing wife. I look at my fellow journalists, most with laptops and phones side by side on the small benches in front of them. I am more old school with just a pen and paper, an A4 sheet I've folded a few times so I can scribble notes.

Guilty of murder. The registrar announces the verdict in a clear voice. 'You say that Richard Satchwell is guilty of the murder of Tina Satchwell.' Sharp breaths are taken across the courtroom and sighs are immediately audible from the back of the court. Members of Tina's family are sobbing. Some members of the jury are now crying. Richard doesn't show much reaction – he's hiding his head in his hands.

Journalists begin tweeting the verdict, racing to be first to tell the country that Richard Satchwell is a murderer, a man whose story of accidentally killing his wife is farcical and had more holes in it 'than a block of Swiss cheese'. For a split second I think of how I ran from court 25 years ago to break the news of Catherine Nevin being convicted of the contract murder of her husband Tom. There was no Twitter or X back then, but there was live radio, where on Today FM I got through to Eamon Dunphy on *The Last Word* and beat RTÉ by breaking the news minutes ahead of them. Now I'm a long-time employee of RTÉ but I know deep down that Richard Satchwell's undoing may be my last big television documentary for the national broadcaster. By now my five-year fixed contract as security correspondent has ended, and RTÉ has not re-advertised the role, while I have now reverted to my original role as multi-media journalist. Only myself and my wife yet know I am thinking about life beyond RTÉ; for now, I know I have a full programme to get to air.

'I thank you sincerely for your service,' Mr Justice McDermott says to the jury. He acknowledges this has been a difficult trial, and he cannot do anything 'other than thank you'. He also excuses them from further jury service for 10 years. The judge says he will impose sentence the following Wednesday and directs Richard Satchwell be further remanded in custody until then. It has all happened very quickly. The prisoner is taken out of court, and the judge leaves the room. Court is adjourned.

I text the programme editors and my producer, Sallyanne Godson, and all the RTÉ colleagues who worked with me in Youghal and Fermoy in 2017 and 2018. I also text my wife, who knows what this means to me. If the jury had failed to reach a verdict there might have been a retrial and I would have had to consider staying in RTÉ a few more years to complete my reporting on Richard. But now it's over. Richard will be going to jail for life, my report will be broadcast soon, and the next stage of my life can begin.

I look at Tina's family, and I feel a mixture of emotions: deep upset at what was done to Tina, but happiness that she is getting justice and that her voice will now be heard through her family. All throughout the trial Tina's loved ones have heard a false narrative spun by Richard Satchwell that his wife was a violent woman, that he was a victim. I know Tina's family will speak outside court within a few minutes. I go downstairs to get ready outside with all the other media.

Tina's family walk out of court en masse, with gardaí behind them, still minding them. Lorraine and Sarah, Tina's sister and niece, immediately address the wrong that has been done to Tina's name. 'During this trial Tina was portrayed in a way that is not true to who she was,' Sarah tells the assembled reporters, who have arranged microphones on stands outside the front of the building. To Sarah's right is Lorraine, who stands beside Tina's mother Mary. Lorraine is keen to thank the prosecution team who have got justice for Tina. Lorraine namechecks barristers Gerardine Small, Imelda Kelly and Maria Brosnan, and DPP solicitor Catherine McAleer. 'Their hard work and professionalism shone through like the classy ladies that you are.' Detective Inspector Ann Marie Twomey, who led the cold-case investigation, and is now a Superintendent, is also thanked by Lorraine, as is Detective Garda Dave Kelleher 'for putting the pieces together and finding Tina'.

That is all the family is saying for now; they will address the court next week when Richard is formally sentenced for murder. I race back to RTÉ, where I have a meeting with the programme editors, and we decide that a 30-second promo ad will run on RTÉ from later tonight advertising a special programme the following Tuesday on how Richard Satchwell was brought to justice, with exclusive imagery from inside the murder scene and exclusive interviews from 2017 and 2018 with the now convicted murderer. I arrange to go on an RTÉ News podcast that afternoon, the *Six One News* with David McCullagh that evening and the *This Week* radio programme on Sunday to speak of my interactions with Richard. I also write a lengthy article for the RTÉ News website.

Then on Tuesday night, I broadcast a full *Prime Time* documentary entitled 'Tina's Truth' that has been a long time in the making. I include information the jury did not know about suspicions that Richard was displaying coercive control over Tina. The programme attracts a huge audience for *Prime Time*.

Immediately after the report airs, and before I have left Donnybrook to head home, Sarah contacts me, expressing happiness with the documentary and asking if I can send her a copy of the video of Tina speaking to the parrot. It dawns on me that I have photographs and video of Tina which her family do not. I have material which Richard let me film, but these are images he never shared with Tina's own loved ones in the years after she had 'disappeared' – another example of his controlling behaviour. I immediately email Sarah a copy of the video of Tina, her clear Cork accent calling out to her beloved parrot Pearl.

33.

Life

The following morning, Wednesday, 4 June 2025, I sit in Court 6 beside RTÉ Legal Affairs Correspondent Orla O'Donnell. I have known Orla for over 20 years – I had actually applied for the job Orla now does, when Mary Wilson left the role in 2006. I had made it to the last three candidates, but Orla got the job. In subsequent years I have recognised that RTÉ's decision had been the right one for both of us. Orla is an excellent court reporter and has expertly covered numerous harrowing cases, including murder, manslaughter, rape and sexual assault. Together with reporter Vivienne Traynor, Orla has spent decades reporting the facts as outlined in court. I had come to realise my talent lies in exploring the hidden elements of cases that make it to court – I am an investigative reporter at heart.

Journalist Alison O'Riordan of Ireland International court reporting agency is sitting in front of us, and in hushed tones the three of us discuss my report of the previous night. A member of the public comes over and shakes my hand, saying well done. I say thank you but try not to meet anyone else's gaze; I feel very self-conscious and also quite emotional.

I think about Tina's mother, Mary, who is sitting behind me. She brought flowers with her as she arrived at court today and has presented them to the volunteers from Victim Support who have been with her over the past month. Such decency and dignity are powerful – they cut through all the noise, all the hype around Tina's case. Tina was loved, Tina is loved.

At 11.21 a.m. Richard Satchwell is brought into court, his head down, and the judge comes into the room soon afterwards. I sense that Dave Kelleher is sitting to my right but I don't look around to check. Gerardine Small stands up and calls Dave to the witness stand, and he gives a quick recap of the investigation which led to Tina's body being found, and the prosecution evidence presented during the murder trial. Everyone in the courtroom already knows this detail, but with today's sentencing hearing, proper dignity is being afforded to the victim, and so a short summation of the evidence is warranted. Dave Kelleher speaks in a clear Cork accent, and I think of how this case has been solved by Cork people, from the gardaí involved to Dr Niamh McCullagh, whose original report advised that 3 Grattan Street should be excavated in the search for Tina.

Dave Kelleher gives details of Richard's previous convictions – 14 from the six-year period of 1999 to 2004. The crimes range from larceny to displaying a false tax disc, theft to driving offences. None of the convictions will impact on the sentence he's about to get – automatic imprisonment for life – but it is important to outline for the record a complete narrative of Richard's previous dealings with Irish courts.

Gerardine then calls Sarah Howard to give a victim impact

statement. I watch Sarah walk in front of Richard and sit into the witness box. I think of how just last night I sent her the video of Tina and how Richard had never shared it with her. Richard had isolated Tina so much and sought to control her both in life and in death.

'Tina was not just my aunt, but my best friend.' Sarah speaks clearly and emotionally into the microphone. 'I am here today to talk about my aunt who was taken in the most tragic and violent way, murdered by someone who claimed to love her.' Sarah's voice rings out across the courtroom; Richard keeps his head down. 'Listening to all the lies in the court was very hard and knowing now all the horrible things that were done to her, such as being wrapped in a piece of plastic and buried in such an undignified way, cause me huge amounts of distress.' Sarah reclaims Tina's dignity and restates the truth. 'Richard Satchwell decided to portray Tina in a way during the trial that is not true to who she was. Tina was not a violent person – she was caring, gentle and loyal to those she loved. Having her name tarnished during the trial was very difficult.'

The personal impact of having to give evidence is now laid bare in Court 6. 'This trial has also ruined the last few weeks of my pregnancy with all the stress from the trial,' Sarah points out. She was quite determined to give evidence on behalf of her aunt, but Sarah wants it noted that Richard Satchwell's web of violence and deception has continued to impact on people. 'Having to leave my baby in the first few weeks of her life to give evidence and be at the trial for Tina was something I shouldn't have had to do.' Sarah points out that it is not just the crime which has caused such aching pain, but the cruelty that followed it, 'the deception, the stolen years, and the false hope he gave us all that one day she might turn up'.

As Sarah leaves the witness box, dignified and strong, she glares at Richard; he does not meet her gaze. Her aunt Lorraine then walks to the witness box and gives an equally powerful statement. She speaks of her murdered sister as someone who always cared so much for animals and who loved fashion – she describes the bridge in the centre of Fermoy as Tina's 'catwalk' and how they loved to walk around the town when they were younger.

Lorraine speaks of the impact of the trial on her mother, Mary, and she expresses upset that her brother Tom's suicide was brought up 'time and time again' during the trial. She also refers to the trauma of being called as a witness by Richard Satchwell. 'Watching me being used to help the defence was like pouring salt into an open wound.'

In the witness box Lorraine nails the issue of control and isolation which has hung over the case. She outlines how, before he murdered Tina, Richard was 'isolating her and alienating her from her many friends'. Lorraine also addresses the narrative put forward by Richard that Tina was a violent woman, saying, 'In fact that couldn't be any further from the truth. I am so thankful that the jury could see through his lies.' Lorraine says she has nightmares over Tina's final moments and what she went through. 'The appalling way my sister was buried, wrapped in plastic, buried beneath soil and concrete, sends shivers down my spine every time I think about it.'

Lorraine's statement takes seven minutes to read, and every word is full of emotion. She glares at Richard as she walks past him back to her seat, but again he doesn't look up.

It's now 11.45 a.m. and the court has been sitting for just over 20 minutes. Defence barrister Brendan Grehan then rises and says three things. His client intends to appeal the guilty verdict, he never intended to kill Tina, and then a final message from the convicted man. Richard is trying to have the last word. Despite everything which was said in court Richard, through his barrister, now wishes to say, 'Tina was a lovely person'. The moment these words are spoken I can hear some sharp intakes of breath behind me.

Mr Justice Paul McDermott then passes sentence. With sentencings for murder convictions, judges are very much a rubber stamp – an automatic life sentence is the punishment for the crime of murder – even if very few convicted murderers actually spend the rest of their lives in prison. There is no tariff system in Irish law to allow a judge to determine how long a murderer should spend in prison before being considered for parole. Although every case is different, the average life sentence is well in excess of 20 years' imprisonment. Journalists in court know that it will be well into the late 2040s before Richard Satchwell might be released. But for now, there is only one sentence to be formally imposed in this courtroom – life imprisonment.

However on this occasion, before this court sitting is over, the judge has something to say. He has heard all the evidence in the case, including Lorraine's testimony about Richard referring to Tina as his 'trophy wife'. The judge knows the charge on the indictment refers to Tina by her married name – the official wording of the crime is 'the murder of Tina Satchwell'. But having imposed the life sentence on Richard, Mr Justice McDermott looks down into the body of the court and says, 'The only other thing to be said is for me to express my condolences to the family of the late Tina Dingivan'.

I smile as I hear the judge's words. He has heard the victim impact statements, he gets it, and he refers to the victim by her maiden name. In that moment I feel a mixture of emotions – sadness and happiness. Tina Dingivan RIP.

And with that the judge is gone from the courtroom, back to his chambers. The next person to leave the room is Richard Satchwell. He gets up the moment the judge has left, and he too leaves the packed courtroom. The prison officers follow him quickly through the custody door, one step behind. I watch Richard leave, wondering if this is the last time I will ever see him in person.

Everybody is now leaving the courtroom, but I stay sitting. I find I need to stay in the room for a moment and take it all in. This marks the beginning of the end of my career in RTÉ. I won't be leaving today or tomorrow, but I know my time is now coming to an end. I feel a heaviness in my chest. I think about sitting on the couch with Richard while Tina's body lay nearby. I'm relieved this case is over, and I'm thankful I helped to play a part, but I feel somewhat heavy with it all.

I come out of the courtroom and see Dave Kelleher. I offer him my hand and as we shake I congratulate him on his work on the case. 'You did a good thing,' I say, patting him on the shoulder as I shake his hand. 'You did a good thing.'

I walk downstairs, where I see Ann Marie Twomey, and I say well done to her too. It might sound like a strange thing to say in such a tragic and distressing case, but it is heartfelt and genuine. There are many lessons for gardaí from the case of Tina Satchwell which will hopefully lead to other cases being solved too. But ultimately it was a fresh team of gardaí, including Ann Marie and Dave, who followed the evidence and pushed for an excavation of 3 Grattan Street.

The cold-case team walk out of court and approach the assembled microphones. Detective Clár Quirke is in the back row, the family liaison officer who has guided Tina's family through this harrowing process. Detectives John O'Connell, John O'Donovan and Dave Barry stand beside her. In front are Detective Superintendent Seán Healy and detectives Dave Kelleher and Dave Noonan. Between the two Daves stands Superintendent Ann Marie Twomey, who makes a short statement on behalf of the team which got justice for Tina Dingivan.

'While no resolution could erase the pain of loss, we sincerely hope the conclusion of the case brings some measure of comfort to Tina's family,' says Ann Marie, addressing the large group of media gathered in front of her. The superintendent thanks the witnesses and the wider community in Youghal and Fermoy who assisted garda enquiries. 'Finally, we, the investigation team, are happy that justice has been served for Tina.' The gardaí turn and walk back into the court building as the media break away to tweet video of the statement and do live radio reports.

I walk to my car, which is parked on Infirmary Road, a journey I have made countless times over recent years. Today

I feel different – I hope that the solving of Tina's case will have a knock-on positive effect. How many more missing people actually lie buried close to where they were last seen? How many searches of properties down the years were not actually completely invasive searches? How many were just surface searches and failed to find bodies buried only feet away? How many unsolved missing persons cases should be gone through with a fine-tooth comb now?

As I sit into my car to drive away, I think of all the families of missing persons who deserve better. I wonder how many families have been assured that thorough and complete searches have been carried out of various properties, when in fact the searches may not have led to any walls being pulled apart or floors dug up. I think of Michael Gaine, the Kerry farmer whose body was found just weeks ago, while Richard Satchwell was on trial. Michael was missing since March, and an extensive search of his farm was conducted within days of his disappearance, but it was a second search, in May 2025, which led to parts of his dismembered body being found in a slurry tank on his property.

I wait a few minutes before driving off, thinking of how I felt after Patrick Quirke was jailed for life in 2019 for the murder of Bobby Ryan, whose body was hidden in an underground tank on a farm in Tipperary. I had really felt after that case, and all my reporting on it, that a full inventory would be ordered by gardaí to establish how many such underground tanks might exist on farms right across the country and whether any other bodies were hidden within them. But no such initiative was forthcoming by gardaí.

I think about how Bill Fennessy's body lay in his car in Fermoy for 12 years, hidden beneath the water and the silt of the river Blackwater. I am in no doubt but that he should have been found sooner, and not in a chance discovery by a local search and rescue team on a training exercise. I think of other such cases of people whose bodies lay hidden for long periods before being found by chance. I remember Stephen Corrigan, whose body lay undiscovered in dense undergrowth in Rathmines for 10 years. How can these things happen in a modern progressive society?

I think of how volunteers with the Cork City Missing Persons Search and Recovery team used sonar equipment to carry out a planned search for Barry Coughlan, who was missing for 17 years. Volunteers like this are simply heroes, they never give up, and their persistence paid off in 2021 when they found Barry's car embedded in the seabed just yards from Hugh Coveney Pier in Crosshaven – only a few feet from where Barry was last seen leaving a pub in 2004.

When Barry's car was retrieved from the water it was upside down, and Barry's body was still in the driver's seat. While the recovery of Barry's remains brought finality to his family's suffering and allowed him to be laid to rest with dignity, the case was yet another example of a missing person who should have been found sooner. It was also notable that Barry had been found in a section of water which had been previously searched.

I have long felt so frustrated at the lack of adequate searching in many missing persons cases, but following Tina's case, I'm feeling slightly more positive. The garda commissioner is talking about the force learning from the case, and the Taoiseach is being asked directly about what more should be done in missing persons cases. In the following days Garda Commissioner Drew Harris will specifically mention me by name to journalists as having brought a number of missing persons cases to his attention down the years which have later been reclassified as murders. The commissioner pointedly refers to the annual National Missing Persons Day event – which I had previously been the host of for 10 years – as an occasion when he and other gardaí have listened carefully to ideas on how to improve garda responses in historical cases.

It's not as simple as having a cadaver dog working within An Garda Síochána, though that would certainly be a start. But it is dedicated and relentless investigators being given the time and resources to properly investigate cold cases that is most needed the length and breadth of the country. With over 900 people long-term missing in Ireland, the discussion needs to be about a root and branch review of what types of searches were done in each case and, more importantly, what type of searches were not done.

As I turn on my engine to drive away from the court and move on to my next story, I say out loud what I'm thinking. 'God rest you, Tina. I hope your legacy is to help find others. Sorry I was so close to you and didn't know. God rest you.'

Quietly the prison van pulls out of the court complex. Everybody else involved in the case has now dispersed. Richard is driven back to his cell in Cloverhill to collect his belongings and is then taken down the M7 to Limerick Prison, where he had been detained before the trial began.

In the following weeks he resumes his job working in the kitchen to while away some hours of the day. There are both male and female sections of the prison; they never mix but they are fed by one kitchen complex, where Richard spends hours making buns and cakes. However, it's soon reported that, in a unique show of solidarity with his murder victim, female prisoners are refusing to consume any of Richard's baked goods.

Two weeks after being given a life sentence Richard marks his 59th birthday in the prison in Limerick. This will be his home for the foreseeable future. However, it is rare that a life-sentence prisoner actually spends the rest of their life in jail. The average life sentence varies, but often lies somewhere above 20 years. However, there is no yardstick to measure the crime of murdering your wife and keeping her hidden under the stairs; there has never been anything quite like it in Ireland – that we know of anyway.

Epilogue: Tina Beams

There is one photograph of Tina which particularly intrigues me. It's an image I filmed as I sat on the couch with Richard at 3 Grattan Street in November 2017. The fact Tina's body lay so close to where I sat has haunted me to this day. I was so physically close to where she was, but so far away from the truth, as I sat with her husband admiring countless photos of his missing wife. One image looked very different to all the others. It was the only one where Tina was in a group.

So many of the photos of Tina were taken by her husband and show a well-dressed woman smiling at the camera. But Tina is alone in most of them. Sometimes one or both of her beloved dogs are in the shot, but very often it is just Tina. Those images are important reminders of a life lived and a life taken violently. The fact the killer took many of the photographs sullies their context, but they are still photographs of a woman who was beloved by so many people.

In her final months Tina's husband isolated her even more. He had moved them to Youghal, far away from friends and family in Fermoy. The couple didn't know anyone in Youghal, and while they would say hello to people on the street, they never engaged in long conversations. The spectre of coercive control hung over the garda investigation into Tina's murder. Gardaí were aware of reported incidents of unsettling behaviour exhibited by Richard towards Tina, but there was no clear proof, nothing to bring to court as part of the murder case. The one significant witness to whatever transpired in the marriage was Tina, and with her violent death so also died the truth of what she had endured married to Richard.

It wasn't always bad, it would seem. Looking at some of the photographs of a younger Richard and Tina it was clear the couple had happy times. Richard was keen to share those photographs with me the night I sat with him in the couple's sitting room. He held the briefcase packed with photographs on his knees, showing me one photograph, and then another, and another. Himself and Tina having a meal at a restaurant on holiday in Sligo, the two of them dressed up for St Patrick's Day, Tina sitting on Richard's lap and both of them laughing.

As I took copies of all the photos – with Richard's permission – I spotted one which looked out of place, or which required more explanation. Richard didn't have the full facts. He just knew that it was taken at the English Market when Tina was doing a chef course. Even that amount of information was intriguing – Tina hadn't worked for many years and at the time of her disappearance had been claiming social welfare benefits. Yet the woman smiling back at me in the photograph was dressed for work and very much in the thick of it.

I didn't have time to study the photograph too much, as

EPILOGUE: TINA BEAMS

Richard quickly handed me other ones. 'There's Tina learning to drive in England,' he said, as he gave me an image of Tina laughing behind the wheel of a car. 'This was taken in the house in Fermoy,' he said about another, which yet again showed Tina on her own, smiling at the camera. But none of the images captured the same smile I saw in the photo from the English Market. I must learn more about that, I thought, as I sat with my colleagues Shirley and Kevin, filming that interview with Richard.

The photo in question shows Tina with two women and a man. It is clear Tina was working at the English Market, and the other three people had stopped by for a photocall. Tina is wearing a chef's uniform, while the other three look like politicians or dignitaries. The man and one of the women wear large chains around their necks, and I recognise the other woman as former Fine Gael TD and MEP Deirdre Clune. I guess the photo was one of a sequence of political and business VIPs meeting local workers in the market.

The Tina in this photograph is nothing like the Tina I've seen in any other image. I send it to my RTÉ colleague Jennie O'Sullivan in Cork. I have previously assisted Jennie with research about the unidentified body of a man in Cork, and I'm now asking Jennie to repay the favour. I tell Jennie I know the two people on the right of the photo, one is Tina and the other is Deirdre Clune, but I don't know the other two. Jennie quickly responds that the man is businessman James O'Sullivan, who passed away in 2017. James had served as president of the Cork Business Association and was well known in business circles and for his charity work in the county.

Another text lands from Jennie. The woman wearing a chain is Patricia Gosch, a former Fine Gael councillor who served as deputy lord mayor of Cork from mid-2008 to mid-2009, so the photograph must date from within that time. Jennie agrees that the image is fascinating and that Tina looks so happy in it.

There's a man in the background of the photo who just happened to be snapped as he was walking past. I ring Deirdre Clune to ask for her help with any information, and I text her a copy of the image. Deirdre agrees it's a 'lovely happy photo', but she doesn't specifically remember it. She didn't know Tina, but is struck that she is captured in a photo with her during a photocall. Deirdre confirms the other two people in the picture are James O'Sullivan and Patricia Gosch. The photo was taken while Deirdre was a TD but she cannot be sure of the exact time.

Deirdre recognises the man in the back of the photo, who is only captured side on. It's Jack Mulcahy of the Chicken Inn, which is based at the English Market. I thank Deirdre and I make contact with Jack's son Tim via LinkedIn and send him the photo. He confirms it's his father in the background, but says Tina wasn't working with the Chicken Inn. He believes it's a uniform which trainees on a State-run catering and tourism course known as CERT wore when assisting with practical work projects at the English Market. A two-day festival used to take place there, where chefs would cook in

EPILOGUE: TINA BEAMS

real time at stalls and the trainees would get on-the-job experience.

Tina is holding a large temperature probe in her left hand and cradling a tub of sterile wipes. The probe is the type used to ensure cooked food is at the correct temperature before serving. Tina's hair is tied back, she wears a black chef's cap on her head and she is dressed in a white kitchen coat with necktie. It looks like the dignitaries have stumbled across her as they move through the market and she has turned to the camera. Deirdre Clune is not looking directly at the photographer, but the other three people are, so there may have been a number of people taking the same image. It's possible Richard actually took this photo, or someone else gave it to Tina later on.

I continue looking for more detail, speaking with a man who worked on the CERT courses in the late 2000s, preparing students for workplace assignments. He doesn't remember Tina but says she may well have been a student. Records of attendees have not been kept after all this time.

I've hit a wall in my research, but I have learned enough to know there was so much more to Tina Dingivan. Something happened in her life to stop her reaching her potential. She had learned to drive, but then didn't drive. She was a talented chef, but didn't pursue it as a career. Tina's prospects became limited from the moment Richard set eyes on her, when she was just 17 years old. The limitations on her life didn't happen immediately, but slowly her life became enclosed, her ability to reach her full potential diminished.

But this photograph captures something, the full extent of

which I do not know. Pictures speak a thousand words; I look at this image and I see Tina as the centre of attention, in a group – she is part of a community, she is active, she is vibrant. Perhaps it's simply because she would have been working with food that day, but I notice that Tina is not wearing her wedding ring.

I look at her face, a face which so many people have come to know, first through an extensive missing person appeal and later through the public realisation of the horrific indignity of how Tina's body lay hidden beneath concrete, wrapped in plastic sheeting, still wearing her pyjamas. I look at Tina working at the English Market. Why she didn't continue on this particular path I may never know. This image was taken eight years before her husband buried her under their stairs.

In this one image, neither with her husband nor alone, Tina seems so happy. I study every bit of it, and I look at Tina's face compared to all the other pictures I have seen. I sense a pride and a confidence which seems to radiate from this photo. I've studied dozens of images of Tina, and I know I'm not reading too much into it – I can see it in her eyes and in her smile. In this photo, this snapshot in time, in a crowded setting, a trainee chef, who is the least dressed up of all four people in the image, seems absolutely thrilled with herself. Tina Dingivan positively beams.

EPILOGUE: TINA BEAMS

Mary Tina Dingivan
30 November 1971 – 20 March 2017

Acknowledgements

Thank you to the family of Tina Dingivan for all your time and trust. Thank you especially to Tina's niece Sarah for assistance from 2017 to the present day. Tina was so loved by all her family and friends.

Thank you to Tina's former teacher Olive, and thank you also to Sara, Tina's friend from car boot sales.

A journalist is nothing without sources. Thank you to the many people who spoke privately with me, people determined that the truth of Tina's life and death be told. Thank you for your trust.

Thank you to my friends and former colleagues in RTÉ. Many are named in this book, and all have shared unique and historic broadcast moments with me. Special thanks to Shirley Bradshaw and Kevin Burns, who were with me inside the house where Tina's body was buried. Kevin and I broadcast two lengthy special reports in 2018 on Tina's disappearance. Thank you also Nick Dolan and Eddie Duffy. Thank you to producer and long-time friend and colleague Sallyanne Godson for working on the lengthy documentary broadcast after the verdict was delivered.

Working in RTÉ for more than two decades was a privilege, made all the more rewarding by my daily interactions with all the camera crews, sounds ops, graphic operators, dubbing operators and video editors who help to provide great television journalism. Thank you to each and every one of you. It was a privilege to work with you all. Thank you to news editors Ray Burke, Barbara Fitzgerald and Mary Campbell (RIP), whom I have worked closely with down through the years. Thank you to former *Prime Time* editors Donogh Diamond and Richard Downes. I have worked on very emotionally challenging stories, often in difficult situations, and always with a wonderful team of supportive colleagues and friends. Thank you to Brídóg Ní Bhuachalla with whom I've worked on a number of missing persons reports. Thank you to John Cunningham, Frank Shouldice, Angela Ryan, Doireann O'Hara, Isabel Perceval, Aaron Heffernan and Lucinda Glynn for collaborations down the years. Thank you also to Aidan McGuinness, Danny McDonald, Steve Farrell, Kieran O'Connell, John Reynolds, Martin Vale, Liz Walsh, Sean Higgins, Billy Kinsella, Dave Perry, John Fay, Brian Walsh, Eoin O'Connor, Olivia Doyle, Paulette O'Connor, Ceri Doyle and Abigail Tuite. Thank you to all my fellow reporters and the wider *Prime Time* team. Some of my *Prime Time* colleagues are no longer with us: *míle buíochas* Office Manager Rhona O'Byrne (RIP) and Deputy Editor Paul Tanney (RIP). Thank you also to RTÉ news journalists Orla O'Donnell, Vivienne Traynor and Paul Reynolds. And thank you Sharon Sorohan and Gavin Leane.

Thank you to my former schools, St Mark's primary and

ACKNOWLEDGEMENTS

secondary in Tallaght, for nurturing my curiosity. Thank you to my first news editor, Barry Flynn in Midlands Radio 3. Thanks also to Declan Meehan at East Coast Radio, John Keogh at 98FM and Conor Kavanagh, Noel Shannon, Ian Noctor, Tom Swift and Cathy Farrell at Today FM. Thank you to Séamus Dooley and all my colleagues in the NUJ.

Thank you to my agent, Faith O'Grady of The Lisa Richards Agency, for realising the unique story I had to tell about my interactions with Richard Satchwell.

Thank you to everyone in Gill Books, including commissioning editor Sarah Liddy, and thank you Margaret Farrelly for all your work on structuring this book and guiding it through the editorial process. Thank you Emma Dunne for the fine-tune editing. Thank you Iollann Ó Murchú for all your work on the photographs, and thank you Charlie Lawlor, Kate O'Halloran and Vada Haberland. This is my sixth book with Gill – thank you to Fergal Tobin (RIP) for setting me on this publishing path. Thank you also Nicki Howard and Teresa Daly. Thank you once again solicitor Kieran Kelly.

Thank you to all my fellow crime and court reporters. It is an important, but often difficult, path we walk and the encouragement and support of such friends and colleagues is essential to work this beat. *Go raibh maith agaibh a chairde go léir.*

Thank you to all the families of missing people who have trusted me down the years with your personal stories. I will continue to do all I can to shine a light.

Thank you to my father, Barry Cummins, and my mother, Patricia O'Neill, and my brother, Mark, for all your support.

Thank you to my wonderful wife, Grace Cappock, for everything from day one, including reading every draft chapter of this book and all the others. You are my rock. Thank you for your constant love, support and encouragement which have ensured I have continued to work in crime journalism for over a quarter of a century. Thank you to our amazing children, Ruby and Conor, for all your constant interest and support.

Finally, I would like to acknowledge the work of every member of An Garda Síochána involved in Tina's case, from 2017 to the present day. I hope the lessons to be learned from the case of Tina Dingivan will inspire more gardaí to revisit cold cases, be relentlessly curious and be brave.

There are more than 900 people classified as long-term missing in Ireland.

This book is for every one of them.